The Early Draft of John Stuart Mill's *Autobiography*

THE EARLY DRAFT OF
JOHN STUART MILL'S
Autobiography

Edited by
JACK STILLINGER

UNIVERSITY OF ILLINOIS PRESS, URBANA, 1961

A grant from the Ford Foundation has helped to
defray the cost of publishing this work

ACKNOWLEDGMENTS

To the Librarians of the University of Illinois Library, Yale University Library, and British Library of Political and Economic Science I am indebted for permission to quote documents in their custody. To the University of Illinois Research Board I am grateful for a summer fellowship and a generous grant that provided, among other things, the services of a research assistant, Mrs. Phyllis Liston, and a typist, Mrs. Vera McCarty. For suggestions and encouragement at the beginning of my project I wish to thank Dr. Gordon N. Ray, former Provost of the University of Illinois, and Professor J. F. Bell, Chairman of the Department of Economics. Among colleagues in the English Department, my greatest single obligation is to Professor G. Blakemore Evans, who gave helpful advice (and some argument) concerning editorial procedures, and read and improved the Introduction. At every stage my wife contributed valuably in matters of judgment. In my work on Mill's text generally I owe a special debt to two British scholars, Dr. Frank Taylor, Keeper of Manuscripts in the John Rylands Library, and Mr. C. G. Allen, Senior Assistant Librarian in the British Library of Political and Economic Science.

J.S.

CONTENTS

1

INTRODUCTION

Three manuscripts of Mill's *Autobiography* were among the collection of letters and papers owned after Mill's death by his stepdaughter Helen Taylor (1831–1907), bequeathed by her to her niece Mary Taylor (d. 1918), and then put up at auction in 1922 by the latter's executors as "the Property of Miss Mary Taylor (deceased), grand-daughter of the wife of John Stuart Mill." They are entered together, "a large parcel," as lot 720 (third day) in Sotheby's sale catalog of 27–29 March 1922: "MILL (John Stuart) Auto. MS. of his AUTOBIOGRAPHY upwards of 220 pp. 4to; with an earlier draft of the same in his hand, and a copy, mostly in the hand of Helen Taylor, *with the suppressed passages.*" The lot was knocked down—six years before the first draft and press copy of Carlyle's *Past and Present* were sold in the same rooms to an American buyer for £2,200 [1]—to Maggs Bros. for £5 5s.

During the next year and a half Maggs resold the manuscripts separately. The "Auto. MS.," the final holograph version of the *Autobiography*, was purchased by Professor John Jacob Coss (1884–1940) for members of the Department of Philosophy at Columbia, who presented it to the Columbia University Library in April 1923. It was used as the basis of an edition published by the Columbia University Press in the following year [2]. The "copy,

[1] Grace J. Calder, *The Writing of "Past and Present"* (New Haven, Conn., 1949), p. 12.

[2] *Autobiography of John Stuart Mill,* [edited by Roger Howson] with a preface by John Jacob Coss (New York, 1924). This edition was reissued in

mostly in the hand of Helen Taylor, *with the suppressed passages*," went to an English buyer. Its whereabouts were unknown until July 1959, when it was discovered in the London salerooms of Messrs. Hodgson by Dr. Frank Taylor, Keeper of Manuscripts in the John Rylands Library, Manchester, and acquired by the Rylands Library shortly afterward. Written mainly in the months just after Mill's death, by Helen Taylor, Mill's youngest sister Mary Elizabeth Colman, and an unidentified French copyist, this manuscript is the press copy of the *Autobiography*, the error-filled transcription of Mill's final draft from which the first edition (1873) was printed. It is valuable in accounting for the differences between the final draft and the first edition, and in thereby establishing the Columbia manuscript as the single authoritative source for the final text of the work.[3]

The "earlier draft," actually the original draft of the *Autobiography*, containing a complete account, as Mill then would have given it, of his life up to his marriage in 1851 (the equivalent of the first 168 pages of the Columbia edition), was bought from Maggs by Jacob Harry Hollander (1871–1940), Professor of Political Economy at Johns Hopkins University. On 13 December 1923, a few months after he had received it, Hollander read a paper on the manuscript before the History of Ideas Club at Johns Hopkins;[4] but it was otherwise unknown until Professor A. W. Levi examined it in 1941, a year after Hollander's death, and published excerpts in two important articles of 1945 and 1951.[5] Between 1941 and 1958 it was inaccessible to scholars, locked up in a Baltimore storage warehouse along with some 4,300 other items—books,

---

1944, 1948, and 1960. Though considerably faulty in minor details, it is still the best—and the only complete—edition available. I have cited it throughout as "Columbia edition."

[3] I have discussed the Rylands manuscript and its relationship to the Columbia draft and the first edition in "The Text of John Stuart Mill's *Autobiography*," *Bulletin of the John Rylands Library*, XLIII (1960), 220–242.

[4] The paper is listed in an appendix to Dorothy Stimson's "The History of Ideas Club," in *Studies in Intellectual History* (Baltimore, Md., 1953), p. 200.

[5] "The 'Mental Crisis' of John Stuart Mill," *Psychoanalytic Review*, XXXII (1945), 86–101; "The Writing of Mill's *Autobiography*," *Ethics*, LXI (1951), 284–296. Both articles quote extracts from R31v–33r; the second also includes passages from fols. 138v–139r and RII.20. The excerpts given by F. A. Hayek, *John Stuart Mill and Harriet Taylor* (Chicago, 1951), pp. 31–32, and Michael St. John Packe, *The Life of John Stuart Mill* (London, 1954), pp. 33, 51, 76, derive from the first of these articles; Hayek, p. 42, quotes a passage from RII.8 based on Levi's own notes.

pamphlets, manuscripts, and letters—that Hollander had collected. In the latter year it was acquired, with the rest of Hollander's library, by the University of Illinois.

After examining it, on its arrival in Urbana in September 1958, I decided that although its text is in many places identical with that of the final draft (a notable fact in itself), its numerous earlier readings canceled or altered in revision, as well as Harriet Mill's alterations and the sometimes complicated reordering of passages and the connections between rejected and revised leaves, could be presented most clearly and concisely—especially for the student of Mill who is not a textual specialist—in relation to a text of the draft itself, rather than as a list of variant readings to the text of the later draft at Columbia. The edition given here, according to principles outlined in the final section of this Introduction, provides a complete text of the early draft, with a selection of earlier readings in the notes and a series of extracts from the rejected leaves. It is intended to present everything of possible significance contained in the draft.

II

The Hollander-Illinois manuscript consists of 169 leaves, comprising 139 leaves of the complete early draft, and thirty leaves of rejected text retained together at the end of the draft. The leaves, which are half-sheets of white laid foolscap measuring 13¼ by 8¼ inches, contain either a Britannia watermark (in about half the leaves, irregularly throughout) or one of three countermarks: "STACEY WISE 1849" (generally in the first thirty leaves, and in a half-dozen leaves between fols. 91 and 104), "C ANSELL 1851" (generally throughout the manuscript beginning with fol. 35), and "C ANSELL 1852" (in additional leaves, e.g. fol. 1, and in some of those replacing the rejected leaves). The paper was apparently that used in the East India Company office where Mill was employed; at the end of the rejected leaves there is a transcript on the same paper (a leaf marked "C ANSELL 1851") of part of an undated letter to a Hyderabad government official. Mill wrote in ink generally on both sides. Before beginning a leaf, he folded it once down the middle, to divide each page into two long halves slightly more than four inches wide; he originally wrote only in the right-hand half, saving the space at left for his revisions and for corrections and comments by his wife.

In the later draft, Mill describes the "double redaction" method by which "all my books have been composed": [6]

They were always written at least twice over; a first draft of the entire work was completed . . . then the whole begun again *de novo;* but incorporating, in the second writing, all sentences and parts of sentences of the old draft, which appeared as suitable to my purpose as anything which I could write in lieu of them. . . . [This system] combines, better than any other mode of composition, the freshness and vigour of the first conception, with the superior precision and completeness resulting from prolonged thought. In my own case, moreover, I have found that the patience necessary for a careful elaboration of the details of composition and expression, costs much less effort after the entire subject has been once gone through, and the substance of all that I find to say has in some manner, however imperfect, been got upon paper. The only thing which I am careful, in the first draft, to make as perfect as I am able, is the arrangement.

In the terms of this passage, the Hollander-Illinois manuscript is Mill's first draft, and the first three-fourths of the Columbia manuscript, in which he copied and rewrote the early draft, is the "second writing." But within the early draft a good deal of revision is evidenced by the frequency of cancellations, interlineations, additional passages written and rewritten at left, and even the perfecting of the original "arrangement." Mill foliated the draft in pencil, and most of the leaves show evidence of having been renumbered one or more times, so that the facts of the addition or reordering of leaves and the substitution of revised for rejected leaves can be determined by the reconstruction of original sequences from the earlier, erased folio numbers.[7] Moreover, except possibly for the revised leaves that replaced the rejected leaves of the original Part II, Harriet Mill read the entire manu-

---

[6] Columbia edition, pp. 155–156.

[7] These facts are given in notes to the text and in headnotes to the extracts from the rejected leaves. Perhaps the most interesting among them is the evidence of Mill's early intention to divide the work into two parts, the first covering his life before he met Harriet Taylor, and "Part II.," beginning with his "first introduction to the lady whose friendship has been the honour & blessing of my existence." Possibly because he wished to introduce her at an earlier point in his account (after his writings of 1832, rather than, as originally, after his writings of 1834 and Molesworth's proposal in that year to establish the *London and Westminster Review*), possibly also because the two parts were of considerably disproportionate lengths (121 vs. 24 leaves), Mill rearranged several paragraphs, condensed the first eight leaves of Part II to three and a half, and discarded the two-part division altogether (see pp. 190–191).

script,[8] marking passages with lines, X's, and question marks in the margin, deleting and sometimes rewriting Mill's text, occasionally commenting in the space at left; and Mill followed many of her suggestions and introduced most of her penciled alterations by rewriting them in ink.

The draft cannot be dated as precisely or as securely as one would wish. The limits set by the factual details of the text seem to be roughly 1853-56—that is, if we interpret Mill's words literally, sometime after October 1852, when the *Edinburgh Review* had lasted "fifty [years] & upwards" [9] since its beginning in October 1802 (p. 91), and before March 1856, when Mill was appointed Chief Examiner in the India House (see p. 85—"this has continued to be my official duty"—and n. 221). It is probably not significant, considering Mill's estimate of him, that John Bowring, who was knighted on 16 February 1854, is called "Mr" (p. 90) rather than, as in the later draft, "Mr. (now Sir John)"; but it is worth noting that in recounting his "longer absences . . . under medical advice" from the India House (p. 87) Mill includes neither his three-months' leave of October-December 1853 nor his nearly nine-months' absence of December 1854-August 1855. We may look to his letters, however, for more specific evidence.

In his extant letters Mill first mentions the early draft on 23 January 1854, four days after recording in a diary entry his bitterness at having "procrastinated in the sacred duty of fixing in writing . . . everything that I have in my mind which is capable

---

[8] Penciled markings, alterations, or comments appear in ninety of the 169 leaves; they are absent most notably in fols. 115–120, 132–133, 137–139 (revised leaves replacing R119–121, RII.1–8, 20, 24). Except for the folio number on each leaf, a query written at left in fol. 52r (see p. 87, n. 228), and the original entering of Coleridge's lines in fol. 82v (see p. 118, n. 339), all penciled writings involving words, letters, or numbers are demonstrably in Harriet Mill's hand. (I am obliged to Mr. G. Woledge, Librarian of the British Library of Political and Economic Science, London, for providing specimens of Harriet's handwriting; the photostat of a letter to Mill dated 14–15 February 1854 has been, because of its date and the fact that it is written in pencil, especially helpful.) Simple markings—lines in the margin, X's, underlinings, and the like—are another matter, but they are uniformly done in ways that differ from Mill's own methods of marking and striking through; and it is an assumption that I have felt strong enough to treat as fact throughout this edition that all pencilings in the draft, with the exceptions just noted, are the work of Harriet Mill.

[9] The words "& upwards" are interlined, but in the same ink as the original writing and apparently with the same pen.

of assisting the destruction of error and prejudice and the growth of just feelings and true opinions." [10] Replying to a letter now lost, he writes to his wife: [11]

I too have thought very often lately about the life & am most anxious that we should complete it the soonest possible. What there is of it is in a perfectly publishable state—As far as writing goes it could be printed tomorrow—& it contains a full writing out as far as anything can write out, what you are, as far as I am competent to describe you, & what I owe to you—but, besides that until revised by you it is little better than unwritten, it contains nothing about our private circumstances, further than shewing that there was intimate friendship for many years, & you only can decide what more it is necessary or desirable to say in order to stop the mouths of enemies hereafter. The fact is there is about as much written as I *can* write without your help & we must go through this together & add the rest to it at the very first opportunity—I have not forgotten what she said about bringing it with me to Paris.

He discusses the subject at length again on 10 February: [12]

I . . . have read through all that is written of the Life—I find it wants revision, which I shall give it—but I do not well know what to do with some of the passages which we marked for alteration in the early part of it which we read together. They were mostly passages in which I had written, you thought, too much of the truth or what I believe to be the truth about my own defects. I certainly do not desire to say more about them than integrity requires, but the difficult matter is to decide how much that is. Of course one does not, in writing a life, either one's own or another's, undertake to tell everything—& it will be right to put something into *this* which shall prevent any one from being able to suppose or to pretend, that we undertake to keep nothing back. Still

---

[10] *The Letters of John Stuart Mill,* ed. Hugh S. R. Elliot (London, 1910), II, 361.

[11] Hayek, p. 190. While referring wherever possible to Hayek's edition of the letters, I have quoted from the original documents in the Yale University Library, and my quotations occasionally differ in minor details from the printed text. In this and the following paragraphs on dating, I am in part going over ground already covered by Professor Levi, who in "The Writing of Mill's *Autobiography,*" p. 293, concludes: "The first draft . . . was undoubtedly begun and probably completed between April, 1853, and April, 1854. I believe it to have been started in Nice in November, 1853, and to have been largely composed during the first three months of 1854." I would agree, give or take a few weeks, with the first statement, but not with the narrower limits proposed in the second.

[12] Hayek, p. 194. Between 23 January and 10 February the "Life" is mentioned briefly in two other letters: "I fancy I see one large or two small posthumous volumes of Essays, with the Life at their head," he writes on 29 January (Hayek, p. 191); and on 4 February he promises to "look again through the Life" when he has finished rewriting "Nature" (Yale University Library).

it va sans dire that it ought to be on the whole a fair representation. Since things appear to me on looking at them now to be said very crudely, which does not surprise me in a first draft, in which the essential was to say everything somehow, sauf to omit or revise afterwards. As to matters of opinion & feeling on general subjects, I find there is a great deal of good matter written down in the Life which we have not written anywhere else, & which will make it as valuable in that respect (apart from its main object) as the best things we have published. But of what particularly concerns *our* life there is nothing yet written, except the descriptions of you, & of your effect on me; which are at all events a permanent memorial of what I know you to be, & (so far as it can be shewn by generalities) of what I owe to you *intellectually*. That, though it is the smallest part of what you are to me, is the most important to commemorate, as people are comparatively willing to suppose all the rest. But we have to consider, which we can only do together, how much of our story it is advisable to tell, in order to make head against the representations of enemies when we shall not be alive to add anything to it. If it was not to be published for 100 years I should say, tell all, simply & without reserve. As it is there must be care taken not to put arms into the hands of the enemy.

Taken together, the two letters show (1) that an early form of the draft, including at least the first eight leaves of the original Part II,[13] largely unrevised since it was first written but nevertheless "in a perfectly publishable state," was finished by 23 January 1854; (2) that Mill and his wife had read an "early part of it" together, marking passages for alteration (those extracted in the section on rejected leaves from R23–25, and possibly Mill's subsequent revisions of them—in $R24^2$–25^2 and R19/20, also marked by her—are more or less specifically mentioned in the second letter); but (3) that Harriet had not yet read any portion of the original Part II, in which she and their relationship are described. Up to this point, therefore, there were at least two periods of composition—one in which he wrote the early part that they read and marked together, the other in which he continued writing in her absence.

---

[13] But apparently not the whole of Part II—or, specifically, not the text of RII.20 (see p. 10)—since Mill says in both letters that he has written nothing of their "private circumstances." Two breaks in the composition of Part II are evident from changes in pen. Following the text of the extract given from RII.1–8 (pp. 191–200), Mill began a new paragraph ("In the years between 1834 & 1840 . . .") with a fresh pen, considerably finer than the first, with which he continued through most of the present fol. 126*v*, the original fol. 14 of Part II, up to the sentence beginning, "I had followed the course of Canadian events . . ." (p. 164). Thereafter, to the end of Part II, he wrote again with a heavier pen.

We have, unfortunately, virtually no biographical documents for the first two years of their marriage, after they had returned from the Continent and settled at Blackheath Park in September 1851.[14] In August 1853 Mill took his wife to Sidmouth, Devonshire, returning to London alone on the 25th—the first time since his marriage that they had been separated. He remained in London through September, and then, presumably at the beginning of October, accompanied his wife to the south of France. When his three-months' grant of absence from the India House had expired, he left her at Hyères, on 27 or 28 December, and arrived back in London on 5 January.

It is unlikely that he worked on the draft between 5 and 23 January (the date of the first letter quoted above). On his return he was occupied with official correspondence that had accumulated in his absence, and of his own work he was primarily concerned with the essay on "Nature." He told Harriet on the 14th, "I am working hard at getting up the arrear of India house business & have taken some of it home to work at tomorrow (Sunday). I hardly feel well or vigorous enough to set about any work of our own yet on Sundays & in the evenings—when I do the first thing shall be to finish the rewriting of the paper on Nature, which I began before we left." [15] Moreover, the tone of his letter of the 23rd ("I too have thought very often lately about the life") does not suggest that he has been writing. What seems most probable, if we assume that he began the draft in London, perhaps even (as he did with other works) during office hours at the India House when correspondence lagged, is that he commenced writing earlier than August 1853; that he and his wife read and marked the early part (at least the first twenty-five leaves) before going to Devonshire in that month; and that he continued writing, through at least the first eight leaves of Part II, in the August-September interval of separation, before joining her for the trip abroad. A large part of the draft, the "publishable" version described in the letter of 23 January, should therefore be dated earlier than October 1853.

On 13 February 1854, still planning to join his wife in Paris, Mill again mentioned bringing the draft with him, and added: "But if we are not to be together this summer it is doubly im-

---

[14] Hayek, p. 183.   [15] Yale University Library

portant to have as much of the life written as can be written before we meet—therefore will you . . . in one of your sweetest
letters give me your general notion of what we should say or imply
respecting our private concerns. As it is, it shews confidential
friendship & strong attachment ending in marriage when you were
free & ignores there having ever been any scandalous suspicions
about us." [16] To his earlier letter of the 10th Harriet replied on
14–15 February: [17]

I feel sure dear that the Life is not half written and that half that is
written will not do. Should there not be a summary of our relationship
from its commencement in 1830—I mean given in a dozen lines. . . .
This ought to be done in its genuine truth and simplicity—strong affection, intimacy of friendship, and no impropriety. It seems to me an
edifying picture for those poor wretches who cannot conceive friendship but in sex—nor believe that expediency and the consideration for
feelings of others can conquer sensuality.

While her letter was in the mail Mill wrote to her again on the
18th that he was "most anxious at present about the Life, but . . .
can do little in the way of addition to it till I hear from her," [18]
and a diary entry of 19 February implies further concern with the
life: "Goethe . . . [called] his autobiography, which tells just
as much about himself as he liked to be known, 'Aus meinem
Leben Dichtung und Wahrheit.' The *Aus* even without the *Dichtung*
saves his veracity." [19] Finally on the 20th, having received her
letter, he was able to report some progress in the work: [20]

As to the Life—which I have been revising & correcting—the greater
part, in bulk, of what is written consists of the history of my mind *up to*
the time when your influence over it began—& I do not think there can
be much objectionable in that part, even including as it does, sketches
of the character of most of the people I was intimate with—if I could
be said to be so with any one. I quite agree in the sort of résumé of our
relationship which you suggest—but if it is to be only as you say a
dozen lines, or even three or four dozen, could you not . . . write it
out your darling self & send it in one of your precious letters—It is one
of the many things of which the *fond* would be much better laid by
you & we can add to it afterwards if we see occasion.

On 5 February Mill had finished rewriting "Nature"; on 5
March, having caught up with the India House correspondence,

---

[16] Hayek, p. 197.   [17] Hayek, p. 196.
[18] Yale University Library. (Mill here, as often in his letters to her, refers to
his wife in the third person.)
[19] *Letters*, II, 373.   [20] Hayek, p. 197.

he began writing "Utility of Religion." [21] Between those dates, and especially around 20 February, when we have seen him "revising & correcting," Mill read over and revised the whole of the draft he had written in 1853, and it was probably then also that he finished writing the original Part II. Professor Levi is surely right in suggesting that a passage from Harriet's letter of 14–15 February ("strong affection, intimacy of friendship . . . an edifying picture for those poor wretches who cannot conceive friendship but in sex—nor believe that expediency and the consideration for feelings of others can conquer sensuality") is echoed in Mill's account of their relationship in the twentieth leaf of Part II:

> . . . our relation to each other was one of strong affection & confidential intimacy, entirely apart from sensuality. . . . [We] disdained, as every person not a slave of his animal appetites must do, the abject notion that the strongest & tenderest friendship cannot exist between a man & a woman without a sensual tie; or that sensuality cannot be put aside when regard for the feelings of others, or even when only prudence & personal dignity require it.[22]

Harriet did not otherwise send him the account he requested, for of the numbered series of Mill's letters to her during this period all but one—a short letter addressed to Marseilles on 13 March—are extant between 20 February and the middle of March, and the draft is not mentioned in any letter after 24 February, when Mill wrote: "We must do what we can while we are alive—The Life being the first thing—which independent of the personal matters which it will set right when we have made it what we intend, is even now an unreserved proclamation of our opinions on religion, nature, & much else." [23]

Harriet returned to London in the middle of April, and it must have been either then or shortly afterward—"the Life being the first thing"—that she read and "improved" the remainder of the draft. Though no useful terminal date for Mill's subsequent corrections can be assigned as fact, it seems most reasonable to suppose that he revised and rewrote the leaves of Part II before leaving on his six-weeks' tour of Brittany (10 June–26 or 27 July 1854), and certainly before setting out on his extended tour of

---

[21] Hayek, p. 192; letter to Harriet of 6 March 1854 (Yale University Library).

[22] Levi, "The Writing of Mill's *Autobiography*," p. 292. The passage from RII.20 was rewritten in fol. 133: see p. 171 and nn. 490–492.

[23] Hayek, p. 200. If Mill's "much else" includes political opinions, the text of fols. 134–135 (see pp. 172–173), the original fols. 21–22 of Part II, must have been written by this date.

France, Italy, and Greece (8 December 1854–late June 1855), during which he was separated from his wife for nearly seven months.

III

"All the earlier part of the Memoir was revised at least twice by Mr Mill himself," Helen Taylor told Alexander Bain on 14 September 1873.[24] She refers to Mill's rewriting of the early draft in 1861, when he copied it into the first 159 leaves of the Columbia draft, and to his efforts of the winter of 1869–70, when he completed the work and presumably gave the whole a final going-over.[25] Between the early draft and the corresponding text of the Columbia draft there are some 2,600 substantive variants, large and small, of which a few may be noticed here.[26]

With the distance gained by the lapse of seven or more years since writing the early draft, Mill viewed the events of his life with increased detachment. He could now write of his heavy dejection during the mental crisis, for example, as "the state . . . in which converts to Methodism usually are, when smitten by their first 'conviction of sin,' " and add, more soberly, "In all probability my case was by no means so peculiar as I fancied it, and I doubt not that many others have passed through a similar state." [27] This new objectivity dictated a number of changes by which earlier outbursts of egotism, contrasting strikingly with the characteristic self-effacement that marks much of the work, were deflated or restrained. "I had now also begun to converse," Mill writes in the early draft—of himself at the age of fifteen or sixteen, exchanging opinions with Ricardo, Grote, and other of his father's friends—

[24] Mill-Taylor Collection (British Library of Political and Economic Science), vol. 4, item 18; Helen Taylor's letter is given in full in the Rylands *Bulletin,* XLIII, 235–237.

[25] The dating is based on Helen Taylor's notes in the 1873 edition, pp. 240, 251; on Mill's own text—"the question now stands (1870)" (Columbia edition, p. 201); and on Helen Taylor's manuscript continuation of the *Autobiography* (Mill-Taylor Collection, box 1, item 32), which begins: "The last portion of this memoir was written, at Avignon, in the winter of 1869–1870" (see the Rylands *Bulletin,* XLIII, 238).

[26] I have not otherwise recorded Mill's changes between the early and later drafts. To facilitate comparison, however, a running series of references to the later text, as printed in both the Columbia edition and the Oxford World's Classics reprint of the first edition, is provided in the headlines in a manner explained below on p. 30.

[27] Columbia edition, pp. 94, 98–99.

"on terms of equality" (p. 79); in the later draft the last four words are rewritten: "on general subjects." Two sentences of the early draft telling that in a debate with the Owenites "I myself spoke oftener than any one else on our side. . . . Ellis & Roebuck took a prominent part" (p. 111) are severely reduced in the later: "Ellis, Roebuck, and I took an active part in the debate"; and parts of his earlier estimation of his speeches in the London Debating Society—"nothing I ever wrote was more carefully elaborated both in matter and expression," and "many of my speeches were of some worth as compositions" (p. 115)—are omitted. Where in 1854 Mill felt that his *Principles of Political Economy* had "both widened the basis of the science itself & made many useful applications of its truths in conjunction with others, to the improvement of human practice, moral, political, & social" (p. 176), in 1861 he more modestly left its evaluation to the reader: "The amount of its worth as an exposition of the science, and the value of the different applications which it suggests, others of course must judge."

Occasionally, for passages first written specifically about himself, Mill substituted generalization. The statement in the early draft, "I have ever felt myself, beyond any modern that I know of except my father & perhaps beyond even him, a pupil of Plato, & cast in the mould of his dialectics" (p. 48), is later applied to anyone who can qualify: "I have felt ever since that the title of Platonist belongs by far better right to those who have been nourished in, and have endeavoured to practise Plato's mode of investigation, than to those who are distinguished only by the adoption of certain dogmatical conclusions. . . ." And many specific details of his life are omitted from the later account: his meeting with the Frenchmen Ternaux, Destutt de Tracy, Dunoyer, and the others (p. 72); "emulation of a little manuscript essay of Mr Grote" in attempting his first argumentative composition (p. 78); writing an early essay replying to Paley's *Natural Theology* (p. 79); keeping a journal, in order to chronicle the activities of the Utilitarian radicals "on the model of Grimm's Correspondence," and contributing three or four articles to Charles Austin's projected "Philosophical Dictionary, suggested by Voltaire's" (p. 101); [28] the

[28] Most of fol. 66r is replaced in the later draft by a single sentence: "No one of the set went to so great excesses in this boyish ambition as I did; which might be shown by many particulars, were it not an useless waste of space and time" (Columbia edition, p. 76).

weekly evening meetings with friends to study elocution (p. 110); his elaborate reply in the Owenite debate to Thirlwall, who was not present to hear it, and his meeting with Thirlwall at Guizot's in 1840 (p. 112); a note on his frequent mistiming of articles (p. 144); the reading of Carlyle's article on Johnson "with enthusiastic admiration" (p. 145); the opinion that among his literary articles in the *London and Westminster Review* "the one which contained most thought was on Alfred de Vigny" (p. 165)—and so on. Some of these details are known through other sources, of course, but by their omission both the texture and the tone of the work are altered. It is a fuller and more varied life that he presents in the early draft.

Here and there Mill toned down his recollections of family relationships and especially of his father. Indirect references to his mother, in speaking of his father's "ill assorted marriage" (p. 66), "to which he had not, & never could have supposed that he had, the inducements of kindred intellect, tastes, or pursuits" (p. 36), are charitably omitted. His father's "authority & indignation" (p. 42) is rewritten as "displeasure"; and the fact that he "often mockingly caricatured" Mill's bad reading (p. 49) is discarded, along with mention of the futile "short sharp contest[s]" between them over differences in opinion (p. 149) and his father's "asperities of temper" (p. 66). In a summary comment on his rigid upbringing, Mill wrote in 1853–54, "It was one of the most unfavourable of the moral agencies which acted on me in my boyhood, that mine was not an education of love but of fear" (p. 66); whether or not his attitude changed, the corresponding passage in the later draft is much less decisive: "As regards my own education, I hesitate to pronounce whether I was more a loser or gainer by his severity." By changes of this sort, with the addition of several sentences comparing his father with Bentham,[29] the later draft comes considerably closer than the earlier to being, in the passages describing him, a eulogy of his father.

The same access of charity is evident in recollections of intimate associates outside his family—if Mill could be said to have been intimate with any of them.[30] The most extensive omissions from the later draft are the greater part of his "character" of Roebuck (most of fols. 91–92, 93v–94r, and a part of 94v, pp. 127–131) and

---

[29] Columbia edition, pp. 142–143.
[30] See the letter of 20 February 1854, quoted on p. 9.

his paragraph of invidious commentary on Sarah Austin (fols. 110v–111v, pp. 147–148), both of whom were still alive when he rewrote the early draft. Roebuck's error, as he later told Bain, lay in "foolishly . . . remonstrating with Mill on the danger to his future prospects from his relation to Mrs. Taylor." [31] Mill, however, attributes the schism between them to disputes over the "culture of the feelings"—Roebuck taking the "unfeeling side"—and he goes on to give a melancholy account of failure in which Roebuck, married and entrapped in "the petty vanities & entanglements of what is called society," gradually became "a panegyrist of England & things English, a conformist to the Church, & in short merged in the common herd of Conservative Liberals." Mrs. Austin, on the other hand, was a gossip, and there had been political differences between them over the Revolution of 1848; [32] but among the faults enumerated in the draft, a principal one, apart from her "very mischievous tongue," was the habitual echoing of her husband's opinions—a fault that some critics have supposed Mill did not recognize in his own wife.

Mill softened his critique of Maurice (pp. 131–132) in the later draft, and rewrote his account of Sterling (p. 133), omitting mention of the vehement encounter between them that resulted in Sterling's withdrawal from the Debating Society and their becoming closer friends privately afterward. A page on Grote's personal deficiencies (fol. 119r, p. 155) was omitted when, seeing "on a calm retrospect" that the radicals in the first Reformed Parliament "were less in fault than we supposed," [33] Mill wrote abstractly of his and his father's failure to find "some competent leader." Other details are left out, such as the claim that Grote began his *History of Greece* "at my father's instigation" (p. 94—Mrs. Grote says it was originally her idea), [34] mention of

---

[31] Alexander Bain, *John Stuart Mill. A Criticism* (London, 1882), p. 39. In his fragmentary autobiography, Roebuck tells that he "most unwisely" sought out Mill at the India House "and then frankly told him what I thought might result from his connection with Mrs. Taylor. He received my warnings coldly, and after some time I took my leave, little thinking what effect my remonstrances had produced." When he called again next day, "the moment I entered the room I saw that, as far as he was concerned, our friendship was at an end. His manner was not merely cold, but repulsive; and I, seeing how matters were, left him" (Robert Eadon Leader, *Life and Letters of John Arthur Roebuck* [London, 1897], p. 39).

[32] Packe, pp. 322–323.   [33] Columbia edition, p. 137.

[34] Harriet Grote, *The Personal Life of George Grote* (London, 1873), p. 49.

the contributions of Praed, Robert Hildyard, Henry Taylor, Vernon and Leveson Smith in the Debating Society (pp. 113–114), Fonblanque's degeneration into "little better than . . . supporter & panegyrist" of the Whigs (p. 156), and Falconer's resignation of the nominal editorship of the *London and Westminster Review* (p. 161)—their omission again contributing to the more formal and generalized character of the later version.

IV

Mill's successive revisions *within* the early draft show the same kind of progress from private to public, and from public to more public, voice. Often at the suggestion of Harriet, he suppressed personal and family details that, had they been kept in the later draft, would have made the *Autobiography* a more recognizably human document, and less of a purely expository account of "thought processes and psychic states": [35] his early imitation of his father's note taking (p. 39, n. 18), his total disregard for his mother's remonstrances (p. 56, n. 105), the arrangement between his father and Bentham in the renting of their house in Queen Square (p. 68, n. 160), a long note on the "mode of life" at Ford Abbey when the Mills visited Bentham (pp. 68–69, n. 163), his walk by the Thames that "insensibly changed my state" in 1828 (p. 125, n. 360), the *Examiner's* loss of nearly two hundred subscribers by his 1832 articles on "Pledges" (p. 144, n. 424), his being made to omit from his review article on Sedgwick two or three pages "which my father considered as an attack on Bentham & on him" (p. 158, n. 463). Again frequently with Harriet's help, by curtailing or emending comment on his "various deficiencies," he gave in many places a better account of his abilities than he had at first put down. His lack of information in modern history is rewritten as a lack of interest (p. 43, n. 43), for example, and his estimation that in natural gifts he was "rather below than above par" originally read, "not only not above par, but decidedly & greatly below it" (p. 54, n. 91).[36] At the other end of the scale of self-opinion, occasional bits of puffery are reduced or omitted, like his notion that "there is nothing for which I am more indebted to my father than for thus effectually

[35] See Wayne Shumaker, *English Autobiography: Its Emergence, Materials, and Form* (Berkeley and Los Angeles, Calif., 1954), pp. 142–146, for extended comment on the *Autobiography's* lack of detail.

[36] See also pp. 48, 70, 72, 79, 93, nn. 61, 166, 174, 201, 245.

preventing the growth of self conceit; for I affirm with confidence that I had not at this period of life, the smallest vestige of it" (p. 56, n. 103)—or that his 1825 articles in the *Parliamentary History and Review* were "fully equal to the best things which had been written on the same class of subjects" (p. 108, n. 302).

More important than any of the separate changes in tone and detail, however, is the way in which the canceled passages in the draft, especially in the rejected leaves, generally illuminate Mill's character and personality in the three areas that he himself considered the major concerns of the work: his early education at the hands of his father; the "successive phases" of his mind, including the mental crisis of 1826; and his intellectual obligations—of which the chief, by his own account, was his debt to his wife. The facts of Mill's extraordinary education, beginning with Greek at the age of three and including Latin at seven, logic at twelve, and a course of political economy at thirteen, are well known. Mill says it was *not* an "education of cram" (p. 54)—"I was not *crammed*; my own thinking faculties were called into strong though but partial play," he told Carlyle [37]—but contemporary opinion prevailed to the contrary.[38] By persistent drilling, demands of the impos-

---

[37] On 22 October 1832 (Iris Wessel Mueller, *John Stuart Mill and French Thought* [Urbana, Ill., 1956], p. 13).

[38] Mill's middle sister Harriet, for example, reminiscing in 1873, called his education a course of "cramming" (Packe, p. 47), and Roebuck recalled that when he first met him (in 1824) Mill "was, as might have been expected, the mere exponent of other men's ideas, those men being his father and Bentham" (Leader, *Life and Letters of . . . Roebuck*, p. 28). Mill himself tells that Sterling and others considered him "a 'made' or manufactured man, having had a certain impress of opinion stamped upon me which I could only reproduce" (p. 132). While he says in one place that his father gave him "the habit of thinking for myself" (p. 149), he writes elsewhere, probably more truthfully, that he gave "implicit credence" to everything his father told him (p. 57), and that "it would have been totally inconsistent with my father's ideas of duty, to allow me to imbibe notions contrary to his convictions" (p. 60); he also speaks of having been "so drilled in a certain sort of mental exercise that I could carry it on when all the spirit had gone out of it" (p. 121). Much of the *Autobiography* is, of course, concerned with showing how he outgrew the narrowness of his "*taught* opinions" (p. 104), and it is worth noting how frequently he mentions, especially in canceled passages, the influence of *teaching* on him: his first contribution to the *Westminster Review* was "a theme written on the ideas which had been instilled into me by my teachers" (p. 93, n. 245); "I had been taught & was thoroughly persuaded . . ." (p. 119, n. 343); "I had been taught & had always been convinced . . ." (p. 119, n. 344); "I had been taught . . ." (p. 120, n. 346); his "early opinions" were, in first writing, those that he "had had the good fortune to be taught" (p. 140, n. 413). Even after his "inauguration as an original & independent thinker" (p. 110), the "thinkers

sible, and "vehement demonstrations of anger" at his failures (p. 55, n. 99), James Mill forced his son through just the sort of educational experiment that Wordsworth condemned as producing "a miracle of scientific lore": "For this unnatural growth the trainer blame, / Pity the tree.—Poor human vanity, / Wert thou extinguished, little would be left / Which he could truly love; but how escape?" [39]

It is similarly well known that this education of fear, under a father who had "scarcely any belief in pleasure," considering human life "a poor thing at best" and passionate emotions "a form of madness" (p. 63), was in some ways defective. "Not what a boy or a girl can repeat by rote, but what they have learnt to love and admire, is what forms their character," Mill wrote in reaction to it afterward.[40] He would not, he told Caroline Fox, recommend such a course to others, because "in most cases it would not answer, and where it does, the buoyancy of youth is entirely superseded by the maturity of manhood, and action is very likely to be merged in reflection": "it is better to let Nature have her own way." [41] His education was not only strenuous and severely passionless (except where his father's temper supplied passion), but entirely abstract, turning him out, as he described himself to Carlyle,[42] "a schoolboy fresh from the logic school, [who] had never conversed with a reality, never seen one, knew not what manner of thing it was." His father trusted exclusively in theory—what he called "the *whole* of the knowledge, which we possess upon any subject"—and believed that good practice could in no case have

---

with whom I was now becoming acquainted" were his "new instructors" (p. 137, n. 404), and, after he met her, Harriet was of course his "main instructor" (p. 153, n. 447) and he "wholly her pupil" (p. 169, n. 485; see also pp. 192, 195). Still later, his stepdaughter became for him an "instructor of the rarest quality" (see p. 27, n. 73).

[39] *The Prelude,* V.315, 328–331.

[40] *London and Westminster Review,* VI and XXVIII (1838), 469; quoted by K. J. Fielding, "Mill and Gradgrind," *Nineteenth-Century Fiction,* XI (1956), 150.

[41] Caroline Fox, *Memories of Old Friends,* ed. Horace N. Pym (London, 1882), p. 85 (journal entry for 10 April 1840).

[42] *Letters,* I, 88 (12 January 1834). Mill is describing his state during the "two or three years" in which "the description commonly given of a Benthamite, as a dry, hard logical machine, was as much applicable to me, as it can well be applicable to any one just entering into life" (p. 101)—a time when, he says in a canceled passage in the draft, he and his friends had "no idea of real culture. In our schemes for improving human affairs we overlooked human beings" (p. 103, n. 279).

any solid foundation without it.[43] The trouble was that his scheme for his son included no theory to cover knot tying, for example, or personal relationships, or a mental crisis; and the theory of education itself was unsound.

Nowhere outside the early draft does Mill write so candidly of "the very considerable drawbacks" with which his education was accompanied—results "which have pursued me through life" (p. 54, n. 93). For one thing, he grew up, he says, "with great inaptness in the common affairs of every day life. I was far longer than children generally are before I could put on my clothes. I know not how many years passed before I could tie a knot. My articulation was long imperfect; one letter, *r*, I could not pronounce until I was nearly sixteen. I never could, nor can I now, do anything requiring the smallest manual dexterity." He was isolated from other boys, and suffered the additional misfortune of "having, in domestic matters, everything done for me" (pp. 178–181). Mill wrote three successive accounts of these deficiencies, lamenting in each that his education was "much more fitted for training me to *know* than to *do*" (R24*r*, 24²*r*, 19/20*r*). At Harriet's insistence the subject was finally dropped altogether from the draft,[44] but his repeated attempts to include some mention of it, and the bitterness of some of his language (references to ungainliness, awkwardness, and "a thoroughly ineffective & bungling manner" occur in one deleted sentence), bear witness to a strong feeling in the matter.

Of two other consequences, itemized among the "many & indelible . . . effects of this bringing-up, in the stunting of my moral growth," one was habitual reserve: "Without knowing or believing that I was reserved, I grew up with an instinct of closeness. I had no one to whom I desired to express everything which I felt; & the only person I was in communication with, to whom I looked up, I had too much fear of, to make the communication to him of any act or feeling ever a matter of frank impulse or spontaneous inclination" (p. 184). The other, the result of being constantly under the rule of a strong will, was "a habit of backwardness, of waiting to follow the lead of others, an absence of moral spontaneity, an inactivity of the moral sense & even to a large extent, of the intellect."

---

[43] *James & John Stuart Mill on Education,* ed. F. A. Cavenagh (Cambridge, Eng., 1931), p. 4.

[44] It was reintroduced in the later draft (see Columbia edition, pp. 25–26).

From being always told what to do, he acquired "a habit of leaving my responsibility as a moral agent to rest on my father, my conscience never speaking to me except by his voice" (p. 185). Both passages tell a good deal about his personal relationships and provide a background for his mental crisis; taken with the earlier one on his lack of practical capacity, they allow some additional insight into his special attachment to his wife and his extraordinary claims of dependence upon her.

The famous mental crisis, beginning in the autumn of 1826, when Mill at the age of twenty paused to ask himself whether he would be happy if all his objects in life were immediately realized, and had to answer from an "irrepressible self-consciousness" that he would not, has been variously explained. Bain thought its causes physical, chiefly "over-working the brain," [45] and there is some vague support in Mill's first account of his condition: "I was, probably from physical causes (connected perhaps merely with the time of year) in a dull state of nerves . . ." (p. 117 and n. 334). What is above all clear, however, is that for the first time he began thinking for himself. The old ideas of good, impressed upon him by his father and always before taken for granted, were now put under analysis, and the shocking result was a breakdown of artificially created associations in which the accustomed pleasurable responses were suddenly stripped away from those ideas, leaving him without purpose in life. "The whole foundation on which my life was constructed fell down. . . . I had nothing left to live for" (p. 117). Except in its severity and duration (it lasted, with relapses, for at least three years), Mill's experience is not an uncommon one for youths approaching manhood. It occupies, however, a central position in the *Autobiography,* as the origin of a transformation that he later called "the only actual revolution which has ever taken place in my modes of thinking." [46]

For his suffering Mill blamed his father. "My education, which was wholly his work, had been conducted without any regard to the possibility of its ending in this result." At this point in the narrative, he laments not so much the fragility of the associations under which he had been brought up, or the inveterate habit of

---

[45] *John Stuart Mill. A Criticism,* p. 38. Sir Leslie Stephen, *The English Utilitarians* (London, 1900), III, 19, connects the crisis with Mill's exhausting editorial work in the preceding year on the five volumes of Bentham's *Rationale of Judicial Evidence.*

[46] Columbia edition, p. 133.

analysis that had been his undoing, as his inability to relieve his condition by communication with others.

> I sought no relief by speaking to others of what I felt. If I had loved any one sufficiently to make the confiding to them of my griefs a necessity, I should not have been in the condition I was. . . . Advice if I had known where to seek it would have been most precious. . . . But there was no one on whom I could build the faintest hope of such assistance. My father . . . was the last person to whom in such a case as this I looked for help. . . . Of other friends I had at that time none to whom I had any hope of making my condition intelligible [pp. 118–119].

But if it was a painful and lonely affair, it had positive results in Mill's mental progress, marking a gain of independence from his father's dominating influence. His recovery began when he read of the death of a father in Marmontel's *Mémoires,* and those who, from this fact, attribute his experience to repressed death wishes against his own father [47] have a good case, at least as it applies to his feelings twenty-five or more years after the event. Mill recalls that he was moved to tears by "the passage where . . . [Marmontel] relates his father's death, the distressed position of his family, & how he, then a mere boy, by a sudden inspiration, felt & made them feel that he would be everything, would supply the place of everything to them" (p. 121). Later in the draft, in his original account of his situation after James Mill's death, he seems to echo the last phrase of the sentence just quoted: "I had now to try how far I might be capable of supplying his place" (p. 160 and n. 470). A few pages before this he had written, of the men associated with the *London and Westminster Review,* "I could not even claim to be the most important individual, especially while my father lived" (p. 158 and n. 461).

In philosophical terms, the crisis came to symbolize a break not only with his father, but with Bentham and the eighteenth-century rationalism they represented. For him, its most important result was that he "now for the first time gave its proper place among the prime necessities of human well being, to the internal culture of the individual. . . . The cultivation of the feelings now became one of the cardinal points in my ethical & philosophical creed" (p. 123). Bowring described the change unsympathetically, saying that Mill "was most emphatically a philosopher, but then he

---

[47] Levi, "The 'Mental Crisis' of John Stuart Mill," and Lewis Samuel Feuer, *Psychoanalysis and Ethics* (Springfield, Ill., 1955), pp. 55–60.

read Wordsworth and that muddled him, and he has been in a strange confusion ever since, endeavouring to unite poetry and philosophy." [48] The new view runs through Mill's letters of the time. "Poetry is higher than logic, and . . . the union of the two is philosophy," he told Carlyle (5 July 1833); and a letter to Bulwer (23 November 1836) explains that the utilitarianism of the *London and Westminster Review* was to comprehend "the whole of human nature . . . [holding] feeling at least as valuable as thought, and Poetry not only on a par with, but the necessary condition of, any true and comprehensive Philosophy." Hostile critics have quickly urged, with Bowring, that poetry and logic produce "strange confusion," and some have held that all Mill's thinking after the crisis was marred by inconsistency. It is well to recall that Mill also recognized, in the letter to Carlyle just cited, that "the same person may be poet and logician, but he cannot be both in the same composition." [49]

His new "manysidedness," a "willingness and ability to learn from everybody," [50] embraced Coleridge and the Coleridgians, Goethe and other German writers, the Saint-Simonians, and Carlyle. But actually his modes of thinking changed less than he admits in the *Autobiography*. Before the crisis he was "speculatively indifferent to poetry, not hostile to it" (p. 103); afterward he was speculatively in favor of poetry, but still only speculatively, and at bottom he remained the remorseless logician. "Mill has singularly little sense of the concrete," Sterling observed in 1840, "and, though possessing deep feeling, has little poetry. He is the most scientific thinker extant." [51] This Mill himself had long known. "The only thing that I believe I am really fit for is the investigation of abstract truth," he had told Sterling nine years earlier, "and the more abstract the better. If there is any science which I am capable of promoting, I think it is the science of science itself, the science of investigation—of method." [52] Accordingly, in his search to unite poetry with philosophy, he turned to others for what he lacked in himself.

In this part of his life, he tells in a canceled passage in the draft, he "was in such a state of reaction against sectarianism of

---

[48] Fox, *Memories of Old Friends*, p. 113 (journal entry for 7 August 1840).
[49] *Letters*, I, 54–55, 103–104.   [50] Columbia edition, p. 172.
[51] Fox, *Memories of Old Friends*, p. 77 (journal entry for 25 March 1840).
[52] *Letters*, I, 8 (20–22 October 1831).

thought or feeling, that those in whom I recognized any kind of superiority I did not judge or criticize at all; I estimated them by that side of their qualities or achievements by which they were admirable & valuable to me, while whatever I saw that seemed criticizable . . . was simply uncounted & disregarded" (p. 145, n. 428). For a while, therefore, Carlyle, who sought him out in 1831 after reading his *Examiner* articles on "The Spirit of the Age," answered many of the requirements. He was a poet and a man of intuition, as Mill was not; his writings served "not as philosophy to instruct but as poetry to animate" (p. 145), and Mill regarded him as "perhaps the only genuine [artist] . . . now living in this country: the highest destiny of all lies in that direction; for it is the artist alone in whose hands Truth becomes impressive and a living principle of action." Mill offered his services "as an auxiliary" to him: "I am rather fitted to be a logical expounder than an artist." [53] But however subordinate Mill's part in their relationship, he was not to be made, as Carlyle had originally hoped, a convert to mysticism. The metaphysical and temperamental differences between them were too great, and Mill finally awoke to judge and criticize—after, he says in the *Autobiography*, Carlyle was interpreted to him "by one far the superior of us both . . . whose own mind & nature included all his & infinitely more" (p. 146).

"She had the same lone thoughts and wanderings, / The quest of hidden knowledge, and a mind / To comprehend the Universe." Byron's Manfred is speaking of Astarte,[54] but the tone is characteristic of Mill's own descriptions of his wife, whom he first met (as Mrs. Taylor) in 1830, and soon felt to be "the most admirable person I had ever known" (p. 151). More a poet than Carlyle, more a thinker than himself, and at least as great a promoter of freedom and progress as his father, she seemed the answer to all his needs (which did not include the physical); his relationship with her was the culminating event of his life, as he presents it in the early draft, for which all before had been preparatory training. She combined, in his eyes, a character of feeling with a vigorous speculative intellect, a poetic and artistic nature, and an eminent practical capacity (p. 199)—"the qualities which in all other persons whom I had known I had been only too happy to find singly"

---

[53] *Letters*, I, 35 (17 July 1832).   [54] *Manfred*, II.ii.109–111.

(p. 152). As he had earlier written of the "humbler" role he would accept in expounding Carlyle's ideas, so he would now—and for the rest of his life—serve "as a sort of prose interpreter of her poetry, giving a logical exposition to those who have more understanding than feeling, of the reasonableness of that which she either knew by . . . experience or divined by . . . intuition" (p. 199).[55] If he fully saw that she derived her opinions by "moral intuition" (p. 153)—by a method that some twenty-five pages later in the draft he described as "the great intellectual support for false doctrines and bad institutions . . . the main doctrinal pillar of all the errors which impede human improvement" (p. 168)—he was not ready to acknowledge any discrepancy in his evaluation; perhaps, as at first with Carlyle, he "did not judge or criticize at all." He had "never known any intellect in man or woman which, taken for all in all, could be compared to hers" (p. 194).

Few readers have suspended disbelief over such extravagant language. Reading proof of the *Autobiography*, Bain (whose acquaintance with Mill dates from 1839) wrote to Helen Taylor on 6 September 1873: [56]

> There is . . . one matter of extreme delicacy, which I have hitherto not remarked upon, but now at last venture to touch: I mean, the terms used in speaking of your mother. Of course, I know well the strength of his admiration for her great and various gifts, and I counted upon his expressing himself very strongly. But I greatly doubt the propriety of your printing those sentences where he declares her to be a greater poet than Carlyle . . . and a greater thinker than himself—and again, a greater leader than his father (or at all events an equal).[57] . . . I venture to express the opinion that no such combination has ever been realised in the history of the human race, and I am sure that many will take the same view: and the whole of his statements will be treated as pure hyperbole, proving, indeed, the strength of his feelings, but not the reality of the case. I think that your mother, yourself and Mr Mill, will all be placed in a false position, before the world by such extreme statements. Of course, I do not wish you now to consider the re-casting of the eulogy, but I would earnestly desire that you should omit those three phrases of comparison. The incredulous world will be sufficiently startled by what still remains, although for all that we were already prepared.

---

[55] See his letter to Carlyle cited in n. 53 above. Compare also his remarks in the draft that he arrived at "the same truths" as Carlyle and "many of the same results" as Harriet (pp. 145, 153) by a different mental process from theirs.

[56] Mill-Taylor Collection, vol. 4, item 15. Helen Taylor's reply is referred to in n. 24 above.

[57] See pp. 146, 160. I have omitted Bain's page references to the first edition.

To give you some idea of the effect produced by the language already published regarding your mother,[58] I may mention the impression made by it on the mind of the gentlest of human kind, and Mr Mill's tenderest friend—Mr Grote. His remark was to the effect that "only John Mill's reputation could have survived such an exhibition". We all admire his courage in avowing his feelings; but if people get the idea that he was liable to exaggerated judgments when the feelings were concerned, they will be apt to set aside his authority on questions generally.

The comparisons were, of course, allowed to stand, and nine years later Bain summed up an opinion that has prevailed ever since:

Unfortunately . . . [Mill] outraged all reasonable credibility in describing her matchless genius, without being able to supply any corroborating testimony. Such a state of subjection to the will of another, as he candidly avows, and glories in, cannot be received as a right state of things. It violates our sense of due proportion, in the relationship of human beings. Still, it is but the natural outcome of his extraordinary hallucination as to the personal qualities of his wife.

The commoner way of representing Harriet's ascendancy—"that she imbibed all his views, and gave them back in her own form, by which he was flattered and pleased"—Bain calls "merest conjecture"; his own explanation is that she set Mill's faculties in motion by "intelligently controverting" his ideas.[59] But according to Harold Laski, Bain told John Morley that Harriet "repeated to . . . [Mill] in the morning what he had said to her the night before and astounded him by the depth of her grasp." And when Justice Holmes innocently inquired about her—"I have a general notion that the world didn't rate her as highly as he did"—Laski replied:

I believe that he was literally the only person who was in the least impressed by her. Mrs. Grote said briefly that she was a stupid woman; Bain said she had a knack of repeating prettily what J. S. M. said and that he told her it was wonderful; Morley told me that Louis Blanc told him he once sat for an hour with her and that she repeated to him what afterwards turned out to be an article Mill had just finished for the *Edinburgh*. I should guess that she was a comfortable and sympathetic person and that Mill, brought up to fight Austin, Praed, Macaulay and

[58] He refers to the dedication inserted in some copies of *Principles of Political Economy* (1848), the dedication of *On Liberty* (1859), and the preface to the reprint of "Enfranchisement of Women" in the second volume of *Dissertations and Discussions* (1859). There was also Mill's inscription on Harriet's grave at Avignon (see Hayek, p. 267).

[59] *John Stuart Mill. A Criticism*, pp. 171, 173.

Grote, had never met a really soft cushion before. If she was what he thought, someone else at least should have given us indications.[60]

No one has given such indications,[61] and the observation of Mill's youngest brother George, who knew Harriet better than anyone else in the family, must be allowed to stand: "Mrs. Taylor was a clever and remarkable woman, but nothing like what John took her to be." [62] Her alterations in the early draft show her to have had some sense of style and propriety of tone, but they do not confirm Mill's estimate of her intellectual qualities. Neither do the letters and documents published by Professor Hayek, in the fullest factual account of their relationship, *John Stuart Mill and Harriet Taylor* (1951). The view of her there is less attractive than any we have had before, and one reviewer remarked that the letters "not only show Mill to have been injudicious about Mrs. Taylor, they show Mrs. Taylor to have been one of the meanest and dullest ladies in literary history, a monument of nasty self-regard, as lacking in charm as in grandeur. . . . Prideful, vain and meanspirited—it is not a pretty picture." [63]

What significantly does emerge from their correspondence, especially from letters and parts of letters omitted by Professor Hayek,[64] is Mill's fantastic dependence upon Harriet's judgment and approval in practical matters. He was virtually helpless in household affairs—having everything done for him was a "fatal" defect in his upbringing (p. 181, n. 18)—and it is not surprising, therefore, that when she was abroad he customarily sought her advice on every bill presented to him and every problem that arose concerning the servants. But his reliance on her went much further: from France she directed the gardening ("I have had the gardener to make it tidy but shall not have him any more till

---

[60] *Holmes-Laski Letters*, ed. Mark DeWolfe Howe (Cambridge, Mass., 1953), I, 471, 668, 675–676.

[61] See Guy Linton Diffenbaugh, "Mrs. Taylor Seen Through Other Eyes Than John Stuart Mill's," *Sewanee Review*, XXXI (1923), 198–204.

[62] Bain, *John Stuart Mill. A Criticism*, p. 166.

[63] Diana Trilling, "Mill's Intellectual Beacon," *Partisan Review*, XIX (1952), 116, 120.

[64] This and the next paragraph are based on Mill's letters to Harriet between August 1853 and July 1854 in the Yale University Library. Hayek rightly ignores much from these letters as too trivial ("Neither their maids' meat consumption, nor their neighbour's rats, nor all the voluminous reports about the momentary state of their health are suitable for printing"—p. 18), but their very triviality is the point of my own discussion here.

you tell me," he writes—"The garden shall be attended to exactly as you say"),[65] and told him where to sit at the supper table, what to eat, what shirts to wear to the doctor's. When (as rarely) he acted independently, she was displeased at his clumsiness. His typical apology to her almost embarrasses us: "I am so sorry the few words I wrote to Powell vexed her—I was much annoyed at having to write or do anything in such a matter without having time to consult her for I know I always miss the proper thing & above all the proper tone." The "matter" was that his neighbor, Powell, thought rats were entering his property through a wall between them. "I shall now do at once what my dearest one recommends . . . & shall write to Powell exactly as she says, & then send for his rat catcher." [66] He relied as heavily on her advice in other matters —in his correspondence, for example. On one occasion he described at length a volume presented to him by the South Carolina legislature, so that she could "judge whether a letter ought to be written in acknowledgment." He later wrote the letter, but sent a draft to her first for improvements.[67] The same procedure was followed in acknowledging a book from a Frenchman; when sending this draft, he asked her, "Shall I date it India House, or Blackheath?" [68]

It is notable, in the correspondence of these two self-styled reformers of the world's opinions, who worried whether there would be any thinkers after them,[69] how seldom *ideas* are touched on. In the letters of January-April 1854 (when he was rewriting "Nature," completing and revising the early draft of the *Autobiography,* beginning "Utility of Religion," and keeping a diary in which he entered at least one thought a day), Mill discusses his and Harriet's health, the prices of food, the quality and size of rooms in the inns he has stopped at, current news from the papers, his work at the India House—but hardly anything approaching a political or philosophical notion. Even in discussing the ballot

---

[65] Letters of 7 and 28 February 1854.

[66] Letter of 18 March 1854. What Mill calls "the Powell affair" is followed up on 3 April: "In answer to my note he sent the ratcatcher's address & offered to send him, but I made no answer & wrote to the man myself. Meanwhile he came again to Powell's & after finding one other rat, came on our premises unasked & Powell also—a piece of great impudence on P's part."

[67] Letters of 29 January, 18 February, and 3 March 1854. His letter "to the Chairman of the Library Committees, South Carolina" is printed in *Letters,* I, 179–180.

[68] Letters of 18 and 28 February 1854.   [69] Hayek, p. 191.

and other reform measures, he focuses on the practical matters of legislation, and not on theory. One feels ultimately that Mill spoke most truly when he said that his intellectual debt to her was "the smallest part of what you are to me."[70] And there is the further interesting point that, in spite of the ordinariness of their letters, he appears to have enjoyed her more as a correspondent than as a companion. In absence, her "words of love" kept his blood circulating, he wrote; without them he "should have only a sort of hybernating existence like those animals found in the inside of a rock."[71] Yet in the spring of 1854, when the time approached to join her in Paris, he delayed, complaining of an "unlucky complication," a boil on his chest; and when she determined to return home instead, he wrote, in a tone suggesting no particular anxiety to see her, "Pray my darling do not attempt the crossing till you feel better—much better. I am going on here with everything that can be done & your presence is not at all *necessary* pleasant as it will be."[72] Less than two months after her arrival he departed for Brittany, where he traveled for six weeks, and later in the same year, after staying home with her for four months, he again embarked alone, this time for a tour of nearly seven months' duration, from which he was notably tardy in returning to her.

What should appear most obvious from these details is that the Harriet of the incomparable intellect—the Harriet of the dedications, the memorial inscription, and the *Autobiography*—was largely a product of his imagination, an idealization, according to his peculiar needs, of a clever, domineering, in some ways perverse and selfish, invalid woman; such an idealization was better thought about and remembered than lived with. From the early draft, especially from the rejected leaves, we may recall those needs. Mill suffered "great inaptness" in practical affairs; Harriet now handled all those affairs for him.[73] Having grown up under a strong

---

[70] See his letter of 10 February 1854, quoted on p. 7.

[71] Letter of 12 September 1853. [72] Letters of 5 and 11 April 1854.

[73] After her death, her daughter took over in the same role, and in the later draft Mill extolled her—"Miss Helen Taylor, the inheritor of much of her wisdom, and of all her nobleness of character . . . another companion, stimulator, adviser, and instructor of the rarest quality"—in the same extravagant terms: all his work was now "the product not of one intellect and conscience, but of three, the least considerable of whom, and above all the least original, is the one whose name is attached to it" (Columbia edition, pp. 184–185; see also pp. 186, 189–190, 214, 216).

will, he lacked initiative and responsibility; she now supplied the strong will, taking up more or less where his father had left off in directing his activities. There was his habitual reserve, resulting in a loneliness that was unrelieved during his first twenty-five years by any completely satisfactory personal relationship; again she answered: "From the time when I could really call her my friend I wished for no other" (p. 193). Finally, in his reaction against the rationalism of his early education, against an abstract mode of theorizing that left out of reckoning the human beings whose good was the ultimate object, she represented, as a character of feeling, poetry, intuition, and humanity, just the qualities that he wished to unite with his own. It was but a short step, by endowing her with his own logical and empirical traits, to make her into a symbol of the perfect mind.

Two sentences from the original Part II of the draft, in a paragraph in which Mill discusses "the influence of this most precious friendship upon my own mental developement," are by their conjunction especially illuminating: "At a very early period of my knowledge of her she became to me a living type of the most admirable kind of human being.[74] I had always wished for a friend whom I could admire wholly, without reservation & restriction, & I had now found one" (pp. 198–199). On both the philosophical and the personal levels, she represented a measure of success in the life he was retracing. Indeed, in the original structure of the *Autobiography*, beginning with his education and proceeding through his mental crisis to a kind of salvation in his friendship and later marriage with her, the philosophical and personal concerns follow a parallel course throughout.[75] By revising and adding the history of twenty more years, Mill somewhat weakened and obscured this structure, and Harriet's place in it, but it is still, in the later draft, the basic scheme around which the account of his life is organized.

V

Every literary manuscript offers its own problems of presentation. The Hollander-Illinois draft, containing Mill's first attempts

---

[74] Similarly, Mill was for Harriet "the type of the possible elevation of humanity" (Hayek, p. 54).

[75] For a discussion of the structure of the *Autobiography* as "the movement of the human hero, John Stuart Mill, from the ægis of one demi-god, his father, to another, his wife, through the very human experience of his crisis," see Keith

at writing his life as well as the successive revisions by which in many passages he arrived at the final text (copied verbatim into the Columbia draft), is a heavily worked-over piece of writing. Theoretically it would be possible, by means of a narrative account of every detail of alteration, deletion, interlineation, and other peculiarity, to enable each reader *almost* accurately to reconstruct the manuscript in his own mind; but to give these details would require the space of perhaps seven or eight hundred pages, and such (at this point in both the study of Mill and the economic history of printing) is out of the question. A facsimile, whether in type or collotype, would for a variety of reasons serve no purpose. Acknowledging Necessity and Utility, therefore—printing costs on the one hand, and my concern for the majority of users of this volume on the other—I have taken some seemingly nonscholarly short cuts in giving only partial information about the manuscript.

The Text. In the section immediately following, the text above the notes represents Mill's final version of text *in the early draft,* reproduced exact and unemended save in the following particulars, all of which involve silent editorial emendations. (1) Superscript letters in "20th," "McCrie's," "Mr," "Dr," and a few other words and numerals have been lowered to the line. (2) Initial capitals of words originally beginning a sentence, but in revision subsequently rearranged into some other position within a sentence, have been reduced (four times) to lower case. (3) Periods have been added (about thirty-five times) to the ends of sentences where none appears—either because Mill did not punctuate at all, as at the end of a line, or because he failed to revise his punctuation when deleting or rewriting as a separate sentence a continuation of the original. (4) Commas have been introduced, as necessary or especially desirable (about 105 times), before and occasionally after interlined phrases or clauses; before deleted conjunctions; and at the ends of lines in the draft. (Many of these emendations simply carry out incomplete revisions; wherever the text was retained, they are, except for the lowering of superscripts, sanctioned by Mill's later version in the Columbia draft. Revisions apart, however, Mill was not especially careful of his punctuation, and like many another nineteenth-century writer he frequently

---

Rinehart, "John Stuart Mill's *Autobiography:* Its Art and Appeal," *University of Kansas City Review,* XIX (1953), 265–273.

used the line ending itself as punctuation, most notably when writing hastily in the middle of a long and involved sentence.) Besides the emendations covered by these general procedures, four other commas and a semicolon have been introduced, in all but one instance to complete Mill's revisions; in four places a word inadvertently left undeleted in revision has been omitted; a closing parenthesis has been inserted on page 116 (the text at the top of fol. 81r); quotation marks at the beginning of lines *within* quotations on pages 77 and 145 have been ignored; and asterisks have been added to Mill's text and note on page 144. Folio numbers, beginning with the verso of the first leaf, are given in the text within square brackets. In the headlines, bracketed page and line references (in the form 13:20 = page 13, line 20) preceded by the abbreviations *Col.* and *W.C.* locate, for every two facing pages of the present text, the beginning of the corresponding text of the later draft as printed in the Columbia edition and the Oxford World's Classics reprint of 1924.

Textual Notes. Disregarding Mill's hope that "nobody would think of reprinting what the writer had purposely rejected," [76] I have presented in the textual notes a selection of canceled readings preliminary to the final form of the manuscript text. The selection (from some four thousand notes originally compiled) is based in each case on the significance of the reading. Ignoring false starts, grammatical entanglements, slips of the pen, repetitions, and the like, I have attempted to give every earlier reading—whether subsequently rewritten or simply deleted—that clarifies, expands, or differs from the final meaning (including, of course, tone) of the text at the point at which the earlier reading occurs. Not every substantive change is recorded. For example, on page 52, for "become a member of the House of Commons" Mill first wrote "go into parliament"; on page 54, for "boy or girl" Mill first wrote "child." Though the earlier readings at one time stood complete in their contexts—the later readings are interlined —neither has been noticed, because neither changes the meaning of the text. My general rule has been to distinguish between alterations by which Mill found a better means of saying what he originally meant, and those by which he said or implied something different from what he originally meant. Once-complete read-

---

[76] Hayek, p. 226.

ings that were discarded in the second kind of alteration have in every instance been recorded, along with a number of readings canceled in the first.

Mainly two forms of note have been employed to give deleted text. In the first, a reading following a lemma and square bracket (e.g. "adequately.] faithfully."—p. 37, n. 7) represents an earlier version of text that was deleted and replaced by the word or words given in the lemma. Because the draft was written and revised in a relatively short period of time, and because it is usually impossible to tell whether an alteration was made in the course of first writing or in revision weeks or months later, I have generally not distinguished between original and intermediate versions of text; there is ample evidence that Mill interlined words in revising before he finished out the original line he was writing, and interlineations, as opposed to alterations made currently, are consequently of no special significance. In no case, however, has a composite reading (that is, a reading combining different states of text) knowingly been given, but every reading following a bracket, unless more than one is given in a note, has the same status—as simply a version earlier than the final text. I have been concerned to represent complete (as opposed to fragmentary) earlier readings, and, where there is no explanation to the contrary, each reading in this kind of note was at one time theoretically complete in its immediate context, and was subsequently replaced or altered by interlineation or some other form of noncurrent writing (as by revision at left—in the left-hand half of the page, which Mill generally left blank). Each individual reading can be substituted for the text that replaced it, although there is no guarantee (and usually no way of knowing) that any two earlier readings on a page ever existed together in the same state of text.

In the second form of note, which contains neither lemma nor square bracket, text is given that was deleted, but not replaced, at the point at which the footnote symbol occurs in the final text. Note 2, on page 35, for example, tells that the deleted words "at least" appear between "has" and "proved." Again I have been concerned to represent complete earlier versions, but for simple cancellations I have generally preferred this form to the first—"has proved] has at least proved"—because it is possible in each instance that Mill deleted his text currently before continuing: in the example given, it cannot be shown that the words "has at least proved" ever existed together in a single state of text. Where the deletion involved a change in punctuation, however, I have used both forms of note, either giving the last word preceding the deletion as a lemma (e.g. "opinions,] opinions on almost all . . ." —p. 35, n. 3) or else introducing the deleted reading with an explanation (e.g. "*Originally continued after a colon:* . . ."—p. 40, n. 23).

In the kinds of note just described, as well as in a number of notes detailing interlineations, later additions of leaves to the draft, connections between draft leaves and the rejected leaves (see below), and Harriet Mill's alterations and markings in the manuscript, editorial explanation is distinguished from canceled readings by the use of italics. (Mill's own occasional italics in the notes are obviously not editorial comment, and I have not thought it necessary to add "[*Mill's italics*]" to readings containing them.) The recording of Harriet's pencilings, designated by the abbreviation *HM*, deserves special explanation here. In notes containing the description "*deleted first by HM*" or "*altered to final form first by HM*" the word "*first*" is significant, for it always indicates that the deletion or alteration noticed was originally made by her, Mill subsequently accepting her change by writing over her penciled markings or interlineations in ink. Where he did not follow her alteration, the note generally will read simply "*deleted by HM*" or "*altered by HM to read:* . . . ." It will be understood, of course, that no change made by her—if Mill did not subsequently alter the text himself—has been included in the final form of the draft printed above the notes.

Rejected Leaves. The final section of this edition presents extracts from the thirty rejected leaves at the end of the manuscript, with headnotes describing the relationships between those leaves and the original and revised leaves of the draft in its final form. Most of the extracts are, in a sense, simply earlier readings too lengthy to print as notes to the main text. Shorter readings from the rejected leaves are (as I have explained in the headnotes) given in notes to the main text, with their source designated as "R23r," "RII.20v," and the like—the folio number appearing on the leaf, preceded by the abbreviation *R* (for rejected folio[s]) or *RII* (rejected folio[s] from the original Part II of the draft). In these notes, unless there is explanation to the contrary, editorial comment following the source designation always refers to alterations made subsequently *in the rejected leaves.*

Index. I have not attempted to include nontextual explanatory notes. The Index, however, identifies all persons and books mentioned in the text and textual notes. It includes three persons not named by Mill: Joseph Lowe (the friend of Mill's father at Caen, p. 72), Donald Maclean (the Oxford orator chosen as the first president of the London Debating Society, p. 113), and Eliza Flower ("a person of genius," pp. 152, 193).

Summary of Editorial Methods and Abbreviations

Bracketed numbers within the text refer to the leaves of the early draft, and mark the division in each leaf between recto and verso sides.

Bracketed numbers in the headlines refer, by page and line, to the corresponding text of the later draft as printed in the Columbia edition (*Col.*) and the Oxford World's Classics reprint (*W.C.*).

Text following a lemma and square bracket in a note represents an earlier reading that was deleted and replaced by the word or words given in the lemma.

Text standing alone in a note represents deleted text appearing after the word to which the footnote symbol is superadded.

Editorial explanation is always printed in italics.

HM = Harriet Mill.

at left = in the normally blank left-hand half of the page.

R = rejected folio(s).

RII = rejected folio(s) of the original Part II of the draft.

2

TEXT OF THE EARLY DRAFT

It [1] seems proper that I should prefix to the following biographical
sketch, some mention of the reasons which have made me think
it desirable that I should leave behind me such a memorial of so
uneventful a life as mine. I do not for a moment imagine that any
part of what I have to relate, can be interesting to the public as
a narrative, or as being connected with myself. But I have thought,
that in an age in which education, & its improvement, are the subject of more if not of profounder study than at any former period
in English history, it may be useful that there should be some
record of an education which was unusual & remarkable, & which,
whatever else it may have done, has [2] proved how much more
than is commonly supposed may be taught, & taught thoroughly,
in those early years which, in the common modes of instruction,
are little better than wasted. It has also seemed to me that in an
age of transition in opinions,[3] there may be somewhat both of interest & of benefit in noting the successive phases of a mind which
was always pressing forward, equally ready to [1v] learn & to un-
learn either from its own thoughts or from those of others. The
reader whom these things do not interest, has only himself to
blame if he reads farther, & I do not desire any other indulgence
from him than that of bearing in mind, that for him these pages
were not written.[4]

---

[1] *Fol. 1 (the first paragraph) is a later addition, after which the original leaves
1–22 were refoliated 2–23*

[2] at least

[3] opinions,] opinions on almost all the great subjects of thought,

[4] The reader whom . . . written.] *two earlier versions of this sentence read:*

[2*r*] I was born in London, on the 20th of May 1806, & was the eldest son of James Mill, the author of the History of British India. My father, the son of a petty tradesman & (I believe) small farmer, at Northwater Bridge, in the county of Angus, was, when a boy, recommended by his abilities to the notice of Sir John Stuart, of Fettercairn, one of the Barons of the Exchequer in Scotland, and was in consequence, sent to the University of Edinburgh at the expense of a fund established by Lady Jane Stuart (the wife of Sir John Stuart) & some other ladies for educating young men for the Scottish Church. He there went through the usual course of study, & was licensed as a Preacher, but never followed the profession; having [5] satisfied himself that he could not believe the doctrines of that or of any other church. For a few years he was a private tutor in various [2*v*] families in Scotland; but ended by going to London, & devoting himself to authorship; nor had he any other means of support until 1819, when he obtained an appointment in the India House.

In this period of my father's life there are two things which it is impossible not to be struck with: one of them, unfortunately a very common circumstance, the other a most uncommon one. The first is, that in his position, with no resource but the precarious one of writing in periodicals, he married & had a large family: conduct, than which nothing could be more opposed, both in point of good sense & of morality, to the opinions which at least at a later period of life, he strenuously upheld; & to which he had not, & never could have supposed that he had, the inducements of kindred intellect, tastes, or pursuits. The other circumstance, is the extraordinary energy which was required to lead the life he did, with the disadvantages under which he laboured from the first, & with those which he brought upon himself by his marriage. [3*r*] It would have been no small thing, had he done no more than to support himself & his family during so many years by writing, without ever being in debt or in any pecuniary difficulty; holding as he did, opinions of extreme democracy, & what is called infidelity, in a generation during which those opinions

---

(1) This brief preliminary indication will, I hope, suffice to prevent the reader from expecting what he will not find. (2) The reader whom these things do not interest, is warned, that he will find nothing else to interest him in the following pages.
[5] at an early period, *underlined and marked with an X in the margin by HM*

were more odious to all persons of influence, & to the common run of prosperous Englishmen, than either before or since: & being a man whom not only nothing would have induced to write against his convictions, but who invariably threw into everything he wrote, as much of his convictions as he thought [6] the circumstances would in any way admit of: being, it must also be said, one who never did anything negligently; never undertook any task, literary or other, on which he did not conscientiously bestow all the labour necessary for performing it adequately.[7] But he, with these burthens on him, planned, commenced, & completed the History of India; & this in the course of about ten years, a [3v] shorter time than has been occupied, (even by writers who had no other employment) in the production of almost any other historical work of equal bulk & of anything approaching to the same amount of reading & research. And to this is to be added that during the whole period, a considerable part of almost [8] every day was employed in the instruction of his children; [9] in the case of one of whom, myself, whatever may be thought of his success, he exerted an amount of labour, care & perseverance rarely if ever employed for a similar purpose, in endeavouring to give according to his own conception the highest order of intellectual education.

A man who in his own practice so vigorously acted up to the principle of losing no time, was likely to adhere to the same rule in the instruction of his pupil. I have no remembrance of [10] the time when I began to learn Greek. I have been told that it was when [4r] I was three years old. My earliest recollection on the subject is [11] of learning what my father termed Vocables, being lists of common Greek words, with their signification in English, which he wrote on cards & gave me to learn by heart. Of grammar I learnt, until some years later, nothing except the inflexions of the nouns & verbs but after a course of vocables, proceeded at

---

[6] he thought] *interlined by HM, then written over in ink by Mill*

[7] adequately.] faithfully. *underlined by HM*

[8] *Mill's interlineations of the qualifiers "about" and "almost" in the preceding sentence, and "almost" here, are typical of many of the changes made while writing. Subsequently such interlineations are not recorded unless they are of especial interest*

[9] none of whom, until they were almost grown up, had any other teacher: &

[10] have no remembrance of] cannot remember the time when I could not read, nor

[11] My earliest . . . is] But I have a distinct recollection

once to translation; & I can faintly remember going through Æsop's
Fables, the first Greek book which I read. The Anabasis [12] was the
second. I learnt no Latin until my eighth year. Before that time
I had read a number of Greek prose authors, among whom I remember the whole of Herodotus, Xenophon's Cyropædia and Memorials of Socrates, some of the lives of the philosophers by Diogenes Laertius, part of Lucian, a little of Isocrates, & [13] I think
part of Thucydides; I also read in 1813 the first six dialogues of
Plato (in the common arrangement) from the Euthyphron to
the Theætetus inclusive, which last dialogue had been better
omitted, as it was utterly impossible I should understand it. But
my father, in all his teaching, demanded & expected [4*v*] of me
not only the utmost that I could do, but much that I could by no
possibility have done. What he was himself willing to undergo
for the sake of my instruction may be judged from the fact, that
I went through the whole process of preparing my Greek lessons
in the same room & at the same table at which he was writing,
and [14] as in those days Greek & English Lexicons were not, & I
could make no more use of a Greek & Latin Lexicon than could
be made without having begun to learn Latin, I was forced to
have recourse to him for the meaning of every word which I did
not know: & this [15] incessant interruption he, one of the most im-
patient of mankind, submitted to, & wrote under that interruption
several [16] volumes of his History & all else that he had to write
during those years.

[5*r*] The only thing besides Greek that I learnt as a lesson
during those years was arithmetic: this also my father taught me:
it was the work of the evenings & I well remember its irksomeness.
But the lessons were not the most important part of the instruction
I was receiving. Much [17] of it consisted in the books I read by my-

---

[12] going through Æsop's Fables . . . The Anabasis] learning the opening
chapters of the Anabasis . . . The Cyropædia
[13] Herodotus . . . &] *originally* Herodotus, a considerable part of Lucian, &
(*in expanding the list, Mill added, in order, the Memorials of Socrates, Isocrates,
Diogenes Laertius, and the Cyropædia*)
[14] the fact, that I went . . . Greek lessons . . . and] what I am about to
relate. I must first mention, that I learned Greek in the common manner: he set
me a portion of a Greek author to make out, as I best could, the meaning, & afterwards construe it verbally to him. Now I not only went through the whole operation of making out the lesson . . . but
[15] (as it must have been)   [16] several] the early
[17] not the most important part . . . Much] but a part & scarcely even the

self & in my father's discourses to me, chiefly during our walks. From 1810 to the end of 1813 we were living at Newington Green, then an almost rustic neighbourhood. My father's health required considerable & constant exercise & he walked habitually before breakfast, generally in the green lanes towards Hornsey. In these walks I always accompanied him, & what I chiefly remember of them, (except the bouquets of wild flowers which I used to bring in) is the account I used to give him daily of what I had read the previous day. [5v] I made notes on slips of paper while reading,[18] & from these I used in the morning walks to tell the story to him. I say the story, for the books were chiefly histories, of which I read in this manner a great number: Robertson's histories, Hume, Gibbon; but my greatest delight, then & for long afterwards, was Watson's Philip 2d & 3d. The heroic defence of the Knights of Malta against the Turks, & of the Dutch revolted provinces against Spain, excited in me an intense & lasting interest. Next to Watson my favorite book of the historical sort was Hooke's History of Rome. Of Greece I had seen at that time no regular history, except school abridgments & the last two or three volumes of a translation of Rollin's Ancient History, from Philip of Macedon to the end. But I read with great delight, Langhorne's translation of Plutarch; & I had Greek history in my daily Greek lessons. For English history beyond the time at which Hume leaves off, I remember reading Burnet's History of his own time, though I cared little for anything in it except the wars & battles—& the historical part of the Annual Register from the beginning to about 1788 where [6r] the volumes my father borrowed for me from Mr Bentham left off. I felt a lively interest in Frederic of Prussia during his difficulties [19] & in Paoli, the Corsican patriot—but when I came to the American War of independence I took my part like a child as I was, on the wrong side because it was called the English side; until set right by my father.[20] In these frequent talks about the books I read, he used as opportunity offered to give

---

principal part of the instruction I received from my fourth to my eighth year. The rest

[18] I made notes . . . reading,] Passing my time in the room in which he wrote, I had fallen into an imitation of many of his ways, & as in reading for his history he made notes on slips [5v] of paper of the main facts which he found in his authorities, I made, as I fancied, similar notes on all the books I read,

[19] in the Seven Years War,

[20] set right by my father.] my father taught me or at least told me better.

me explanations & ideas respecting civilization, society, government, morality, mental cultivation, which he required me afterwards to restate to him in my own words.[21] He also made me read,
& give him a verbal account of, many books which would not
have interested me sufficiently to induce me to read them of myself: I particularly remember Millar's Historical View of the English Government, a book of great merit for its time, & which he
much valued: also Mosheim's Ecclesiastical History, McCrie's Life
of Knox,[22] & even Sewell's & Rutty's histories [6v] of the Quakers.
Of voyages & travels I remember as part of my constant reading
Anson's Voyage which is so delightful to most young persons,
& a Collection in four octavo volumes, (Hawkesworth's I believe
it was) of Voyages round the World, from Drake to Cook & Bou-
gainville.[23] I read few books of amusement properly so called:
of children's books, any more than of playthings, I had scarcely
any, except an occasional gift from a relation or acquaintance—
among those I had, Robinson Crusoe was preeminent & continued to delight me through all my boyhood. It was no part however of my father's system to exclude books of amusement: though
he allowed them very sparingly. Of such books he possessed, at
that time, next to none, but an early friend & companion of his,
Dr Thomson the chemist, had many, & some of those he borrowed
purposely for me—those which I remember are the Arabian Nights,
Cazotte's Arabian Tales,[24] Don Quixote, & a book of some reputation in its day, Brooke's Fool of Quality.[25]

[7r] In my eighth year I commenced learning Latin by means
of teaching it to a younger sister, who afterwards repeated the
lessons to my father. From this time other sisters & brothers being
successively added as pupils, a considerable part of my day's work

---

[21] restate . . . words.] give him an account of, in order to shew whether I had
understood what he had told me & to ensure my remembering it.

[22] McCrie's Life of Knox,] *interlined*

[23] *Originally continued after a colon:* & I have a faint remembrance of some
folio collection in which I read an account of the first circumnavigation of the
globe, by Magellan.

[24] Cazotte's Arabian Tales,] *interlined*

[25] *The last three lines of fol. 6v give the deleted beginning of a new paragraph:*
One of my favorite amusements at this time as well as for some years later (*probably the sentence was continued on another sheet now lost; cf.* "one of my greatest amusements . . . experimental science" *on p. 45). The next paragraph, on
fol. 7r, began with a sentence now deleted:* I continue the, as it were, mechanical
detail of my course of instruction in order to finish it before entering on the influences of a more general kind under which I was placed in my early years.

consisted of this preparatory teaching; & it was a part which I especially disliked. The principal [26] advantage which, as far as I am aware, arose from it, was that I myself learnt more thoroughly & retained more lastingly the things which I had to teach as well as learn; perhaps too, the practice it afforded in explaining difficulties to others, may even at that age have been useful.[27] [7v] In other respects the experience of my boyhood is not favorable to the plan of teaching children by means of one another. The teaching, I am sure, is very inefficient as teaching, & I well know that the relation between teacher & taught [28] is a most unfavourable moral discipline to both.[29] I went through the grammar & [30] part of Cornelius Nepos & Cæsar's Commentaries in this manner, but afterwards added to the superintendance of these [31] lessons, much longer ones of my own which I repeated to my father in the usual manner.[32]

In the same year in which I began Latin I made my first commencement in the Greek poets with the Iliad. After I had made some progress in this, my father put Pope's translation into my hands: it was the first English verse I had cared to read, & became [8r] one of the books in which for many years I most delighted: I think I must have read it from twenty to thirty times through. I should not have thought it worth while to mention a taste apparently so natural to boyhood if I had not, as I think, observed that the keen enjoyment of this brilliant specimen of narrative & versification, is not so universal with boys as I should have expected both a priori & from my individual experience. Soon after this time I commenced Euclid, & somewhat later, algebra, still under my father's tuition.

From my eighth to my twelfth year the Latin books which I remember reading were the Bucolics of Virgil, & the first six books of the Æneid; all Horace; the fables of Phædrus; the first five books of Livy, (to which from my love of the subject I voluntarily added at my leisure, the remainder of the first decad); all Sallust; a con-

---

[26] principal] only real

[27] *Originally continued after a comma:* though of this I am not sure, because [7v] I am not certain that I did remove any difficulties.

[28] (the teacher also being without any real authority) *deleted first by HM*

[29] But to return to my Latin lessons: [30] a great

[31] in this manner, but . . . these] with my sister but . . . her *altered to final form first by HM*

[32] in the usual manner.] with my Greek lessons.

siderable part of Ovid's Metamorphoses; some plays of Terence;
two or three books of Lucretius; some of the orations of Cicero &
of his writings on oratory; [33] also his letters to Atticus, my father
taking the trouble to translate to me from the French the historical
explanations in Mongault's notes. Tacitus I do not think I meddled
with till my thirteenth year.[34] In Greek [8v] I read the Iliad &
Odyssey through; one or two plays of Sophocles, Euripides &
Aristophanes, but by these I profited little; all Thucydides; Xenophon's Hellenics; a great part of Demosthenes, Æschines &
Lysias; Theocritus; Anacreon; part of the Anthology; a little of
Dionysius; [35] the first two or three books of Polybius; & lastly,
Aristotle's Rhetoric, which as the first expressly scientific treatise
on any moral or psychological subject which I had read & containing, besides, many of the best observations of the ancients on
human nature & human affairs, my father made me study with
peculiar care & throw the matter of it into synoptic tables.[36] During
the same years I learnt elementary geometry & algebra thoroughly;
the differential calculus & other portions of the higher mathematics not thoroughly; [37] for my father not having kept up this
part of his early acquired knowledge, could not spare time to
qualify himself for removing my difficulties & left [9r] me to deal
with them with little other aid than that of books; at the same time
continually calling on me, with authority & indignation, to solve
difficult problems for which he did not see that I had not the
necessary previous knowledge.

As to my private reading, I can only speak of what I remember.
History continued to be my strongest predilection. Mitford's
Greece I used to be continually reading.[38] My father had put me
on my guard against the [39] Tory prejudices of this writer, & his
perversions of facts for the glorification of despots & discredit [40]

---

[33] *In this list "the fables of Phædrus" and "all Sallust" are interlined additions;
the rest of the sentence is an addition written at left*

[34] *Originally continued after a semicolon:* as well as part of Juvenal, & a great
part of Quintilian.

[35] *In this list Thucydides, Xenophon, and Dionysius are interlined additions;
for "a great part of Demosthenes," Mill originally wrote:* all Demosthenes (except
the private orations, which I read later)

[36] tables.] tables like those in some of the treatises on the scholastic logic &
metaphysics.

[37] not thoroughly;] not thoroughly, but very much the reverse;

[38] *Originally continued after a semicolon:* no book ever delighted me more.

[39] intense   [40] discredit] calumny

of popular institutions. These points he used to discourse upon, exemplifying them from the Greek orators & historians [41] with such effect that in reading Mitford my sympathies always were on the contrary side to those of the author, & I could, to some extent, have argued the point against him; yet this did not diminish the ever new pleasure with which I read the book. Ferguson's Roman history was also a favorite.[42] Another [9v] book which notwithstanding what is called the dryness of the stile I took great pleasure in was the Ancient Universal History: through the incessant reading of which I had my head full of details of the history of the obscurest ancient people, while in modern history with the exception of detached passages such as the Dutch war of independence I was at this time little interested.[43] A voluntary exercise to which I was throughout my boyhood much addicted, was what I called writing histories: of course [44] in imitation of my father—who used to give me the manuscript of part of his history of India to read. Almost as soon as I could hold a pen I must needs write a history of India too: this was soon abandoned, but what I called a Roman history, picked out of Hooke, I continued for a long time to employ myself in writing: after this an abridgment of the Ancient Universal History: then a History of Holland, compiled [10r] from my favorite Watson & from an anonymous history which somebody who knew my liking for the subject, picked up at a book stall & gave to me. But in my eleventh & twelfth year I occupied myself with writing what I flattered myself was something serious, & might be made fit to be published; this was no less than a history of the Roman Government, compiled (with the assistance of Hooke) from Livy & Dionysius: of which I wrote as much as would have made an octavo volume, extending to the epoch of the Licinian laws. It was in fact an account of the struggles between the patricians & plebeians, which now engrossed all the interest in my mind that I had previously felt in the mere wars & conquests of the Romans. I discussed all the constitutional points as they arose, vindicated the Agrarian law on the evidence of Livy

[41] which I read as my daily lessons: & he did this

[42] Ferguson's . . . favorite.] *interlined*

[43] detached passages . . . I was at this time little interested.] a few detached passages . . . I was very far from being similarly well informed. *altered to final form first by HM. The next sentence originally began:* This is the place to mention a sort of voluntary exercise . . .

[44] of course] This fancy was of course taken up (*"fancy" is underlined by HM*)

(though quite ignorant of Niebuhr's researches) & upheld [45] to the best of my capacity the Roman democratic party. A few years later in my contempt of my childish efforts I destroyed all these papers, not then [10v] anticipating that I could ever have any curiosity about my first attempts at writing or reasoning. My father encouraged me in this useful amusement, though, as I think judiciously, he never asked to see what I wrote, so that I never felt that in writing it I was accountable to any one, nor had the chilling sensation of being under a critical eye.

But though these histories were never a compulsory lesson, there was another kind of composition which was so, namely writing verses & it was one of the most irksome of my tasks. Greek or Latin verses I never wrote, nor learnt the prosody of those languages. My father,[46] thinking this not worth the time it required, was contented with making me read aloud to him & correcting false quantities. I never composed at all in Greek, even in prose, & but little in Latin. But I wrote many English verses; beginning from the time of my first reading Pope's Homer, when I ambitiously attempted [47] to write something of the same kind, & [11r] achieved as much as one book of a continuation of the Iliad. The exercise, begun by choice, was continued by command.[48] Conformably to my father's usual custom of explaining to me the reasons for what he required me to do, he gave me, for this, two reasons which were highly characteristic of him. One was that some things could be expressed better & more forcibly in verse than in prose: this he said was a real advantage: the other was, that people in general attached more value to verse than it deserved, & the power of writing it was therefore useful & worth acquiring. He generally left me to choose my own subjects which as far as I remember were mostly odes to some mythological personage or allegorical abstraction: but he made me translate into English verse many of Horace's shorter poems. I remember his giving me Thomson's "Winter" to read, & afterwards making me attempt to write something myself on the same subject. I had read very little English poetry at this time. Shakespeare [11v] my father had put

---

[45] upheld] glorified   [46] very rationally
   [47] I ambitiously attempted] nothing would satisfy me but attempting *altered by HM to read:* I attempted
   [48] The exercise . . . command.] For some years after, my father made me keep up the practice of attempting to write verses.

into my hands, at first for the sake of the historical plays, from which however I went on to the others.[49] My father was never a great admirer of Shakespeare the English idolatry of whom, he used to attack in unmeasured terms. He had little value for any English poetry except Milton, Goldsmith, Burns, & Gray's Bard, which he preferred to his Elegy: perhaps I may also add Beattie.[50] I remember his reading to me (unlike his usual practice of making me read to him) the first book of the Fairie Queene: but I took little pleasure in it. The poetry of the present century he set no value on—& I hardly saw any of it till I was grown up to manhood, except Walter Scott's metrical romances, which he borrowed for me & which I was much delighted with—as I always was with all animated narrative.[51] Dryden's Poems were among my father's books & many of these he made me read, though I never cared for any of them except Alexander's Feast, which like the songs in Walter Scott I used to sing internally, to a music of my own. Cowper's short poems [12r] I read with some pleasure but never got far into the longer ones—& nothing in the two volumes interested me like the little prose account of his three hares. In my thirteenth year I met with the poems of Campbell, among which Lochiel, Hohenlinden, the Exile of Erin & some others gave me sensations I had never before received from poetry. Here too I made nothing of [52] the longer poems, except the opening of Gertrude of Wyoming, which appeared to me the perfection of pathos.

During this part of my childhood one of my greatest amusements was experimental science; not however trying experiments, a kind of discipline which I have often regretted not having had —[53] but merely reading about the experiments of others. I never remember being so wrapt up in any book as I was in Joyce's Scientific Dialogues, & I devoured treatises on chemistry, especially

[49] *Originally continued after a colon:* I was of course like all persons young or old, pleased & interested with them.

[50] *He had little value . . . Beattie.]* Milton's poetry he did admire but did not think me of an age to comprehend.

[51] animated narrative.] narrative in which there was spirit & verve.

[52] made nothing of] *Mill altered to read:* skipped *but later, after HM underlined the new word, restored the original reading*

[53] a kind of discipline . . . had—] which would have been a kind of discipline eminently useful to me,

Dr Thomson's, for years before I ever attended a lecture or saw an experiment.[54]

[12v] From about the age of twelve I entered into another and more advanced stage in my course of instruction— [55] in which the main object was no longer the aids & appliances of thought, but the thoughts themselves. This commenced with Logic, in which I began at once with the Organon & read it to the Analytics inclusive, but profited little by the Posterior Analytics, which belong to a branch of speculation I was not yet ripe for. Contemporaneously with the Organon my father made me read the whole or parts of several of the Latin treatises on the scholastic logic; giving each day to him, in our walks, a minute account of the portion I had read & answering his numerous & searching questions. After this I went through in the same manner the "Computatio sive Logica" of Hobbes, a work of a much higher order of thought than the books [13r] of the school logicians & which he estimated very highly; in my opinion beyond its merits great as these are. It was his invariable practice, whatever studies he exacted from me, to make me as far as possible understand & feel the utility of them: & this he deemed peculiarly fitting [56] in the case of the syllogistic logic, its usefulness having been impugned by so many [57] writers of authority. Accordingly I well remember how, in his usual manner, he first attempted by questions to make me think on the subject, & frame some conception of what constituted the utility of the syllogistic logic, & when I had failed in this, to make me understand it by explanations. I do not believe that the explanations made the matter at all clear to me at the time; but they were not therefore useless; they remained as a nucleus for my observations & reflexions to crystallize upon: his general remarks being interpreted to me by the particular instances which occurred to myself afterwards. My own consciousness & experience ultimately led me to appreciate quite as highly as he did the value of an early practical [13v] familiarity with the school logic. I know of nothing, in my education, to which I

---

[54] This was a very easy & pleasant part of my mental education & by no means the least valuable part of it.

[55] another and more advanced . . . instruction—] what may be called the third of the stages into which my course of instruction may be divided—that

[56] fitting] desirable

[57] impugned by so many] so strenuously denied by many

think myself more indebted for whatever capacity of thinking I have attained. The first intellectual operation in which I arrived at any skill was dissecting a bad argument & finding in what part the fallacy lay: & though whatever success I had in this I owed entirely to the fact that it was an intellectual exercise in which I was most perseveringly drilled by my father; yet it is also true that the school logic, & the mental habits acquired in studying it, were among the principal instruments of this drilling. I am persuaded that nothing, in modern education, tends so much when properly used, to form exact thinkers, who attach a definite meaning to words & propositions, & are not imposed on by vague, loose, or ambiguous terms.[58] It is also a study peculiarly adapted to an early stage in the education of students in philosophy, since it does not presuppose the slow process of acquiring by experience & reflection, valuable thoughts of their [14r] own. They may become capable of seeing through confused & self contradictory thinking before their own thinking powers are much advanced; to the great benefit of those powers in their subsequent developement.[59]

During this time the Latin & Greek books which I continued to read with my father were chiefly such as were worth studying not merely for the language, but for the thoughts. This included much of the orators & the whole of Demosthenes, some of whose principal orations I read several times over, & wrote out, by way of exercise, an analysis of them. My father's comments on these orations when I read them to him were very instructive to me: he not only drew my attention to the knowledge they afforded of Athenian institutions, & to the principles of legislation & government which they illustrated, but pointed out the skill & art of the orator—how everything important to his purpose was said exactly at the moment when he had brought the minds of his hearers into the [14v] state best fitted to receive it; how he made steal into their minds, gradually & by insinuation, thoughts which if expressed directly would have [60] roused their opposition. Most of these reflexions were beyond my capacity of full comprehension at

---

[58] terms.] language.

[59] to the great benefit . . . developement.] & nothing can more aid development by clearing the path of the thinker from the mists of vague & sophistical language.

[60] repelled them or

the time,[61] but they left seed behind. I also read through Tacitus,
& Quintilian. The latter, owing to his obscure [62] stile & to the
scholastic details of which many parts of his treatise are made up,
is little read & seldom sufficiently appreciated. His book is a kind
of encyclopædia of the thoughts of the ancients on education &
culture: & I have retained through life many valuable ideas which
I can trace to my reading of it, even at that age. I read, too, at
this time, some of the most important dialogues of Plato, especially
the Gorgias, the Protagoras, & the Republic. There is no author to
whom my father thought himself more indebted for his own mental
culture, than Plato, & I can say the same of mine. The Socratic
method, of which the Platonic dialogues are the chief example, is
unsurpassed as a discipline for abstract thought on the most difficult subjects. [15r] Nothing in modern life & education, in the
smallest degree supplies its place. The close, searching *elenchus*
by which the man of vague generalities is absolutely compelled
either to express his meaning to himself in definite terms, or to
confess that he does not know what he is talking about—the
perpetual testing of all general statements by particular instances
—the siege in form which is laid to the meaning of large abstract
terms, by laying hold of some much larger class-name which includes that & more, & *dividing down* [63] to the thing sought, marking out its limits & definition by a series of accurately drawn
distinctions between it & each of the cognate objects which are
successively severed from it—all this even at that age took such
hold on me that it became part of my own mind; & I have ever
felt myself, beyond any modern that I know of except my father
& perhaps beyond even him,[64] a pupil of Plato, & cast in the mould
of his dialectics.[65]

[16r] In going through Demosthenes & Plato, as I could now

----

[61] beyond my capacity . . . time,] of course lost on me *altered to read:* of
course in a great measure lost on me

[62] obscure] bad   [63] (if I may so speak)

[64] beyond any modern that I know of . . . him,] (what I still believe that I
am in a greater degree than any modern I know of, except my father)

[65] *Fol. 15v contains a deleted paragraph beginning:* The strong moral impressions yielded by the writings of Plato also took great effect on me, nor was their
inculcation neglected by my father. Even at the very early age at which I read
with him the Memorabilia of Xenophon . . . *and continuing with substantially
the same text as the paragraph on fol. 29r (p. 62, all but the third sentence
of the paragraph), where Mill recopied it when he decided that the moral impressions of Plato took effect "at a later period"*

read these authors as far as the language was concerned with perfect ease, I was not required to construe them sentence by sentence but to read them aloud to my father, answering questions when asked: but the particular attention which he paid to elocution (in which his own excellence was remarkable) made this reading aloud to him a most painful task.[66] Of all things which he required me to do, there was none which I did so constantly ill, or in which he so perpetually lost his temper with me. He had thought much on the principles of the art of reading, especially the part of it which relates to the inflexions of the voice, or *modulation* as writers on elocution call it (in contrast with *articulation* on the one side, & *expression* on the other) & had reduced it to [67] rules, grounded on the logical analysis of a sentence. These rules he constantly impressed upon me, & severely took me to task for every violation of them: but I even then remarked (though I did not [16v] venture to [68] make the remark to him) that though he reproached me when I read a sentence ill, & *told* me how I ought to have read it, he never *shewed* me: he often mockingly caricatured my bad reading of the sentence, but did not, by reading it himself, instruct me how it ought to be read. It was a defect running through his modes of instruction as it did through his modes of thinking that he trusted too much to the intelligibleness of the abstract when not embodied in the concrete.[69] It was at a much later time of life when practising elocution by myself or with companions of my own age, that I for the first time thoroughly understood his rules & saw the psychological grounds of them; & at that time I & others followed out the subject into its ramifications & could have composed a very useful treatise grounded on my father's principles. He himself left those principles & rules unwritten, & unwritten they still remain.

My [70] private exercises in composition during my thirteenth & fourteenth year changed from historical to dramatic; though indeed they were historical still, for my dramatic attempts were on historical subjects. Like most youthful writers I wrote tragedies: the first was on the Roman emperor Otho, the attraction to me not

---

[66] a most painful task.] the *supplice* of every day.

[67] a set of excellent   [68] did not venture to] dared not

[69] *Originally continued after a semicolon:* a mistake closely connected with his own mental characteristics. (*Mill deleted this when he interlined* "as it did through his modes of thinking" *just above*)

[70] *This paragraph is written at left*

being the character or fortunes of the hero, but the movement & bustle of that portion of Roman history, as related by Tacitus. I wrote a play [71] on the story of the Danaides, & began two more, one on a subject from Tacitus, another from Thucydides. What kindled my dramatic aspirations was not so much Shakespeare as the plays of Joanna Baillie, among which "Constantine Paleologus" appeared to me one of the most glorious of human compositions. I have read it since & I still think it [72] one of the best dramas of the last two centuries.

[17r] A book which contributed very much to my education was my father's History of India. It was published in the beginning of 1818. During the year previous it was passing through the press, & I used to read the proofsheets to him; or rather, to read the manuscript to him while he corrected the proofs. The number of new ideas which I received from this remarkable book, & the impulse & stimulus as well as guidance given to my thoughts by its criticisms & disquisitions [73] on society & civilization in the Hindoo part, on institutions & the acts of governments in the English part—made my early familiarity with this book eminently useful to my subsequent progress. And though I can perceive deficiencies in it now as compared with a perfect standard, I still think it [74] the most instructive history ever yet written, & one of the books from which most benefit may be derived by a mind in the course of making up its opinions.

[17v] The Preface to the History, one of the most characteristic of my father's writings, as well as one of the richest in materials for thought, gives a picture entirely to be depended on, of the sentiments & expectations with which he wrote the book. Saturated as the book is with the principles & modes of judgment of a democratic radicalism [75] then regarded as extreme; & treating with a severity then most unusual the English constitution, the English law, & all parties & classes who possessed at that time any influence in this country, he may have expected reputation but certainly not advancement in life from its publication, nor could he have supposed that it would raise up anything but enemies for him in powerful quarters, least of all could he have expected favour from the East India Company, on the acts of whose government

---

[71] a play] another tragedy   [72] really
[73] criticisms & disquisitions] searching criticisms & instructive disquisitions
[74] by far   [75] democratic radicalism] democracy

he had made so many severe comments: though in various parts of his book he bore a testimony in their favour, which he felt to be their due, viz. that if the acts of any other government [18r] had the light of publicity as completely let in upon them, they would probably still less bear scrutiny; & that no government on record had on the whole given so much proof (to the extent of its lights) of good intention towards its subjects.

On learning however in the spring of 1819, about a year after the publication of his History, that the East India Directors desired to strengthen that part of their establishment which was employed in carrying on the correspondence with India, my father declared himself a candidate for that employment, & to the credit of the Directors, successfully. He was appointed one of the Assistants of the Examiner of Indian Correspondence; officers whose duty it is to prepare drafts of despatches to India in the principal departments of administration. In this office & in that of Examiner which he subsequently attained, the [76] influence which his talents, his reputation, & his decision of character gave him, enabled him to a great extent to throw into his [18v] drafts of despatches, & to carry through the ordeal of the Court of Directors & Board of Control without having their force much weakened, his real opinions on Indian subjects. Those despatches, in conjunction with his History, did more than had ever been done before to promote the improvement of India, & teach Indian officials to understand their business. If a selection of them were published, they would, I am convinced, place his character as a practical statesman quite on a level with his reputation as a speculative writer.

This new employment [77] caused no relaxation in his attention to my education. It was in this same year 1819 that he went through with me a course of political economy. His loved & intimate friend, Ricardo, had shortly before published the book which made so great an epoch in political economy; a book which [78] would never have been published or written, but for the earnest [19r] entreaty & strong encouragement of my father; for Ricardo, the most modest of men, though firmly convinced of the truth of his

---

[76] the] he continued during the remainder of his life. The

[77] employment] occupation, relieving him from the necessity of writing for subsistence,

[78] book which made so great . . . which] great work which gave to political economy so new & improved a form & foundation. This book, it may be remarked incidentally,

doctrines, believed himself so incapable of doing them justice in point of exposition & expression, that he shrank from the idea of publicity. The same friendly encouragement induced Ricardo, a year or two later, to become a member of the House of Commons, where during the few remaining years of his life, unhappily cut short in the full vigour of his intellect, he rendered so much service to his & my father's opinions both in political economy & on other subjects.

Though Ricardo's great work was already in print, no didactic treatise [79] embodying its doctrines, in a manner fit for learners, had yet appeared. My father therefore instructed me on the subject by a sort of lectures,[80] which he delivered to me in our walks. He expounded to me each day a part of the [19v] subject, & I gave him next day a written account of it which he made me write over & over again until it was clear, precise & tolerably complete. In this manner I went through the whole subject; & the written outline of it which resulted from my daily *compte rendu*,[81] served him afterwards as notes from which to write his Elements of Political Economy. After this I went through Ricardo, giving an account daily of what I read, & discussing in the best manner I could, the collateral points which were raised as we went on. On money, as the most intricate part of the subject, he made me read in a similar manner Ricardo's admirable pamphlets, published during what was called the Bullion controversy.[82] I afterwards went through Adam Smith, & in this reading it was one of my father's main objects [83] to make me apply to Smith's more superficial view of political economy the superior lights of Ricardo, & detect with logical exactness what was fallacious in Smith's arguments or erroneous in his conclusions. Such a system of instruction was [20r] excellently suited to form a thinker; but it required to be worked by a thinker, as close & vigorous as my father.[84] The path was a thorny one even to him, & I am sure it was so to me, though I took the strongest interest in the subject. He was continually provoked by my failures both where success could, & where

---

[79] didactic treatise] properly didactic work on political economy
[80] if they may be so called,
[81] resulted from . . . *rendu*,] he had made me draw up,
[82] controversy.] Committee.
[83] one of my father's main objects] my father's main object
[84] father.] father to have much chance of being successful.

it could not,[85] have been expected: but in the main his method was right, & it succeeded. I do not believe that any scientific teaching ever was more thorough, or better calculated for training the faculties, than the mode in which logic & political economy were taught to me by my father. He not only gave me an accurate knowledge [86] of both subjects but made me a thinker on both; who thought for myself almost from the first, & occasionally thought differently from him, though for a long time only on minor points, & making his opinion the ultimate standard. If I could not convince him that I was right I always supposed I must be wrong, but it sometimes happened that I did convince him, & that he [20v] altered his opinion on points in the detail of political economy which he had not much considered from representations & arguments of mine. I state this to his honor, not my own; it at once exemplifies his perfect candour & the real worth of his method of teaching.

At this point concluded what can properly be called my lessons. When I was about fourteen I left England for more than a year & after my return though my studies went on under my father's general direction he was no longer my schoolmaster. I shall therefore pause here & turn back to matters of a more general nature connected with the part of my life & education included in the preceding reminiscences.

In the education which I have partially retraced, the point most superficially apparent is the great effort to give, during the years of childhood, an amount of knowledge [87] in what are considered the higher branches of education, which is seldom acquired (if acquired at all) until the age of manhood. [21r] The experiment shews the [88] ease with which this may be done, & places in a strong light the wretched waste [89] of so many precious years as are spent in acquiring the [90] modicum of Latin & Greek commonly taught to schoolboys—a waste, which has led so many of the reformers of education to propose discarding those languages altogether from

---

[85] both where success could . . . not,] where success could not
[86] gave me an accurate knowledge] made me most accurate in my knowledge
[87] an amount of knowledge] *an incomplete version deleted three lines earlier in the draft reads:* a large amount of book knowledge
[88] great
[89] wretched waste] *an incomplete version deleted seven lines earlier in the draft reads:* utter [21r] absence of the smallest necessity for the waste
[90] wretched

general education. If I had been by nature extremely quick of apprehension, or had possessed a very accurate & retentive memory, or were of a remarkably active & energetic character, the trial would not be decisive: but in all these natural gifts I am rather below than above par.[91] What I could do, could assuredly be done by any boy or girl of average capacity & healthy physical constitution: & it is most encouraging to the hopes of improvement for the human race, that education can do so much for persons of not more than the ordinary [92] natural gifts.[93]

[21v] There is one cardinal point in my education which more than anything else, was the cause of whatever good it effected. Most boys or youths who have had much knowledge drilled into them, have their mental faculties not strengthened but overlaid by it. They are crammed with mere facts & with the opinions or phrases of others, & these are accepted as a substitute for the power to form opinions of their own. And thus the sons of eminent fathers, who have spared no pains in their education, grow up mere parroters of what they have learnt, incapable of any effort of original or independent thought. Mine, however,[94] was not an education of cram. My father never permitted anything which I learnt, to degenerate into a mere exercise of memory. He strove to make the understanding not only go along with every step of the teaching but if possible precede it. His custom was, in the case of everything which could be found out by thinking, to make me strive & struggle to find it out for myself [22r] giving [95] me no more help

---

[91] but in all these natural . . . par.] I am, as all are aware who have intimately & closely observed me, not only not above par, but decidedly & greatly below it. *In an intermediate version, the corresponding text of R19/20r—*"But in every one of these natural gifts, as all are aware who have intimately or closely observed me, I am, to say the least, rather below than above par."—*HM altered* "every one of" *to read* "all", *and deleted* "as all are . . . observed me," *and* "to say the least". *See p. 182 for an additional passage, subsequently rejected, in* R19/20

[92] not more than the ordinary] no considerable R19/20v

[93] it is most encouraging . . . gifts.] I am satisfied also that it could be done without the very considerable drawbacks with which in my case it was accompanied & which have pursued me through life. *Mill then began the next paragraph (fol. 21v):* One drawback, which if it had existed would have rendered the whole of the intellectual education worthless, did not exist in my case. [*the sentence is marked with a line in the margin by HM*] Most boys or youths . . .

[94] Mine, however,] Such was not the character of my education. It *deleted first by HM, who interlined* "Mine" *above* "It"

[95] giving] before he would tell it to me, & to [22r] give

than was positively indispensable. As far as I can trust my remembrance, I acquitted myself very lamely in this department; my recollection of such matters is almost wholly of failures, hardly ever of successes. It is true, the failures were often in things in which success was almost impossible. I remember at some time in my twelfth or thirteenth year,[96] his indignation at my using the common [97] expression that something was true in theory but required correction in practice: & how, after making me vainly strive to define the word theory, he [98] explained its meaning & shewed the fallacy of [22v] the form of speech which places practice & theory in opposition: leaving me fully persuaded that in being unable to give a definition of Theory, and in speaking of it as something which might be opposed to practice I had shewn unparalleled ignorance. In this he seems, & perhaps was, very unreasonable; but I think, only in being angry [99] at my failure. A pupil from whom nothing is ever demanded which he cannot do, never does all he can.

One of the evils [100] most liable to attend on any sort of early proficiency, & which often fatally blights its promise, my father most sedulously guarded against. This was self conceit. He kept me, with extreme vigilance, out of the way of hearing myself praised, or of being led to make self complimentary comparisons between myself & others. From his own intercourse with me I could derive none but a very humble opinion of myself; & the standard of comparison he always held up to me, was not what other [23r] people did, but what could & ought to be done. He completely succeeded in preserving me from the sort of influences he so much dreaded. I was not at all [101] aware that my attainments were anything unusual at my age. If as unavoidably happened I occasionally had my attention drawn to the fact that some other boy knew less than my-

---

[96] when I happened to use the word idea, he asked me what an idea was: & with much displeasure at my ineffective attempts to define the word, at last gave me a definition which, allowing it to be correct, had never been given by any metaphysician except Hartley. viz. that an idea is the type or remembrance of a sensation. A little before or after the same time I recollect *deleted first by HM*

[97] common] vulgar   [98] at last

[99] being angry] his vehement [*altered by HM and then Mill to read:* the vehemence of his] demonstrations of anger

[100] One of the evils] Another evil

[101] I was not at all] Through my whole boyhood I never was in the smallest degree

self, I supposed, not that I knew much, but that he for some reason
or other knew little: [102] or rather that the things he knew were different.[103] My state of mind was no more arrogance than it was
humility. I never thought of saying to myself, I am, or I can do,
so & so. I neither estimated myself highly or lowly: I did not think
of estimating myself at all. I was sometimes thought to be self conceited, probably because I was disputatious, & did not scruple to
give direct contradictions to what was said. [23v] I suppose I acquired this manner from [104] having been encouraged in an unusual
degree to talk on matters beyond my age, & with grown persons,
while I never had inculcated on me the usual respect for them.
My father did not correct this ill breeding & impertinence, probably from not seeing it, for I was always too much in awe of
him to be otherwise than extremely subdued & quiet in his presence.[105] Yet with all this I had no notion [106] of any superiority in
myself. I remember the very place in Hyde Park where, in my
fourteenth year, on the eve of my leaving my father's house for a
year's absence, he told me,[107] that I should find, as I got acquainted
with new people, that I had been taught many things which youths
of my age did not commonly know; [24r] & that many people

---

[102] knew much . . . knew little:] was above par . . . was below it,

[103] *Originally continued after a comma:* for I was always conscious that I could
not do many things which others could. There is nothing for which I am more
indebted to my father than for thus effectually preventing the growth of self conceit; for I affirm with confidence that I had not at this period of life, the smallest
vestige of it. *The first fifteen words, to the end of the sentence, are marked with
a line in the margin by HM. The next three sentences in the text are written at
left, originally as an addition to this canceled passage*

[104] I was sometimes thought to be self conceited . . . from] *written at left on
fol. 23r (over several lines in HM's hand now erased and largely illegible) and
interlined on fol. 23v to replace Mill's original continuation of the canceled passage given in the preceding note:* I have, however, since found that those who
knew me in my early boyhood thought me greatly & most disagreeably self-
conceited; the reason of which was, that I was disputatious, & made no scruple
to give direct contradictions to what was said on things which I knew nothing
whatever about. How I came by this detestable [*deleted and replaced inter-
lineally by* offensive] [23v] habit, I do not know. Probably from being on the
one hand, accustomed to lay down the law to my younger sisters, & having no
other companions to withstand me, & on the other hand (*HM deleted "on things
which I knew nothing whatever about" and the beginning of the last sentence,
and with several words written at left on fol. 23v, now erased, probably supplied
Mill with the new beginning of the sentence*)

[105] My mother did tax me with it, but for her remonstrances I never had the
slightest regard. *deleted first by HM*

[106] had no notion] never had the slightest idea

[107] told me,] gave me the following admonition: he said

would be disposed to talk to me of this, & to flatter me about it.[108] What other things he said on this topic I remember very imperfectly; [109] but he wound up by saying, that whatever I did know more than others, could not be ascribed to any merit in me, but to the very unusual advantage which had fallen to my lot, of having a father who was able to teach me, & willing to sacrifice the necessary trouble & time; that it was no matter of praise to me, to know more than those who had not had a similar advantage, but the utmost disgrace to me if I did not. I have a distinct remembrance, that the suggestion thus for the first time made to me that I knew more than other youths who were considered well educated, was to me a piece of information; to which as to all other things which my father told me, I gave implicit credence, but which did not at all impress me as a personal matter. I felt no disposition to glorify myself upon the circumstance that there were other persons who did not know what I knew, nor had I been accustomed to flatter myself that my acquirements, whatever they were, were any merit of mine: but now when my attention was called to the [24v] subject, I felt that what my father had said respecting my peculiar advantages was exactly the truth & common sense of the matter, & it fixed my opinion & feeling from that time forward.[110]

In my, as in all other education, the moral influences, which are so much more important than all others, are at the same time the most complicated, & the most difficult to specify with any approach to exactness.[111] I shall not attempt to enter [112] into the detail of the circumstances by which in this respect my character may have been shaped. I shall confine myself to a few leading points, which are essential to a correct account of my education.

I was brought up from the first without any religious belief, in

---

[108] *In the corresponding text of R23r (see p. 178) the sentence was originally continued after a colon:* & he then represented the folly it would be to let myself be puffed up & made vain by such flattery.

[109] very imperfectly;] too imperfectly to risk writing them down; *R23r, subsequently altered to final form*

[110] *See pp. 178–181 for two additional paragraphs following the text at this point in R23v–25v*

[111] *For the remainder of this paragraph R25v reads, after a colon:* but what I can I will do towards describing the circumstances under which in this respect I grew up from childhood, both as to direct teaching, & the indirect operation of the moral atmosphere in which I lived.

[112] fully

the ordinary meaning of the term. My father, educated in the creed
of Scotch presbyterianism, had by his own studies & reflections
been early led to reject not only all revealed religion but the belief
in a supreme governor of the world. I have heard him say that the
turning point of his mind on this subject was his reading Butler's
Analogy. That work, of which he always continued to speak with
respect, kept him, as he said, a [25*r*] believer in Christianity for
(if I remember right) a whole year; by shewing him that whatever are the difficulties in believing that the Old & New Testaments
proceeded from a perfectly wise & good being, there are the same,
& even greater difficulties in conceiving that a wise & good being
could have been the maker of the universe. He considered Butler's
argument conclusive against the only opponents for whom [113] it
was intended, those who, rejecting revelation, adhere to what is
called Natural Religion: Those who admit an omnipotent & all-
benevolent maker & ruler of such a world as this, can say little [114]
against Christianity but what can be [115] retorted against themselves.
Finding, therefore, no halting place in Deism, he remained in a
state of perplexity, until, doubtless after many struggles, he yielded
to the conviction, that of the origin of things nothing whatever can
be known. These particulars are important, because they shew that
my father's rejection of all religious belief was not, as many might
suppose, primarily a matter of logic & evidence; the grounds of
it were moral, still more than intellectual. He found it [116] impossible to believe [25*v*] that a world so full of evil was made by a
being of perfect goodness. His intellect spurned the subtleties by
which men attempt to elude this open contradiction. His aversion
to religion was like that of Lucretius: he regarded it with the feelings due not to a mere mental delusion but to a great [117] moral evil.
He looked upon religion as the greatest enemy of morality: first,
by setting up factitious excellencies, belief in creeds, devotional
feelings & ceremonies, not connected with the good of human kind
& causing them to be accepted as substitutes for real virtues: but
above all by radically vitiating the standard of morals; making it
consist in doing the will of a being on whom it lavishes the most

---

[113] the only opponents for whom] Deists, for whom alone
[114] little] nothing *altered to final reading first by HM*
[115] triumphantly *deleted first by HM* [116] utterly
[117] he regarded it . . . great] it was odious to him, not as an intellectual inconsistency or absurdity but as a

servile [118] phrases of adulation but whom in sober truth it depicts
as eminently hateful. I have a hundred times heard him say, that
all ages & nations have represented their gods as wicked, in an
increasing progression; that mankind have gone on adding trait
after trait till they reached the most perfect conception of wickedness which the human mind could devise, & called this God &
prostrated themselves before it. This ne plus ultra [119] [26r] he
considered to be embodied in the idea of God as represented in
the Christian creed. Think (he used to say) of a being who would
make a Hell—who would create the human race with the infallible
foreknowledge & therefore with the intention that the great majority
of them were to be consigned to infinite torment.[120] The time, I too
believe, is not very far distant when all persons with any sense of
moral good & evil will regard this horrible conception of an object
of worship with the same indignation with which my father regarded
it. That they have not done so hitherto, is owing to the infantine
state of the general intellect of mankind, under the wretched cultivation which it has received. Such however [121] is the facility with which
mankind believe at one & the same time contradictory things; &
so few are those who draw from what they receive as truths, any
consequences but those recommended to them by their feelings;
that multitudes have held the belief in an omnipotent author of
Hell, & have nevertheless identified [122] that Being with the best
conception they knew how to form of perfect goodness. Their
worship was not paid to the demon which such [26v] a Being
as they imagined would really be, but to their own ideal of excellence. The evil is, that such a belief keeps the ideal wretchedly
low; & crushes all thought which has any tendency to raise it.
Believers shrink [123] from every train of thought which would lead
to a clear conception & an elevated standard of excellence, because they feel, (even when they do not distinctly see), that any
such would [124] conflict with many of the dispensations of nature,

---

[118] the most servile] all *altered to final reading first by HM*

[119] ne plus ultra] God of Christianity *altered currently to read:* consummation [26r] of wickedness

[120] infinite torment.] this hell for all eternity.

[121] The time, I too believe, is not very far . . . however] *written at left to
replace:* Human imagination, he said, never formed an idea of wickedness com-
parable to this. Assuredly this is a conception worthy of all the indignation
with which he regarded it. But (it is just to add) such

[122] identified] invested   [123] terrified   [124] necessarily

& with many doctrines of the Christian creed. And thus morality
continues a matter of blind tradition, with no consistent principle
or feeling to guide it.

It would have been totally inconsistent with my father's ideas
of duty, to allow me to imbibe notions [125] contrary to his [126] convictions & feelings respecting religion: & he impressed upon me
from the first [127] that the manner in which the world came into
existence was a subject on which nothing was known; that the
question "Who made me?" [27r] cannot be answered, because we
have no experience from which to answer it; & that any answer
only throws the difficulty a step further back,[128] since the question immediately presents itself, Who made God? He at the same
time took care that I should be [129] acquainted with what had
been thought by mankind on these impenetrable [130] problems. It
has been seen how early he made me a reader of ecclesiastical
history: & he taught me to take the strongest interest in the Reformation, as the great & decisive contest against priestly tyranny
& for liberty of thought.

I am thus one of the very few examples, in this country, of one
who has, not thrown off religious belief, but never had it.[131] I grew
up in a negative state with relation to it. I looked upon the modern
exactly as I did upon the Greek religion,[132] as something which
in no way concerned me. It did not seem to me more strange that
English people should believe what I did not believe, than that
the men whom I read about in Herodotus should have done so.[133]
[27v] History had made the variety of opinions among mankind
a fact familiar to me, & this was but a prolongation of that fact.
This point in my early education, however, had incidentally one
bad consequence deserving notice. In giving me an opinion contrary to that of the world, my father thought it necessary to give
it as one which could not prudently [134] be avowed to the world.
This lesson of keeping my thoughts to myself at that early age,

---

[125] notions] impressions   [126] strong

[127] impressed upon me from the first] indoctrinated me from the first with
the opinion

[128] without at all diminishing it,   [129] well

[130] impenetrable] impracticable   [131] From the first

[132] Greek religion,] Pagan mythology *altered currently in the course of first
writing*

[133] It never occurred to me to [27v] look down upon them for it: *deleted first
by HM*

[134] prudently] wisely

could not but be morally prejudicial; though my limited inter-course with strangers, especially such as were likely to speak to me on religion, prevented me from being placed in the alternative of avowal or hypocrisy. I remember two occasions in my boyhood on which I felt placed in this alternative & in both cases I avowed my disbelief & defended it. My opponents in both cases were boys, considerably older than myself; one of them I certainly staggered at the time, but the subject was never renewed between us; the other, who seemed surprised & somewhat shocked, did his best to convince me, but it is hardly necessary to say, without effect.

[28r] [135] The great advance in liberty of discussion which is one of the points of difference between the present time & that of my childhood, has greatly altered the moralities of this question; & I think that few men of my father's intellect & public spirit, hold-ing with such intensity of moral conviction as he did, unpopular opinions on religion or on any other of the great subjects of thought, would now either practise or inculcate the withholding of them from the world; unless in those cases, becoming rarer every day, in which frankness on these subjects would risk the loss of means of subsistence. On religion in particular it appears to me to have now become a duty for all who being qualified in point of knowl-edge, have on mature consideration satisfied themselves that the current opinions are not only false but hurtful, to make their dis-sent known. At least those are bound to do so whose station, or reputation, gives their opinion a chance of being attended to. Such an avowal would put an end, at once & for ever, to the vulgar prejudice that what is called, very improperly, unbelief, is con-nected with any bad qualities either of mind or heart. The world would be astonished if it knew how great a proportion of its bright-est ornaments, of those most distinguished both for wisdom & vir-tue, [28v] are complete sceptics in religion; many of them [136] re-fraining from avowal, less from personal considerations, than from a conscientious though in my opinion a most mistaken apprehen-sion lest by speaking out what would tend to weaken existing be-liefs they should do harm instead of good.

Of unbelievers (so called) as well as of believers, there are

---

[135] *Fol. 28 (the next two paragraphs) is a later addition, after which the leaf headed "24—25" (see p. 178) and the original fols. 26–28 were refoli-ated 24–27*

[136] them] them, it should be said to their credit,

many species, including almost every variety of moral type. But
the best among them, as no one who has opportunities of knowing
will hesitate to say (believers rarely have that opportunity) are
more genuinely religious, in the best sense of the word religion,
than those who exclusively arrogate to themselves the title. Though
they may think the proofs insufficient that the universe is a work
of design, and assuredly believe that it cannot have a Creator &
Governor who is perfect both in power & in goodness,[137] they have
that which constitutes the principal worth of all religions whatever,
an ideal conception of a perfect character which they take as the
guide of their conscience; [138] & this ideal of good [139] is usually far
nearer to perfection than the objective Deity of those, who think
themselves obliged to find perfection in the author of a world so
crowded with suffering & so deformed by injustice.

[29r] My [140] father's moral convictions, entirely dissevered from
religion, were very much of the character of those of the Greek
philosophers: & were delivered with the force & decision which
characterized all that came from him. Even at the very early age
at which I read with him the Memorabilia of Xenophon, I imbibed from that book & from his comments a deep respect for the
character of Socrates; who stood in my mind as a model of ideal
excellence: & I remember how, at the same time of life, my father
impressed on me the lesson of the "Choice of Hercules." At a later
period the lofty moral standard exhibited in the writings of Plato,
took great effect on me. My father's moral inculcations were at all
times mainly those of the "Socratici viri": justice, temperance,
veracity, perseverance; readiness to brave pain & especially labour;
regard for the public good; estimation of persons according to
their merits, & of things according to their intrinsic usefulness; a
life of exertion, in contradistinction to one of self indulgent indolence. These & other moralities were mostly [29v] conveyed by
brief sentences, uttered as occasion arose, of stern reprobation or
contempt.

---

[137] or the world would not be what it is,

[138] have that which constitutes . . . conscience;] pay a truly religious hom-
age to an ideally perfect Being, to whose approbation they habitually refer
every thought & action (*"whose approbation" altered by HM to read:* which)

[139] of good] God *altered to final reading first by HM*

[140] *This paragraph originally followed the third paragraph above (see p. 61,
n. 135), and its first nine words, here interlined, were originally written at the
bottom of fol. 27v. An earlier version of it was written and deleted in fol. 15v
(see p. 48, n. 65)*

But though direct moral teaching does much, indirect does more; & the effect my father had on my character, did not depend merely on what he said or did with that direct object, but also, & still more, on what manner of man he was.

In his views of life he partook of the character of the Stoic, the Epicurean, & the Cynic. In his personal character the Stoic predominated: his standard of morals was Epicurean, in so far as that it was utilitarian, taking as the sole test of right & wrong, the tendency of actions to produce pleasure or pain. But he had (& this was the Cynic element) scarcely any belief in pleasure; at least in his later years, of which alone on this subject I can speak confidently. He deemed very few pleasures worth the price which at all events in the present state of society, must be paid for them. The greatest miscarriages in life he considered attributable to the overvaluing of pleasures. Accordingly, temperance in the large sense intended by the Greek philosophers—[30r] stopping short at the point of moderation in all indulgences—was with him as with them, almost the cardinal point of moral precept. His inculcations of this virtue fill a large place in my childish recollections.[141] He thought human life a poor thing at best,[142] after the freshness of youth & of unsatisfied curiosity had gone by. This was a topic on which he did not often speak, especially, it may be supposed, in the presence of young persons: but when he did, it was with an air of profound & habitual conviction. He would sometimes say that if life were made what it might be, by good government & good education, it would then be worth having: but he never spoke with anything like enthusiasm even of that possibility. He never varied in rating intellectual enjoyments above all others, even in their value as pleasures, independently of ulterior consequences. The pleasures of the benevolent affections he placed high in the scale; & used to say, that he had never known a happy old man, except those who were able to live over again in the pleasures of the young. For passionate emotions of all sorts, & for everything which has been said or written in [30v] exaltation of them, he professed the greatest contempt: he regarded them as a form of madness; "the intense" was with him a bye-word of scornful disapprobation. He regarded as an aberration of the moral standard of modern

---

[141] *Originally continued after a semicolon:* applied, as in childhood they necessarily were, chiefly to over indulgence in amusement.

[142] human life a poor thing at best,] the most fortunate human life very little worth having;

times, compared with that of the ancients, the great stress laid
upon feeling. Feelings, as such, he considered to be no proper
subjects of praise or blame; Right & wrong, good & bad, he regarded as terms having reference only to conduct; to acts & omissions; there being no feeling which may not lead, & does not frequently lead, either to good or to bad actions: even conscience,
even the desire to act right, often leading people to act wrong.
Consistently carrying out the doctrine, that the object of praise &
blame should be the discouragement of wrong conduct & the encouragement of right, he refused to let his praise or blame be influenced by the motive of the agent. He blamed as severely what
he thought bad actions when the motive was a sense of duty [143]
[31r] as if the agents had been consciously evil doers. He would
not have accepted as a plea in mitigation for inquisitors, that they
conscientiously believed burning heretics to be a sacred duty. But
though he did not allow sincerity of purpose to soften his disapprobation of actions, it had its full effect on his estimation of
characters; [144] no one prized conscientiousness & rectitude of intention more highly, or was more incapable of valuing [145] any
person in whom he did not feel assured of it. But he disliked
people quite as much for any other deficiency, provided he thought
it equally likely to make them act ill. He disliked, for instance, a
fanatic in any bad cause, as much or more than one who adopted
the same cause from self interest,[146] because he thought him still
more likely to be practically mischievous.[147] And thus his aversion
to many intellectual errors, or what he regarded as such, partook,
in a certain sense, of the character of a moral feeling.[148] This senti-

---

[143] (if opposed to *his* standard) *R31r* (*see p. 182*), *deleted by HM*
[144] He would not have accepted as a plea . . . characters;] Such considerations however, though he did not suffer them to influence his praise or blame
in particular instances, influenced his general estimation of persons: *R31r; at
left HM penciled a question mark and several words, now erased, of which*
"of them influenced his dislike of particular persons" *can be made out. Just
above, opposite the ending of the preceding sentence, she wrote the word*
"*Inquisitors*"
[145] valuing] liking *R31r; altered to final reading in fol. 31r*
[146] one who adopted . . . interest,] a hypocrite *R31r, subsequently altered
to final form*
[147] *In R31r HM commented at left, beginning opposite the last word of this
sentence:* "It is indeed generally true that knaves do less mischief in the world
than fools   a dishonest man stops when he has got what he wanted a fool
carries on his foolishness thro his own & his descendants"
[148] In this surely he was fundamentally right. *R31r, deleted. For the rest of
this paragraph R31 reads:* This sentiment, though by persons who do not care

ment, though persons who do not care about opinions may confound it with intolerance, is inevitable to any earnest mind. Those who, holding opinions which they deem immensely important & their contraries prodigiously hurtful, have any strong feeling of care for the general good, will necessarily dislike those who think wrong what they think right, & right what they think wrong. They will not, or at least they ought not, to desire to punish them for their sincere opinions,[149] [31v] & this forbearance, flowing not from indifference but from a conscientious sense of the [150] importance to mankind of freedom of opinion, is the only kind of tolerance which is [151] commendable. I grant that an earnest person may dislike others on account of opinions which do not merit dislike.[152] But if he neither himself does them any ill office, nor connives at its being done by others, he is not intolerant; nor does he err [153] because he judges them by his own standard, but because his own standard is wholly or partially wrong; & because his antagonism to the opinions he dislikes is a stronger principle than his desire to enlarge & rectify his own doctrines.

Personally [154] I believe my father to have had much greater capacities of feeling than were ever developed in him. He resembled almost all Englishmen in being ashamed of the signs of feeling, & by the absence of demonstration, starving the feelings

---

about opinions it may be confounded with intolerance, is natural to all who do; & inevitable in those who, holding opinions which they deem immensely important & their contraries prodigiously hurtful, have any strong feeling of care for mankind. We must try actions & characters by our own standard, not by that of the person we judge of. If our standard is right, we ought to like or dislike others according to its dictates. [R31v] If persons err in their judgments by following this rule, or rather obeying this necessity, it can only be because their own standard is wholly or partially wrong: & because they do not strive to enlarge & rectify their standard by appropriating what of good there may be in those of others. *The last twenty-four words* ("& *because they do not* . . . *others.") are written at left to replace:* an inquisitor judges a heretic to deserve the fire in this world & damnation in the next. When my father erred it was where his standard was too narrow, & omitted some of the elements of right judgment which might have been found scattered among the judgments of those whom he condemned.

[149] punish them for their sincere opinions,] do [31v] them harm, as they would in the case of those who act with conscious evil intention:

[150] great   [151] reasonable or

[152] on account of opinions . . . dislike.] unjustly on account of their opinions or in other words may be a bigot.

[153] does he err] is he to be blamed

[154] *For an earlier version of this paragraph and the first two sentences of the next, in R31v–34r, see pp. 183–186*

themselves. In an atmosphere of tenderness & affection he would have been tender & affectionate; but his ill assorted marriage & his asperities of temper disabled him from making such an atmosphere. [32r] It was one of the most unfavourable of the moral agencies which acted on me in my boyhood, that mine was not an education of love but of fear. I do not mean, for I do not believe, that boys can be induced to apply themselves with vigour, & what is so much more difficult, perseverance, to dry & irksome studies, by the sole force of persuasion & soft words. Much must be done & much must be learnt by children, for which rigid discipline & known liability to punishment are indispensable as means. It is no doubt a very laudable effort, in the improved methods of modern teaching, to render as much as possible of what the young are required to learn, easy & interesting to them. But when this principle is pushed to the length of not requiring them to learn anything but what has been made easy & interesting, one of the chief objects [155] of education is sacrificed. I rejoice in the decline of the old brutal & tyrannical system [32v] of teaching, which however did enforce habits of application; but the new, as it seems to me, is training up a race of men incapable of doing anything which is disagreeable to them. I do not believe that fear, as an element in education, can be dispensed with; but I am sure that it ought not to be the predominant element; & when it is carried so far as to preclude love or confidence on the part of the child to those who should be the unreservedly trusted advisers of after years, & perhaps to seal up altogether the fountains of frank & spontaneous communicativeness in the child's character, it is an evil for which a large abatement must be made from the benefits, moral & intellectual, which may flow from any other part of the education.

During this first period of my life, the habitual frequenters of my father's house were limited to a very few persons, mostly little known, but whom personal worth, & more or less of congeniality with his opinions (not so frequently to be met with then as since) disposed him to cultivate; & his conversations with them I listened to with interest & instruction. My being an [33r] habitual inmate of my father's study, made me acquainted with the most intimate & valued of his friends, David Ricardo, who by his benevolent countenance & kindliness of manner was very attractive to young persons, & who after I became a student of political economy,

---

[155] one of the chief objects] the most important part

sometimes invited me to breakfast & walk with him in order to converse on the subject. I was a more frequent visitor (from about 1817 or 1818) to Mr Hume, who, born in the same part of Scotland as my father, & having been, I rather think, a younger schoolfellow or college companion of his, had after his return from India renewed their old acquaintance, & who coming like many others greatly under the influence of his intellect & energy of character, was induced partly by that influence to go into Parliament, & there to adopt the line of conduct by which he has earned an honorable place in the history of his country. Of Mr Bentham I saw much more, owing to the close intimacy which subsisted between him & my father.[156] I do not know at what time they became first acquainted. But my father was the earliest Englishman of any great mark who thoroughly understood & in the main adopted Bentham's general views of ethics, government, & law: & Bentham accordingly valued his society highly & they became intimate companions [157] [33v] in a period of Bentham's life during which he admitted much fewer visitors than was the case subsequently. At this time Mr Bentham passed some part of every year at Barrow Green House, in a beautiful part of the Surrey hills, a few miles from Godstone, & there I each summer accompanied my father on a long visit. In 1813 Mr Bentham, my father & I made an excursion, which included Oxford, Bath & Bristol, Exeter, Plymouth, & Portsmouth.[158] In this journey I saw many things which were [159] instructive to me, & acquired my first taste for natural scenery, in the elementary form of fondness for a

---

[156] close intimacy which . . . father.] greater closeness of my father's connexion with him. *R34v; HM underlined and queried "connexion", and then wrote at left the version that Mill copied into fol. 33r*

[157] they became intimate companions] made an intimate companion of him *R34v, altered by HM to read:* they became very intimate companions

[158] At this time Mr Bentham passed . . . Portsmouth.] When we lived in Newington Green my father used to dine with Mr Bentham (at the very [R35r] considerable distance of Queen Square Place) every Tuesday. During each of seven or eight years Mr Bentham passed some part of the year in the country & my father with the whole or part of his family (I being always one) used to accompany him. At first the time occupied by these annual excursions was from one to three months & the place was Barrow Green House, in a beautiful part of the Surrey Hills a few miles from Godstone. In 1813 part of the time usually passed at Barrow Green was devoted to a three weeks tour in which my father & I accompanied Mr Bentham & which included Oxford, Bath & Bristol, Exeter, Plymouth, & Portsmouth. *R34v–35r, deleted and altered by HM to produce the two sentences that Mill copied into fol. 33v*

[159] even then *R35r, deleted by HM*

"view." In the following winter we left Newington Green, & moved into a house which my father rented of Mr Bentham, in Queen Square, Westminster.[160] From 1814 to 1817 Mr Bentham lived during half of each year at Ford Abbey,[161] in Somersetshire (or rather in a parish of Devonshire surrounded by Somersetshire) & these intervals I had the advantage of passing at that place.[162] This sojourn was, I think, an important circumstance in my education. Nothing contributes more to nourish elevation of sentiments in a people, than the large & free character of their habitations. The middle age architecture, the baronial hall & the spacious & lofty rooms of this fine old place, so unlike the mean and cramped externals of English middle class life, gave the feeling of a larger & freer existence, & were to me a sort of poetic [34*r*] culture, aided also by the character of the grounds in which the Abbey stood; which were riant & secluded, umbrageous, & full of the sound of falling waters.[163]

---

[160] In the following winter . . . Westminster.] In the next following winter, we left Newington Green & moved into the house No 1 Queen Square, looking into Mr Bentham's garden & rented by him, which he allowed my father to occupy at the rent he himself paid for it. In this house we lived until 1831. [R35*v*] My father paid the rent direct to the head landlord so that Mr Bentham's participation was simply equivalent to being security for the rent. I am particular in mentioning these circumstances because statements have been made exaggerating greatly my father's personal obligations to Mr Bentham. The only obligation, in money or money's worth, which he ever, to the best of my knowledge & belief, received from Mr Bentham, consisted of the visits to the country which I have mentioned, & these visits were of no remarkable length until the four years subsequent to 1813. *R35; HM penciled "by Dr Bowring" in the margin opposite "statements have been made" (in the fourth sentence), and "maliciously" opposite the next word, "exaggerating"—and then deleted and altered the text to produce the single sentence that Mill copied into fol. 33v*

[161] near Chard, *R35r; deleted in fol. 33v*

[162] these intervals I had . . . place.] during those months my father & the whole family were domiciled with him. *R35v, altered by HM to read:* each summer I passed in the beautiful scenery of this place.

[163] were riant & secluded . . . waters.] though[a] not picturesque, were riant & secluded, & full of the sound of falling waters.[a] *R36r, altered by HM to produce the version that Mill copied into fol. 34r. There follows in R36 a note, which HM first altered in several places, then deleted entirely and marked "omit":* (a) Note   The mode of life at Ford Abbey was the following. Mr Bentham & my father studied & wrote in the same large room, (a different room however in summer & in winter). My father commenced at about seven, summer & winter: & as Mr Bentham did not make his appearance till some time after nine, I & the other children worked at our lessons in the same room during those two hours. The general hour of breakfast was nine, but Mr Bentham always breakfasted at one oclock among his books & papers, his breakfast

I owed another of the fortunate circumstances in my education, a year's residence in France, to Mr Bentham's brother, General Sir Samuel Bentham. I had seen Sir Samuel Bentham & his family at their house near Gosport at the time of the tour before mentioned, (he being then Superintendant of the Dockyard at Portsmouth) & also during a stay of a few days which they made at Ford Abbey shortly after the peace, before going to live on the Continent. In 1820 they invited me for a six months visit to them in the South of France, ultimately prolonged to nearly a twelvemonth.[164] Sir Samuel Bentham, though of a character of mind very different from his illustrious brother, was a man of considerable attainments & general mental powers, with a decided genius [165] for mechanical art. His wife, a daughter of the celebrated chemist Dr Fordyce, was a woman of strong will & determined character, much general knowledge, & great practical good sense in the Edgeworth stile: she was the ruling spirit of the household, which she was well qualified to be. Their family consisted of one son (the eminent botanist) & three daughters, the youngest about

---

being laid early in the morning on his study table. The party at the general breakfast consisted of my father & mother, Mr Bentham's amanuensis for the time being, & the visitors, if, as not unfrequently happened, any were staying in the house. Before his one oclock breakfast Mr Bentham regularly went out for the same invariable walk, a circuit of about half an hour, in which my father almost always joined him. The interval between breakfast & this walk my father [R36v] employed in hearing lessons, which when weather permitted, was always done in walking about the grounds. The hours from one to six my father passed in study & this was the time regularly allotted to us children for learning lessons. Six was the dinner hour, & the remainder of the evening Mr Bentham passed in social enjoyment, of which he had a keen relish. I was never present on these evenings except a few times when Mr Bentham good-naturedly sent for me to teach me to play at chess. (End of Note).

[164] I owed another of the fortunate circumstances . . . twelvemonth.] It was to Mr Bentham's interest in me that I was indebted for another of the fortunate circumstances in my education, a year's residence in France. For it could only be on Mr Bentham's account that his brother, General Sir Samuel Bentham, invited me at the age of fourteen, for a six months visit to him in the South of France, ultimately prolonged to nearly a twelvemonth: Sir Samuel & his family being only slightly acquainted with my father, & having seen me only twice, the first time at their house near Gosport, in the three weeks tour before mentioned (Sir Samuel being then Superintendant of the Dockyard at Portsmouth): the second time on a visit of a few days which they paid to Ford Abbey shortly after the peace, before going to live in France. *R37r; HM deleted the first sentence, and altered the rest to produce (except in minor particulars and the order of the sentences) the second and third sentences of this paragraph in fol. 34r*

[165] (if such a word may be so used) *R37r, deleted*

two years my senior. I am indebted to [34v] them for much instruction, & for an almost parental interest in my improvement.[166] When I first joined them, in May 1820, they occupied the Chateau of Pompignan (still belonging to a descendant of Voltaire's enemy) on the heights overlooking the plain of the Garonne between Montauban & Toulouse. I [167] accompanied them on an excursion to the Pyrenees, including a stay of some duration at Bagnères de Bigorre, a journey to Pau, Bayonne, & Bagnères de Luchon, & an ascent of the Pic du Midi de Bigorre. In October we proceeded by the beautiful [35r] mountain route of Castres & St Pons from Toulouse to Montpellier, in which last neighbourhood (a few miles north of Montpellier) they had just bought the estate of Restinclière, which they set about vigorously to improve.[168] During this sojourn in France I acquired a familiar knowledge of the French language & considerable acquaintance with French books; I took lessons in various bodily exercises, in none of which however I made any proficiency; & at Montpellier I attended the excellent winter courses of lectures at the Faculté des Sciences of the University, those of M. Anglada on chemistry, of M. Provençal on zoology, & of M. Gergonne, on logic, under the name of Philosophy of the Sciences. I also went through a course of the higher branches of mathematics under the able private tuition of M. Lenthéric, a professor at the Lycée of Montpellier.[169] But the greatest advantage which I derived from this episode in my life was that of having breathed for a whole year the free & genial atmosphere of Continental life. This advantage I could not then judge [35v] & appreciate, nor even consciously feel, but it was not the less real. Having so little experience of English life, & the few people I knew being mostly such as had at heart public objects of a large & personally disinterested kind, I was then ignorant of

---

[166] I am indebted to them . . . improvement.] They treated me in every respect like a child of the family, & did all that advice & admonition could do to correct many of my various deficiencies & render me fitter for the ordinary purposes & intercourse of life. I wish that their judicious kindness had had all the effect which it deserved & which they had reason to expect. *R37r; before deleting the whole, HM altered the first sentence to read:* They did all that advice & admonition could do to correct my various deficiencies.

[167] I] After a few weeks they removed to Toulouse, taking me with them, & early in August I *R37v; HM deleted all but the last four words*

[168] Their headquarters however during the whole time of my stay with them were at Montpellier, where I remained with them until the middle of April. *deleted first by HM*

[169] *Originally continued without punctuation:* & a most excellent teacher.

the low moral tone of English society generally; the habit of, not indeed professing, but taking for granted in all modes of implication, that conduct is of course always directed towards low & petty objects; the absence of high feelings which manifests itself by sneering depreciation of all demonstrations of them, & by general abstinence (except among the more fanatical religionists) from professing any high principles of action at all, except in those preordained cases in which such profession is put on as part of the costume or formalities of the occasion. I could not then know or estimate the difference between this *manière d'être* & that of a people like the French with whom elevated sentiments are the current coin of human intercourse both in writing & in private life; & though doubtless [170] often evaporating in profession, are yet, in the nation at large, kept alive by constant exercise, & stimulated by sympathy so as to form an active & living part of the existence of multitudes [36r] of persons & to be recognized & understood by all. Neither could I then appreciate that general culture of the [171] understanding which results from the habitual exercise of the feelings & which is thus carried down into the most uneducated classes of the Continent to a degree not equalled in England among the so called educated. I did not know how, among the English, the absence of interest in things of an unselfish kind, except sometimes in a special thing here & there, & the habit of not speaking to others, nor much even to themselves, about the things in which they *are* interested, makes both their feelings & their intellectual faculties remain undeveloped, or develope themselves only in some single & very limited direction, & reduces them to a kind of negative existence. All this I did not perceive till long afterwards: but I even then felt, though without stating it clearly to myself, the contrast between the frank sociability & amiability of French personal intercourse, & the English mode of existence in which everybody acts as if everybody else (with perhaps a few individual exceptions) was either an enemy or a bore. In France, it is true, the bad as [36v] well as the good points of individual character come more to the surface & break out more fearlessly in ordinary intercourse, than in England, but the general manner of the people is to shew, as well as to expect, friendly feeling wherever there is not some positive cause for its opposite. In

---

[170] much oftener professed than felt, & when felt, *deleted first by HM*
[171] the] superiority of

England it is only of the best bred people (either in the upper or middle ranks) that as much can be said.[172]

In my way through Paris to the South I stayed some days & in my return several [173] weeks in the house of M. Say, the political economist, who was a correspondent of my father, having become acquainted with him on a visit to England a year or two after the peace. I remembered M. Say as a visitor to Ford Abbey. He was a man of the later period of the French Revolution, a fine specimen of the best kind of old French republican, one of those who had never bent the knee to Bonaparte though courted by him; a thoroughly upright & [37*r*] brave man. He lived a quiet & studious life, made, I should think, happy by warm affections, public & private. He was acquainted with many of the chiefs of the Liberal party: but the only one of them whom I remember seeing at that time was M. Ternaux, the manufacturer, who then lived at the beautiful place formerly Necker's at St Ouen. The other persons of note whom I saw were M. Destutt-Tracy; M. Dunoyer; M. Duméril the zoologist; M. Clement-Desormes, the chemist; a more eminent chemist Berthollet, who was a friend of Sir S. Bentham but not of M. Say, being on the opposite side in politics; & I have pleasure in the recollection of having once seen Saint Simon, not then known as the founder either of a philosophy or of a religion but considered only as a clever *original*. The chief fruit which I carried away from the society I saw, was [174] a strong interest in Continental Liberalism, of which I always afterwards kept myself *au courant* as much as of English politics.[175] After passing a few weeks at Caen with an early [176] friend of my father's, I returned to England in July 1821.

[37*v*] For the next year or so I continued my old studies, with the addition of some new ones. When I returned my father was just finishing for the press his Elements of Political Economy & he made me perform as an exercise on the manuscript, what Mr

---

[172] *Originally continued after a comma:* & only so far as such feeling & demeanour can be maintained by a few, among a multitude incapable of making suitable response. *marked with a line in the margin by HM*

[173] several] as much as three *altered to final reading first by HM*

[174] The chief fruit which . . . was] Inexperienced as I was, I carried away little from the society I saw, except (*the first four words, "little", and "except" are underlined by HM*)

[175] as much as of English politics.] to the extent of my opportunities. *underlined by HM*

[176] early] old college

Bentham practised on all his own writings, namely, making what he called "marginal contents"; a short abstract of every paragraph, to enable the writer more easily to judge of, & improve, the order of the ideas, & the general character of the exposition. Shortly after this, my father put into my hands Condillac's Traité des Sensations, & the logical and metaphysical [177] volumes of his Cours d'Etudes; [178] [38r] the first (notwithstanding the superficial resemblance between Condillac's psychological system & my father's own theory) rather as a warning than as an example. I am not sure whether it was in this winter or the next that I first read a history of the French Revolution. I learnt with astonishment that the principles of democracy then apparently in so insignificant & hopeless a minority everywhere in Europe, had borne down everything before them in France thirty years earlier, & had been the creed of the nation. [38v] As may be supposed from this, I had previously had a very vague idea of that great commotion. I knew nothing about it except that the French had thrown off the absolute monarchy of Louis 14th & 15th, had put the king & queen to death, guillotined many persons, one of whom was Lavoisier,[179] & had ultimately fallen under the despotism of Bonaparte. But from this time the subject took an immense hold of my feelings. It allied itself with all my juvenile aspirations to the character of a democratic champion. What had happened so lately, seemed as if it might easily happen again: & the greatest glory I was capable

---

[177] logical and metaphysical] first four (the logical & metaphysical)

[178] *Originally continued:* M. Gergonne's lectures had already given me Condillac's view of the analysis of the mind. I read these books in a useless, ineffectual way, not seeing any fallacy in them, but not gaining from them any grasp or command of the subject. When my father afterwards questioned me & made me give him an account of Condillac's system he shewed me that Condillac's seeming analyses of all mental phenomena into sensation [38r] amounted to nothing, that he paid himself in words, & that I had proved myself quite willing to be paid in words. I remember the impression which this phrase, which was then new to me, of paying in words, made on me. *Mill rewrote the passage at left on fol. 37v:* I was not then capable of perceiving, until it was explained to me, the superficiality & fallacy of Condillac's psychological theory; so radically inferior to Hartley's, notwithstanding the apparent resemblance. My father pointed out to me, that Condillac's seeming analyses of all mental phenomena into sensation, amounted to nothing, & that he paid himself & endeavoured to pay others in words. (*In several places HM attempted alterations, and in the second version she underlined* "until it was explained to me" *and* "My father pointed out to me, that".) *The rest of the sentence in the final text (*"the first . . . example.") *is written at left on fol. 38r*

[179] Lavoisier,] Lavoisier the great chemist,

of conceiving was that of figuring, successful or unsuccessful, as a
Girondist in an English Convention.

In the course of the winter of 1821/2 Mr Austin, with whom
at the time when I went to France my father had but lately become acquainted, allowed me to read Roman law with him. At
this time my father, notwithstanding his abhorrence of the chaos
of barbarism called English law, had turned his thoughts towards
the bar as on the whole less ineligible for me than any other profession: & these readings of Roman law [39r] with Mr Austin, who
had made Bentham's best [180] ideas his own & added many others
to them, were not only a valuable introduction to legal studies but
an important branch of general education. With Mr Austin I
went [181] through Heineccius on the Institutes, his Roman Antiqui-
ties, & part of his exposition of the Pandects; with the addition of
a considerable part of Blackstone. It was on this occasion that my
father, as a needful accompaniment to these studies, put into my
hands Bentham's principal [182] speculations, as interpreted to the
Continental world & indeed to the world in general by Dumont,
in the Traité de Législation. The reading of this book was an event
in my life; one of the turning points of my mental history.

My previous education had been, in a great measure, a course
of Benthamism. The Benthamic standard of "the greatest happiness" was that which I had always been taught to apply; I was
even familiar with an abstract discussion of it contained in a
manuscript dialogue on government, written by my [39v] father
on the Platonic model.[183] Yet in the first few pages of Bentham it
burst on me with all the force of novelty. What thus impressed me
was the chapter in which Bentham examined the common modes
of reasoning on morals & legislation, deduced from phrases like
"law of nature" "right reason" "the moral sense" "natural rectitude"
& the like, & characterized them as dogmatism in disguise, imposing its own sentiments upon other people by the aid of sound-
ing phrases which [184] convey no reason for the sentiment but set
up the sentiment as its own reason. This struck me at once as true.
The feeling rushed upon me that all previous moralists were superseded, & [185] that here indeed was the commencement of a new era

---

[180] Bentham's best] all Bentham's   [181] carefully   [182] principal] greatest
[183] *Originally continued after a comma:* which I had diligently studied.
[184] when their meaning is analysed,
[185] The feeling rushed . . . &] I immediately conceived a sovereign contempt
for all previous moralists; & felt

in thought. This impression was strengthened by the manner in which Bentham gave a scientific form to the application of the happiness principle to the morality of actions, by analysing the various classes & orders of consequences. But what most of all impressed me was the Classification of Offences; [40r] which is much more clear, compact, & imposing in Dumont's *redaction* than in the original work of Bentham from which it was taken. Logic & the Dialogues of Plato, which had formed so large a part of my intellectual training, had given me a great relish for accurate classification; this taste had been strengthened & enlightened by the study of botany, on the principles of the so called Natural Method which I had taken up with great zeal [186] during my stay in France: & when I found scientific classification applied to the large & complex subject of Punishable Acts, under the guidance of the ethical principle of Pleasurable & Painful Consequences followed out in the method of detail introduced into these subjects by Bentham, I felt taken up to an eminence from which I could survey a vast mental domain & see stretching out in the distance, intellectual results beyond all computation. As I proceeded farther, to this intellectual clearness there seemed to be added the most inspiring prospects of practical improvement in human affairs. To Bentham's general views of the construction of a body of law I was not altogether a stranger, having read with attention [40v] that admirable compendium, my father's article "Jurisprudence": but I had read it with little profit, & almost without interest, no doubt on account of its extremely general & abstract character, & also because it concerned the form more than the substance of the *corpus juris,* the logic rather than the ethics of law. But Bentham's subject was Legislation, of which Jurisprudence is only the formal part; & at every page he seemed to open a clearer & larger conception of what human opinions & institutions *ought* to be, how far removed from it they *were,* & how they might be made what they ought to be. When I laid down the last volume of the Traité I was a different being. The "principle of utility," understood as Bentham understood it, & applied in the manner in which he applied it through these three volumes, fell exactly into its place as the keystone which held together the detached & fragmentary portions of my knowledge & beliefs. It gave unity to my conceptions of things. I now had opinions; a creed, a doctrine, a philosophy; in one (&

---

[186] as a mere amusement *deleted first by HM*

the best) sense of the word, a religion; the inculcation & diffusion of which could be made the principal outward aim of a life. And I had a grand conception laid before me of [41r] changes to be made in the condition of mankind by that doctrine. The Traité de Législation winds up with what was to me a most impressive picture of human life as it would be made by such opinions & such laws [187] as are recommended in the book. The anticipations of practicable improvement are studiously moderate, deprecating & discountenancing as reveries of vague enthusiasm much which will one day be so natural to human beings that they will be apt to ascribe intellectual & even moral obliquity to those who could ever think such prospects chimerical. But in my state of mind this apparent superiority to illusions added to the effect of Bentham's doctrines on me, by heightening the impression of mental power. And the vista of improvement which he did open was large enough, & brilliant enough, to light up my life, as well as to give definiteness to my aspirations.

After this I read from time to time the most important of the other works of Bentham which had at that time been published, either as written by himself or as edited by Dumont. This I did for my own satisfaction; while under my father's direction my studies were carried into the [41v] higher branches [188] of analytic psychology. I read Locke's Essay on the Human Understanding & wrote out an account of it, consisting of a full abstract of every chapter, with such remarks as [189] occurred to me: this was read by, or (I think) to, my father, & discussed throughout. I went through the same process, of my own motion, with Helvetius "De l'Esprit"; a book which I greatly admired.[190] This writing of abstracts, subject as it was to my father's censorship, was a most valuable exercise, by compelling precision in conceiving & expressing philosophical [191] doctrines, whether received as truths or merely as the opinions of writers. After Helvetius, my father made me study what he deemed the really master-production in the philosophy of mind, Hartley. This book, though it did not constitute an era in my existence, like the Traité de Législation, made a

---

[187] laws] institutions   [188] higher branches] more difficult parts

[189] such remarks as] any criticisms which

[190] of my own motion . . . admired.] with Helvetius "De l'Esprit"; in which case I remember that my own strong wish to read the book was the moving impulse.

[191] philosophical] abstract

very similar impression on me in regard to its immediate subject. Hartley's explanation, incomplete as in many parts it is, of the more complex mental phenomena by the law of association, commended itself to me [192] as a real analysis, & made me feel by contrast the insufficiency [42r] of the mere verbal generalizations of Condillac, & even of the instructive gropings & feelings-about for psychological explanations, of Locke. It was at this very time that my father commenced writing his Analysis of the Mind, which carried Hartley's mode of explaining the phenomena to so much greater length & depth. He could only command the concentration of thought necessary for this work during the complete leisure of his annual holiday of a month or six weeks & he commenced it in the summer of 1822, the first holiday he passed at Dorking; in which neighbourhood from that time to the end of his life, with the exception of two years, he lived (as far as his official duties permitted) for six months of every year.[193] He worked at the Analysis during several successive holidays, & allowed me to read the manuscript portion by portion as it advanced.[194] The first instalment of it I read in this same summer.[195] [42v] The other principal English writers on mental philosophy I read afterwards as I felt inclined, particularly Berkeley, Hume's Essays, Dugald Stewart, Reid,[196] & Brown on Cause & Effect. Brown's Lectures I did not read till two or three years later, nor at that time had my father himself read them.

Among the things read in the course of this year which contributed materially to my developement I should mention a book, written on the foundation of some manuscripts of Bentham & published under the pseudonyme of Philip Beauchamp, entitled "Analysis of the Influence of Natural Religion on the Temporal Happiness of Mankind." This was an examination not of the truth, but of the usefulness of religious belief, in the most general sense, apart from any supposed special revelation; which, of all the

---

[192] at once

[193] (as far as his . . . year.] for about six months of every year, as much as circumstances permitted, namely passing from the Saturday or oftener the Friday afternoon to the Monday morning of each week, & the whole of the annual holiday.

[194] *Originally continued after a comma:* so that I was cognizant of these speculations not merely when complete, but in the process of their formation.

[195] *At this point Mill interlined and subsequently deleted:* (the last which I passed in the country).

[196] Dugald Stewart, Reid,] *interlined*

portions of the discussion respecting religion, is the most important in this age, in which real belief in any religious doctrine is feeble, but the opinion of its necessity for moral & social purposes almost universal; & when those who reject revelation very generally take refuge in an optimistic deism, a worship of the order of Nature or of Providence at least as full of contradictions, & as perverting to the moral sentiments, as any of the received forms of Christianity; for if the world has [43r] a ruler, & but one ruler, that one is certainly far less deserving of worship than[197] the author of the Sermon on the Mount. Yet very little of a philosophical character has been written by sceptics against the usefulness of the belief in this Being. The volume bearing the name of Philip Beauchamp, which was shewn to my father in manuscript & by him given to me to read and make a marginal analysis of, as I had done of the Elements of Political Economy, made a great impression on me,[198] & gave me much instruction both on its express subject & on many collateral topics. On reading it lately after an interval of many years, I find it to have the defects as well as the merits of the Benthamic modes of thought, & to contain many weak arguments, but with a great overbalance of sound ones, & much good material for a more philosophic & conclusive treatment of the subject.

I have now, I believe, mentioned all the books which had any considerable effect on my early mental developement. From this point I began to carry on my own mental cultivation by writing still more than by reading. In the summer of 1822 I wrote my first argumentative essay: [43v] I remember very little about it except that it was an attack on what I regarded as the aristocratic prejudice that the rich were, or were likely to be, superior in moral excellence to the poor. I set about this task unprompted, except by emulation of a little manuscript essay of Mr Grote.[199] I recollect

---

[197] that one is certainly . . . than] the character of that one must be atrocious, & the worship of such a Being more morally degrading, if not more intellectually contemptible, than almost any adoration which is capable of being directed to

[198] *Originally continued after a period:* It is now many years since I have read it, but it remains in my memory as a most searching & substantial piece of argument, far superior to any other discussion of the subject which I have seen, & abounding in incidental instruction on important collateral topics. *After canceling this sentence, Mill wrote the new conclusion to the paragraph* ("*& gave me . . . subject.*") *at left*

[199] *Originally continued without punctuation:* which I had been allowed to read.

that my performance was entirely argumentative without any of the declamation which the subject would admit of, & might be expected to suggest to a young writer. In that department however I was & remained very inapt. Dry argument was the only thing I could manage, or willingly attempted: though passively I was very susceptible to the effect of all composition, whether in the form of poetry or oratory, which appealed to the feelings on any basis of reason. My father was well satisfied with this essay, & as I learnt from others, even much pleased with it; but, perhaps from a desire to promote the exercise of other mental faculties than the argumentative, he advised me to make my next exercise in composition one of the oratorical kind; & accordingly availing myself of my familiarity with Greek history & ideas & with the Athenian orators, I wrote two speeches, one an accusation, the other a defence of Pericles on a [44r] supposed impeachment for not marching out to fight the Lacedæmonians on their invasion of Attica. My next essay, suggested by my father, was a reply to [200] Paley's Natural Theology: & after this I went on writing papers often on subjects very much beyond me, but with great benefit both from the exercise itself, & from the discussions with my father to which it led.[201]

I had now also begun to converse on terms of equality, with the instructed men with whom I came in contact: & the opportunities of such contact naturally became more numerous. The two friends of my father from whom I derived most, & with whom I most associated,[202] were Mr Grote & Mr Austin. The acquaintance of both with him was recent, but had ripened rapidly into intimacy. Mr Grote was introduced to my father by Ricardo, I believe in 1819 (being then about twenty five years old) & sought assiduously his society & conversation. Already a highly instructed man, he was yet, by the side of my father, a tyro on the great subjects of human opinion; but he rapidly [44v] seized on my father's best ideas, & made them his own: & in the department of political opinion he signalized himself as early as 1820 by a pamphlet in defence of Radical Reform, in reply to a celebrated article by Sir James Mack-

---

[200] reply to] formal refutation of

[201] me, but with great benefit . . . led.] my knowledge & capacity but which led to discussions with my father that shewed me when my ideas were confused, & helped to clear them up. *marked with a line in the margin by HM*

[202] & with whom I most associated,] who were his most frequent visitors, & whose houses I most frequented, *the last six words deleted first by HM*

intosh, then lately published in the Edinburgh Review. Mr Grote's
father, the old banker, was I believe a thorough Tory & his mother
intensely Evangelical, so that for his liberal opinions he was in no
way indebted to home influences. But, unlike most persons who
have the prospect of being rich by inheritance, he had, though
actively engaged in business as a banker, devoted a great portion
of time to philosophic studies, & his intimacy with my father decided the character of his subsequent mental progress. Him I often
visited, & my conversations with him on politics, ethics, religion &
philosophy, gave me, in addition to much instruction, some useful
practice in expressing myself & carrying on discussion by word of
mouth.

Mr Austin, a man four or five years older than Mr Grote, was the
eldest son of a retired miller in Suffolk who had made money by
contracts during the war & who I think [45r] must have been [203] a
man of remarkable qualities, from the fact that all his sons are of
more than common ability & all eminently gentlemen. At least I
can affirm this of three out of the four, & have reason to believe the
same of the remaining one with whom as he went early to live
abroad I was never much acquainted. The one of whom I am now
speaking was for some time an officer in the army, & served in
Sicily under Lord William Bentinck. After the peace he sold his
commission & studied for the bar, to which he had been called &
was endeavouring to get into practice at the time when my father
became acquainted with him. He could not, like Mr Grote, be
called [204] a disciple of my father, but had already formed by reading or thought, many of the same opinions, modified however by his
own individual character. He was a man of great intellectual
powers, which in conversation appeared still greater: from the
energy & richness of expression with which, under the excitement
of discussion, he was accustomed to assert & to defend some view
or other of most subjects; & from an appearance of [205] [45v] not
only strong but deliberate & collected will; tinged with a certain

---

[203] think must have been] am sure [45r] must have been (for though he is,
I believe, still alive I never saw him)

[204] could not . . . called] was not, like Mr Grote, in some measure *altered
to read:* was . . . Grote, what might almost be called

[205] an appearance of] a manner of delivery [45v] which as in others of this
remarkable family conveyed an impression of immense strength of will. In him
it appeared (*HM deleted the original ending of the sentence, after the semicolon in "subjects;" and struck through "it" in the beginning of the new
sentence*)

bitterness, partly derived from temperament, partly perhaps from personal circumstances, & partly from the general course of his feelings & reflexions. The dissatisfaction with life and the world, felt more or less in the present state of society by every discerning & conscientious mind, was in his case, I think, combined with habitual dissatisfaction with himself, giving a generally melancholy cast to the character, very natural to those whose passive moral susceptibilities are much more than proportioned to their active energies. For it must be said, that the strength of will of which his manner seemed to give such strong assurance, expended itself in manner, & appeared to bear little active fruits except bitterness of expression.[206] With great zeal for human improvement, a strong sense of duty, & habitual precision both in speech & in action, he hardly ever completed any intellectual task of [207] magnitude. He had so high a standard of what ought to be done, so exaggerated a sense of deficiencies in his own performances & was so unable to content himself with the degree of elaboration which the occasion & the purpose required [46r] that he not only spoiled much of his work by overlabouring it, but spent so much time & exertion in superfluous study & thought that when his task ought to have been completed he had generally worked himself into an illness without having half finished what he undertook. From this mental infirmity combined with liability to frequent attacks of disabling though not dangerous ill health, he accomplished through life very little compared with what he seemed capable of; though like Coleridge he might plead as a set off that he had exercised, through his conversation, a highly improving influence on many persons, both as to intellect & sentiments. On me his influence was most salutary. It was moral in the best sense. He took a sincere & kind interest in me, far beyond what was to be expected towards a mere [208] youth from a man of his age, standing, & what seemed austerity of character. There was in his conversation & demeanour a tone of what I have since called high-mindedness, which did not shew itself so much, if the quality existed as much, in any of the [46v] other persons with whom at that time I associated.[209] My intercourse with him

---

[206] expended itself in manner . . . expression.] was more apparent than real.
[207] the smallest *altered to read:* any   [208] mere] raw
[209] *Originally continued after a comma:* not even in my father; although my father was as high principled as Mr Austin & had a stronger will; but Mr Austin was both a prouder man, & more a man of feeling than my father. *deleted first by HM*

was the more beneficial to me owing to his being of a different mental type from any of the other intellectual men whom I frequented, & his influence was exerted against [210] many of the prejudices & narrownesses which are almost sure to be found in a young man formed by a particular school or a particular set.

His younger brother, Charles Austin, of whom at this time & for the next year or two I saw much,[211] had also a great effect on me though of a different kind.[212] He was but six years older than myself, & at that time had just left the University of Cambridge where he had shone with great éclat as a man of intellect & especially of brilliancy both as an orator & as a converser. His influence among his Cambridge contemporaries deserves to be regarded as an historical event; for to it may in no small degree be traced the tendency towards Liberalism in general, & towards the Benthamic & politico-economic form of [47r] Liberalism, which shewed itself among a [213] portion of the more active minded young men of the higher classes, from this time to 1830. The Union Debating Society, then at the height of its reputation, was an arena where what were then thought extreme opinions, in politics and philosophy, were weekly asserted, face to face with their opposites before audiences consisting of the élite of the Cambridge youth: & though many persons afterwards of more or less note (Mr Macaulay perhaps the most conspicuous) gained their first oratorical laurels in these debates,[214] the really influential mind among these intellectual gladiators was Charles Austin. He continued after leaving the University to be by his conversation & personal ascendancy a leader among the same class of young men who had been his associates there; & he attached me among others to his car. Through him I became acquainted with Macaulay, Hyde & Charles Villiers, Strutt, & various other young men who afterwards became known in literature or in politics, & among whom I heard discussions on many topics to a certain degree new to me.[215] None of them however had any effect on my developement except Austin: whose influence over me differed from

---

[210] was exerted against] tended to correct

[211] & for the next . . . much,] I saw much, & who indeed made a sort of companion of me, to a certain extent, for the next year or two,

[212] His was the influence of a young man over a young man.

[213] great

[214] I have always heard that *deleted first by HM*

[215] discussions on many topics . . . me.] a much wider range of topics than I had previously been used to.

that of the persons whom I have hitherto mentioned, in being not that of a man over a boy but of an older contemporary.[216] [47v] It was through him that I first felt myself not a pupil with teachers but a man among men.[217] He was the first person of intellect whom I met on a ground of equality, though obviously & confessedly my superior on that common ground. He was a man who never failed to make a great impression on those with whom he came in contact, even when their opinions were the very opposite of his. The impression which he gave was that of unbounded strength, together with talents which, combined with such apparent force of will & character, seemed made to dominate the world. Those who knew him, whether friendly to him or not, always anticipated that he would play a [218] conspicuous part in public life. It is seldom that men produce so great an immediate effect by speech unless they in some degree lay themselves out for it, & he did so in no ordinary degree. He loved to strike, & even to startle. He knew that decision is the greatest element of effect & he uttered his opinions with all the decision he could throw into them, never so well pleased as when he could astonish any one by their audacity. Very unlike his brother, who made war on [48r] the narrower interpretations and applications of the principles they both professed, he on the contrary presented the Benthamic doctrines in the most startling form of which they were susceptible, exaggerating everything in them which tended to consequences offensive to any one's preconceived feelings. All which, he defended with such verve & vivacity, & carried off by a manner so agreeable as well as forcible, that he always came off victor, or divided the honours of the field with any, however formidable antagonist. It is my belief that much of the popular notion of the tenets & sentiments of what are called Benthamites or Utilitarians, had its foundation in paradoxes thrown out by Charles Austin. It is but fair to add, however, that his example was followed, *haud passibus æquis,* by younger proselytes, & that to *outrer* whatever was by anybody considered offensive in the doctrines & maxims of Benthamism, became at one time the badge of a certain, not very numerous, coterie of youths. All of them however who had anything in them, myself among others, quickly outgrew this boyish

---

[216] differed from that of the persons . . . contemporary.] was not that of a man over a boy but of an older contemporary & had an equality in it combined [47v] with its superiority, which rendered it highly stimulating to me.

[217] *Originally continued after a comma:* forming & defending my own opinions.

[218] much more

vanity; & those who had not, became tired of differing from other
people, & left off both the good & the bad of the [48*v*] heterodox
opinions they for some time professed.

It was in this winter of 1822/23 that I formed the plan of a little
society, to be composed of young men agreeing on fundamental
principles—that is, acknowledging utility as their first principle in
ethics & politics, & a certain number of the principal corollaries
drawn from it in the philosophy I had accepted; & meeting once a
fortnight to read essays & discuss questions conformably to the
premises thus agreed on. This fact would be hardly worth mentioning but for the circumstance, that the name I gave to the little
society I had planned was the Utilitarian Society. It was the first
time that any one had taken the title of Utilitarian, & the word
made its way into the language from this humble source. I did not
invent the word, but found it in one of Galt's novels, the "Annals
of the Parish." [219] In one sentence of this book (if my remembrance
is correct) the Scotch clergyman of whom it is the supposed autobiography, [49*r*] finding heretical doctrines creeping into his parish
about the time of the French Revolution, warns some parishioner
not to leave the gospel & become an utilitarian. With a boy's fondness for a name & a banner I seized on the word, & for some years
called myself & others by it as a sectarian appellation: & it came to
be a little used (though never very much) by some others holding
the opinions which it was intended to designate. As those opinions
attracted more notice the term came to be repeated by strangers &
opponents, & got into rather common use just about the time when
those who had originally assumed it laid down that along with
other sectarian characteristics. The society so called consisted at
first of only three members, one of whom being Mr Bentham's
amanuensis we obtained permission to hold our meetings in his
house. The number never I think reached ten & the society was
broken up in 1826. It had thus an existence of about three years &
a half. The chief effect of it as regards myself, over & above practice in oral discussion,[220] was its bringing me in contact with young
men less [49*v*] advanced than myself, among whom, as they professed the same opinions, I became a sort of leader or chief, either

[219] *Originally continued apparently without punctuation:* a book by the way,
much admired by my father as a picture of Scotch village life. *deleted first
by HM*
[220] oral discussion,] speech-making (for our discussions were in the form of
speeches)

directing for the time, or much influencing, their mental progress. Any young man of education who fell in my way, whose opinions were not incompatible with those of the society, I endeavoured to press into its service: & several others I probably should never have known had they not joined it. Those of the members who became my intimate companions were William Eyton Tooke, the eldest son of the eminent political economist, a young man of singular worth both moral & intellectual, lost to the world by an early death; his friend William Ellis, now known by his apostolic exertions for the improvement of education; George Graham, now an official assignee of the Bankruptcy Court; & (from the time when he came to England to study for the bar, in 1824 or 1825) a man who has made considerably more noise in the world, John Arthur Roebuck.

In May 1823 my professional [50r] occupation & status were decided by my father's obtaining for me an appointment from the East India Company, in the office of the Examiner of Indian Correspondence, immediately under himself. I was appointed in the usual manner at the bottom of the list of Clerks, to rise by seniority; but with the understanding that I should be employed from the first in preparing drafts of despatches; & be thus trained up as a successor to those who then filled the higher departments of the office. My drafts of course required at first much revision from my immediate superiors, but I soon became well acquainted with the business & by my father's instructions & the general progress of my own powers I was in two or three years qualified to be, & practically was, the chief conductor of the correspondence with India in one of the leading departments, that of the Native States: & this [221] has continued to be my official duty up to the present time. I know no occupation among those by which a subsistence is now gained more suitable than such as this to any one who, not being pecuniarily independent, desires to devote a part of the twenty four [50v] hours to intellectual pursuits. The attempt to earn a living by writing for the press, can be recommended to no one qualified to accomplish anything in the higher departments of literature or speculation: for (not to speak of the uncertainty of such a means of livelihood, especially if the writer has a conscience & will not consent to serve any opinions but his own) it is evident

---

[221] & this] which in the successive characters of Clerk & Assistant Examiner, *deleted and altered to final form first by HM*

that the writings by which one can live are not the writings which
themselves live, or those in which the writer does his best. The
books which are to form future thinkers take too much time to
write, & when written come in general too slowly into notice &
repute to be a resource for subsistence. Those who have to support
themselves by literature must depend on literary drudgery, or at
best on writings addressed to the multitude, & can employ in the
pursuits of their choice only such time as they can spare from those
of necessity; generally less than the leisure allowed by office occupations, while the effect on the mind is far more enervating &
fatiguing. For my own part I have through life found office duties
an actual rest from the occupations which I have carried on simultaneously with them.[222] [51r] They were sufficiently intellectual
not to be an onerous drudgery, without being such as to cause any
strain upon the mental powers of a person used to abstract thought
or even to the labour of careful literary composition. The drawbacks, for every mode of life has its drawbacks, were not, however,
unfelt by me. The absence of the chances of riches & honours held
out by some professions, particularly the bar (which had been as
I said the profession thought of for me) affected me little. But I
was not indifferent to exclusion from Parliament & public life: &
I felt very sensibly the more immediate unpleasantness of confine-
ment to London, the holiday allowed by India-house practice not
exceeding a month in the year, while my taste was strong for a
country life & my year in France had left behind it an ardent desire for travelling. But though these tastes could not be freely indulged they were at no time entirely sacrificed. I passed most Sundays throughout the year in the country, often in long walks.[223]
[51v] The month's holiday was for a few years spent at my father's

---

[222] While they precluded all uneasiness about the means of subsistence, they
occupied fewer hours of the day than almost any business or profession, they
had nothing in them to produce anxiety, or to keep [51r] the mind intent on
them at any time but when directly engaged in them. *deleted first by HM*

[223] I passed most Sundays . . . walks.] I continued during the summer half
of every year to pass the Saturday [51v] afternoon & Sunday in the country,
returning to town with my father on Monday morning; generally in one of
the most beautiful districts of England, the neighbourhood of Dorking, in the
finest part of which (the vale of Mickleham near the foot of Box Hill) my
father after some years occupied a cottage permanently. During the last months
of winter & the first of spring I used every Sunday when weather permitted
to make a walking excursion with some of the young men who were my companions; generally walking out ten or twelve miles to breakfast, & making a
circuit of fourteen or fifteen more before getting back to town.

house in the country: afterwards a part or the whole was passed in tours, chiefly pedestrian, with some one or more of the young men who were my companions: [224] and from 1830 onwards the greater part of it was in most years employed in visits to friends whose acquaintance I made in that year, or in journeys or excursions [225] in which I accompanied them.[226] France, Belgium, & Rhenish Germany have been within easy reach of the annual holiday: & two longer absences, one of three, the other of six months, under medical advice, added Switzerland, the Tyrol, & Italy [227] to my list. Fortunately also both these journeys occurred rather early, so as to give [52r] the benefit & charm of the remembrance to a large portion of life.

The occupation of so much of my time by office work did not relax my attention to my own pursuits, which were never carried on more vigorously.[228] It was about this time that I began to write in newspapers. The first writings of mine which got into print were two letters published towards the end of 1822 in the Traveller evening newspaper, on I forget what abstract point of political economy. The Traveller, (which soon after grew into the "Globe & Traveller" by the purchase & incorporation of the Globe) was then the property of the well known political economist Colonel Torrens, & under the editorship of an able man, Mr Walter Coulson (who after being an amanuensis of Bentham, became a reporter, then an editor, next a barrister & conveyancer, & is now counsel to the Home Office) had become one of the most important newspaper organs of liberal politics. Col. Torrens himself wrote much of the political economy of his paper, & had at this time made an attack on some opinion of [52v] Ricardo & my father to which at my father's instigation I wrote an answer & Coulson out of consideration for my father & good will to me, inserted it. There was a reply by Torrens to which I again rejoined. I soon after attempted [229] something more ambitious. The prosecutions of Richard Carlile &

---

[224] some one or more . . . companions:] some of the same companions; *altered by HM to read:* different men of my age

[225] the greater part of it was . . . excursions] it was in most years employed in journeys or excursions. *expanded and altered to final form first by HM*

[226] The northern half of *underlined by HM*

[227] as far as Pæstum, *deleted first by HM*

[228] *Originally continued without punctuation:* than during the next few years. HM *underlined* "few", *and Mill penciled a query, now erased, at left:* "meaning of this mark?"

[229] of my own accord *deleted first by HM*

his wife & sister for publishing books hostile to Christianity, were then exciting much attention, & nowhere more than among the people I frequented. Freedom of discussion even in politics, much more in religion, was at that time far from being, even in theory, the conceded point which it at least *seems* to be now; & it was necessary for the holders of obnoxious opinions to be always ready to argue & reargue for liberty to express them. I wrote a series of five letters, under the signature of Wickliffe, going over the whole length & breadth of the question of free publication of all opinions on religion, & offered them to the Morning Chronicle. The first three were published in January & February 1823; the others contained things too outspoken for that journal & never appeared at all. But a paper which I wrote some time [53r] after on the same subject, a propos of a debate in the H. of Commons, was inserted as a leading article: & during the whole of this year, 1823, I sent a considerable number of contributions to the Chronicle & Traveller, sometimes notices of books, but oftener letters commenting on some nonsense talked in parliament, or some defect of the law or misdoings of the magistracy or the courts of justice. In this last department the Chronicle was now rendering signal service. After the death of Mr Perry, the whole editorship & management of the paper had fallen into the hands of Mr John Black, long a reporter on its establishment, a man of most extensive reading & information, great honesty & simplicity of mind; a particular friend of my father, imbued with many of his & Bentham's best ideas which as a writer he reproduced together with many other valuable thoughts, with great facility & skill. From this time the Chronicle ceased to be the merely Whig organ it was before, & became to a very considerable extent, for the next ten years, a vehicle of the opinions of the utilitarian radicals. This was mainly by Black's own articles, with some assistance from Fonblanque, [53v] who first shewed his eminent qualities as a writer by articles & jeux d'esprit in the Chronicle. The defects of the law & of the administration of justice were the subject on which that paper rendered most service to improvement. Up to that time hardly a word had been said, except by Bentham & my father, against that most peccant part of English institutions & of their administration. It was the almost universal creed of Englishmen, that the law of England, the judicature of England, the unpaid magistracy of England, were models of excellence. I express my sober conviction when I say that after

Bentham who supplied the whole materials, the greatest share of the glory of breaking down this miserable superstition belongs to Black, as editor of the Morning Chronicle. He kept up an incessant fire against it, exposing the absurdities & vices of the law & the courts of justice, paid & unpaid, until he forced some sense of them into people's minds. On many other important questions he became the organ of opinions much in advance of any which had ever before found regular advocacy in the newspaper press; only avoiding any direct radical confession of faith which would have brought the paper [54r] into a collision with all who called themselves Whigs, fatal to its prosperity & influence. Black was a frequent visitor of my father,[230] & Mr Grote used to say that he always knew by the Monday morning's article, whether Black had been with my father on the Sunday. Black was one of the most influential of the many channels through which my father's conversation & personal influence made his opinions tell on the world; cooperating with the effect of his own writings in making him a power in the country such as no individual has since exercised, in a private station, by mere force of intellect & character; & a power which was often acting the most efficiently when it was least seen or suspected. I have already noticed how much of what was done by Ricardo, Hume, & Grote was done at his prompting & persuasion; he was [54v] the good genius by the side of Brougham in all he ever did for the public, either on education, law reform, or any other subject. And his influence flowed in minor streams too numerous to be specified. This influence now received a great extension by the foundation of the Westminster Review.

Contrary to what might be supposed, my father was in no degree a party to the setting up of the Westminster Review.[231] The need of a Radical review to make head against the Edinburgh & Quarterly (then in the period of their greatest reputation & influence) had been a topic of conversation between him & Mr Bentham many years earlier, & it had then been [232] part of their *chateau en Espagne*

---

[230] often going to Mickleham on Saturday (the weekly holiday of the editors of morning newspapers) & returning to town on Sunday afternoon, in time for the editorial duties of Monday's paper: *deleted first by HM*

[231] *Originally continued after a comma:* nor was his opinion asked on the subject.

[232] Bentham many years . . . been] Bentham; & in their speculations on what might be done for its establishment if the pecuniary means were forthcoming, it was (*"on what might be done . . . forthcoming," deleted by HM, then altered by Mill to read:* on the mode of carrying on such an organ)

that my father should be the editor, but the idea had never assumed a practical shape.[233] In 1823 however Mr Bentham determined to establish the review at his own cost, & offered the editorship to my father, who declined it, as being incompatible with
his India House appointment. It was then entrusted to Mr Bowring,
at that time engaged in mercantile business.[234] [55r] Mr Bowring
had for two or three years previous been an assiduous frequenter
of Bentham, to whom he was recommended by many personal good
qualities, by an ardent admiration for Bentham, a zealous adoption of many though not all of his opinions, & not least by an extensive acquaintanceship & correspondence with Liberals of all
countries, which seemed to qualify him for being a powerful
agent in spreading Bentham's fame & doctrines through all quarters of the world. My father had seen little of Bowring,[235] but knew
enough of him to be convinced that he was a man [55v] of an entirely different type from what my father deemed suitable [236] for
conducting a political & philosophical review: & he augured so ill
of the enterprise that he regretted it altogether, feeling persuaded
not only that Bentham would lose his money, but that [237] discredit
would be brought upon radical principles. Since however it was to
be attempted he could not refuse to write for it.[238] He consented

---

[233] editor, but the idea . . . shape.] editor; this was before his appointment
to the India House.

[234] In 1823 however Mr Bentham determined . . . business.] *written at left
to replace:* Some time in the summer of 1823 when as still frequently happened
my father was dining with Mr Bentham, or when as often happened Mr Bentham [55r] had stepped across his garden to speak to my father at his study
window, he reminded my father of this old project & announced to him "the
money is found." About the source of it he said nothing, & my father was
never told, though he never had any doubt of the fact, that the money was
Bentham's. He was never asked for an opinion, but only for cooperation. The
editorship was offered to him, but he declined it as being incompatible with his
India house appointment. On his refusal he was asked to write for the review,
& was informed that Mr Bowring was to be the editor. *In the first sentence Mill
deleted "when as still frequently . . . window, he" and interlined "I do not
know on what occasion, Bentham". HM marked the second sentence ("About
. . . Bentham's.") with a line in the margin, and opposite the last seven words
of the last sentence wrote at left: "the editorship was entrusted to Mr Bowring
at that time engaged in"*

[235] & knew but little of his qualifications: [236] suitable] necessary

[237] nothing but

[238] Since however it was . . . it.] Since however not only no desire was shewn
for his advice but such a mere *secret de la comédie* as where the money was
to come from, was not confided to him, he doubtless felt that it would be an
impertinence in him to obtrude his opinion. Probably also he saw that it would

therefore to write an article for the first number: & as it had been part of the plan formerly talked of between him & Bentham that a portion of the work should be devoted to reviewing the other Reviews, this article of my father's was a general review [56r] of the Edinburgh. Before he began writing it he put my services in requisition, to [239] read through all the numbers of the Edinburgh Review from its commencement, or at least as much of them as seemed important (this was not then so onerous a task as it would be now, the review having only lasted twenty years of the fifty & upwards which it now reckons) making notes for him of the articles which I thought he would wish to examine, either on account of their good or their bad qualities. The article is I think one of the most striking of all his writings, both in conception & in execution. He began with an analysis of the tendencies of periodical literature in general; pointing out that since it cannot, like a book, wait for success, but must succeed immediately or not at all, it is almost certain to [240] profess & inculcate the opinions already held by the public to which it addresses itself, instead of attempting to rectify them. He next, by way of characterizing the position of the Edinburgh Review as a political organ, entered into a complete analysis of the British Constitution. He commented on its thoroughly aristocratic composition; the nomination of a majority of the H. of Commons [56v] by a few hundred families; the different classes which this narrow oligarchy was obliged to admit to a share of power; & finally, what he called its two props, the Church, & the legal profession. He then pointed out the natural tendency of an aristocratic body of this composition, to group itself into two parties, one of them in possession of the executive, the other seeking to become so, & endeavouring to supplant the former & become the predominant section by the aid of public opinion. He described the course likely to be pursued, & the political ground occupied, by an aristocratical party in opposition, coquetting with popular principles for the sake of popular support. He shewed how this idea was realized in the conduct of the Whig party, & of the Edinburgh Review, as the chief literary organ of

---

be of no use. At the same time, the terms he was on with Bentham made it impossible for him to refuse to write for the review. *The first two sentences are marked for deletion by HM. In the last, for "refuse" Mill originally wrote "mortify him by refusing"*

[239] put my services in requisition, to] made me *altered to read:* asked me to
[240] certain to] a condition of its existence that it should

that party. He noted as their principal characteristic what he termed "seesaw"; writing alternately on both sides of every question which touched the power or interest of the governing classes: sometimes in different articles, sometimes in different parts of [57*r*] the same article. And this he illustrated by copious specimens. So formidable an attack on the Whig party & policy had never before been made; nor had so great a blow ever been struck, in this country, for radicalism: & there was not, I believe, any person living who could have written that article except my father.[(a)]

(a) [241] The continuation of this article, in the second number of the review, was written by me under my father's eye, & (except as practice in composition, in which respect it was, to myself, very useful) was of little or no value.

In the meantime the nascent review had formed a junction with another project, of a purely literary periodical to be edited by Mr Henry Southern, afterwards known as a diplomatist, then a literary man by profession.[242] The two editors agreed to unite their corps & to divide the editorship, Bowring taking the political, Southern the literary department. Southern's review was to have been published by Longman, & that firm, though part [243] proprietors of the Edinburgh, were willing to be the publishers of the new journal. But when all the arrangements had been made, & the prospectuses sent out, the Longmans saw my father's attack on the Edinburgh & drew back. My father was now appealed to for his interest with his own publisher, Baldwin; to whom he spoke accordingly with a successful result. And so, amidst anything but hope on my father's [57*v*] part, & that of most of those who afterwards aided in carrying on the review, the first number made its appearance.

That number was an agreeable surprise [244] to us. The average of the articles was of much better quality than had been expected. The literary & artistic department had rested chiefly on Mr Bingham, a barrister on the Western Circuit (subsequently a Police Magistrate) who had been some years a frequenter of Bentham, was a friend of both the Austins, & had adopted with great ardour

---

[241] *Mill added this note at left after deleting the paragraph given in n. 245 below*

[242] *Originally continued after a comma:* & editor of the Retrospective Review.

[243] part] half

[244] surprise] disappointment

Mr Bentham's philosophical opinions. Partly I believe from accident, there were in the first number no less than five articles by Bingham; & we were extremely pleased with them. I well remember the mixed feeling I myself had about the Review; the joy at finding, what we did not at all expect, that it was sufficiently good to be capable of being made a creditable organ of those who held the opinions it professed; & extreme vexation, since it was so good in the main, at what we thought the blemishes of it: there were two articles in particular which I individually took extremely to heart. When however, in [58r] addition to our favourable opinion of it on the whole, we found that it had an extraordinarily large sale for a first number, & that the appearance of a Radical Review of pretensions equal to those of the established organs of parties had excited considerable attention, there was no room for hesitation, & we all became eager in exerting ourselves as much as possible to strengthen & improve it.[245]

---

[245] *Originally followed by a new paragraph:* My first contribution to the review was in the second number. In my father's article the detailed shew-up of the Edinburgh Review had been left unfinished, & he wished me to attempt to finish it. I had one qualification for doing so, a strong indignation at many of the articles which I had read in my course of reading & notetaking for my father's use. But I can now see that there was something ridiculous in this pretension of a youth, not yet 18, to sit in judgment on some of the principal writers of the time. The thing however was written & published, & what seems strange, many if not most of its readers did not suspect that the continuation was by a different hand from the first article. So incapable are most people, when the *fond* of the thoughts is the same, & the manner imitated, to distinguish [58v] the borrowed from the original. The article of course was not, & could not be, anything more than a theme written on the ideas which had been instilled into me by my teachers. The stile was bony & wiry, very unlike the writing of a young person, but with a certain degree of vigour & of polish. No one but myself wrote any part of it, or even corrected it; but it went through an incredible amount of elaboration from myself under my father's eye, he giving it back to me repeatedly part by part to be amended, or cancelled & begun again, either to throw in more & better thoughts or to bring them out more pointedly in the expression. I suppose there are few sentences that were not rewritten with great pains & effort nearly a dozen times. The article was worth little enough in any other respect but to me it was very valuable as practice in composition. *In the second sentence, for "wished me to attempt to" Mill first wrote (and HM underlined, and penciled "wished" opposite): "determined to see whether I could". At the beginning of the fourth sentence, for "But I can now see" (apparently supplied by HM) Mill first wrote and HM underlined: "In every other respect the subject was so much above me". In the same sentence, "youth, not yet 18," was interlined in pencil by HM and written over in ink by Mill to replace the original word "boy". In the sixth sentence HM deleted "& the manner imitated," and "the borrowed from the original"; and she marked the seventh sentence with a line in the margin. In*

[58*v*] My father continued to write occasionally. First the Quarterly Review received its exposure, as a sequel to that of the Edinburgh: of his other contributions the most important were an attack on Southey's Book of the Church [59*r*] in the fifth number, & a political article in the twelfth. Mr Austin only contributed one article, but one of great merit, an argument against [246] primogeniture, in reply to an article then lately published in the Edinburgh Review by McCulloch. Grote also was a contributor only once, all the time he could spare being already taken up by his History of Greece, which he had commenced at my father's instigation. The article he wrote was on his own subject, & was a very complete exposure & castigation of Mitford. Bingham & Charles Austin continued to write for some numbers; Fonblanque was a frequent contributor from the third number. Of my particular set, Ellis was a regular writer up to the ninth number & about the time when he left off others of the set began: Eyton Tooke, Graham, & Roebuck. I myself was the most frequent writer of all, having contributed from the second number to the eighteenth, thirteen articles; chiefly [247] reviews of books on history and political economy, or discussions on special political topics, as corn laws, game laws, law of libel. Occasional articles of merit came in from other acquaintances [248] of my father's & in time, of mine; [59*v*] & some of Dr Bowring's writers turned out well. On the whole however, the conduct of the review was never satisfactory to any of the persons strongly interested in its principles with whom I came in contact. Hardly ever did a number come out which did not contain several things extremely offensive to us, either in point of opinions, or of taste, or by mere want of ability. The unfavourable judgments passed by my father, Grote, the two Austins & others, were reechoed with exaggeration by us younger people: & as our youth-

---

the ninth she deleted "or even corrected it;" and then marked the whole of it and the next sentence ("No one but myself . . . dozen times.") with a line in the margin; apparently as an alternate to them or as a trial replacement for some part of them, Mill wrote and deleted at left: It was wholly my own writing, but was written under my father's eye. *See n. 241 above.*

The next paragraph originally began: In the same number of the review there were also articles by Charles Austin & Ellis; & gradually most of the writing radicals of my father's or my acquaintance were brought into play. My father continued to write . . .

[246] argument against] attack on

[247] articles; chiefly] articles. These were on subjects much more level than my first with my acquirements & experience:

[248] acquaintances] friends

ful zeal[249] rendered us by no means backward in making complaints, we led the two editors a sad life. From my remembrance of what I then was, I have no manner of doubt that we were at least as often wrong as right; & I am very certain that if the review had been carried on according to our notions (I mean those of the juniors) it would have been no better, perhaps not even so good as it was. But it is a fact of some interest in the history of English radicalism, that its chief philosophical organ was from the beginning extremely unsatisfactory to those, whose opinions it was supposed especially to represent.

In the meanwhile however the review made a considerable [60r] noise in the world, & gave a recognized *status* in the arena of opinion & discussion to the Benthamic type of radicalism quite out of proportion to the [250] number of its adherents & to the personal merits or abilities at that time, of any but some three or four of them. It was a time, as is well known, of rapidly rising Liberalism. When the fears & animosities accompanying the war against France[251] were ended, & people had room in their minds for thoughts on home politics, the tide began to set towards reform. The renewed oppression of the Continent by the old reigning families, the countenance given by the English Government to the conspiracy against liberty called the Holy Alliance, & the enormous weight of the national debt & of taxation occasioned by so long & costly a war, rendered the government & the parliament very unpopular: & Radicalism, under the lead of the Burdetts & Cobbetts, had assumed a character which seriously alarmed the Administration.[252] Their apprehensions had scarcely been temporarily allayed by the Six Acts, when the trial of Queen Caroline excited a still wider & deeper feeling of hatred: [60v] & though the outward signs of this hatred passed away with its exciting cause, there arose on all sides a spirit which had never shewn itself before, of opposition to abuses in detail. Mr Hume's persevering scrutiny of the public expenditure, forcing the House of Commons to a division on every objectionable item in the estimates, had begun to tell with great force on public opinion. Political economy had asserted itself with great vigour in public affairs, by the Petition of the Merchants of London for Free Trade drawn up in 1820

---

[249] youthful zeal] zeal (I am speaking of the juniors & especially myself)
[250] very small   [251] France] Napoleon
[252] seriously alarmed the Administration.] made the government tremble.

by Mr Tooke & presented by Mr Baring; & by the noble exertions of Ricardo during the few years of his parliamentary life. His writings, following up the impulse given by the Bullion Controversy, & followed up in their turn by the expositions & comments of my father & McCulloch, had drawn general attention to the subject, making converts, partially at least, even among the ministers; & Huskisson, backed by Canning, had already commenced that gradual demolition of the protective system, which one of their colleagues virtually completed in 1846. Mr Peel,[253] then Home Secretary, was entering, though very cautiously, into the untrodden and [61r] peculiarly Benthamic path of Law Reform. At this time when Liberalism seemed to be becoming the tone of the times, when improvement of institutions was preached from the highest places, & a complete change of the constitution of parliament was loudly demanded from the lowest, it is not wonderful that attention was roused by the regular appearance in controversy of what seemed a new school of writers, claiming to be the philosophers & legislators of this new tendency. The air of strong persuasion [254] with which they wrote, while scarcely any one else seemed to have as strong faith in as definite a creed; the boldness [255] with which they ran full tilt against the very front of both the existing political parties; their uncompromising profession of opposition to many of the most generally received opinions; the talent & verve of at least my father's articles, & the appearance of a corps behind him sufficient to carry on a review: & finally the fact that the review sold & was read,[256] made the so called [61v] Bentham school in philosophy & politics fill a greater place in the public mind than it ever had done before or has done since. As I was in the headquarters of it, knew of what it was composed, & as one of the most active of its very small number might even say, *quorum pars magna fui,* it belongs to me more than to most others, to give some account of it.

This supposed school, then, had no other existence than was constituted by [257] the fact that my father's writings & conversa-

---

[253] Mr Peel,] That same colleague, *marked with a line in the margin by HM, who interlined "Sir R Peel"*

[254] persuasion] persuasion, amounting to arrogance,

[255] boldness] unreserved manner

[256] & continued to support itself; these things (*the five words before the semicolon deleted first by HM*)

[257] had no other existence . . . by] never had any unity, concert, or any existence at all beyond

tion drew a certain number of young men round him who had already imbibed, or who imbibed from him, a greater or less portion of his very decided political & philosophical opinions. The notion that Bentham was surrounded by a band of disciples who received their opinions from his lips, is a fable which my father [258] exposed in his "Fragment on Mackintosh" & is ridiculous to all who knew anything of Mr Bentham's habits of life & manner of conversation. But what was [259] false of Bentham was to some extent true of my father: He *was* sought for the vigour & instructiveness of his conversation & did [62r] use it largely as an instrument for the diffusion of his opinions. I have never met with any man who could do such ample justice to his opinions in colloquial discussion. His perfect command of all his great mental resources, the terseness & expressiveness of his language & the intellectual force & moral earnestness of his delivery, made him one of [260] the most striking of all argumentative conversers; while he was also full of anecdote, a hearty laugher, & when with people whom he liked, a most lively & amusing companion. It was not solely or even chiefly in diffusing his mere intellectual convictions, that his power shewed itself; it was still more through the influence of a quality of which I have only since learnt to appreciate the extreme rarity, especially in England: that exalted public spirit, & regard above all things to the good of the whole, which warmed into life & activity every germ of similar virtue that existed in the minds he came in contact with; the desire he made them feel for his approbation, the shame at his disapproval; the moral support which his conversation, & his [62v] very existence, gave to those who were aiming at the same objects, through their respect for his judgment; & the encouragement he afforded to the faint hearted or desponding among them by the firm confidence which (though the reverse of sanguine as to the results to be expected in any one particular case) he always felt in the power of reason, the general progress of improvement, & the good which could always be done by judicious effort.

My father's opinions were those which gave the distinguishing character to what was then regarded as the Benthamic or utilitarian tone of speculation. His opinions fell singly scattered from him in all directions but they flowed from him in a continued stream principally through three channels. One was through me, the only

---

[258] fully   [259] ludicrously   [260] one of] *interlined*

mind directly formed by his instructions, & through whom considerable influence was exercised [261] over various young men who
became in their turn propagandists orally & by writing. A second
was through some of the contemporaries at Cambridge of Charles
Austin, who either initiated by him [63r] or through the general
mental impulse which he gave, had adopted opinions much allied
to those of my father, & some of the more considerable of whom
afterwards sought my father's acquaintance & frequented his house:
among these may be mentioned Strutt, since known as a radical
member of parliament, & the present Sir John Romilly, with whose
father, Sir Samuel, my father had of old been on terms of friendship. The third channel was that of a younger generation of Cambridge undergraduates [262] contemporary not with Austin but with
Eyton Tooke, drawn to him by affinity of opinions & by him introduced to my father: the most notable of these was Charles Buller. Various other persons individually received & transmitted a
considerable amount of my father's influence: for example, Black
(as before mentioned) & Fonblanque: but most of these we ac-
counted only partial allies; Fonblanque for instance was widely
divergent from us on many important points. But indeed there
was by no means complete unanimity among any portion of us nor
had any of us [263] adopted [63v] implicitly all my father's opinions.
For example, the paragraph in his Essay on Government,[264] in
which he maintained that women might without compromising good
government be excluded from the suffrage because their interest is
the same with that of men—from this I & all those who formed my
chosen associates, most positively dissented. It is due to my father
to say that he always denied having intended to say that women
should be excluded, any more than men under the age of forty,
concerning whom he maintained in the very next paragraph an
exactly similar thesis. He was, as he truly said, not discussing
whether the suffrage ought to be restricted to less than all, but,
(assuming that it is to be restricted) what is the utmost limit of
restriction which does not involve a sacrifice of the securities for
good government. But I thought then, as I have always thought
since, that even the opinion which he acknowledged was as great an

---

[261] through whom . . . exercised] who had considerable influence
[262] (each Cambridge generation lasting just three years)
[263] us] us, even myself,
[264] the worst in point of tendency he ever wrote, that

error as any of those which his Essay combated; that the interest of women is exactly as much & no more involved in that of men, as the interest of subjects is involved in that of kings, & that every reason which exists for [64r] giving the suffrage to anybody, imperatively requires that it be given to women. This was also the general opinion of the younger proselytes: & it is pleasant to be able to say that Bentham on this most important point, was wholly with us.[265]

But though none of us, probably, agreed in everything with my father, yet as I said before, his opinions gave the general character & colour to the band, or set, or whatever else it may be called; which was not characterized by Benthamism, in any sense which has relation to Bentham as a guide, but rather by a combination of Bentham's point of view with that of the modern political economy, & with that of the Hartleian metaphysics. Malthus's population principle was quite as much a banner,[266] & point of union among us, as any opinion specially belonging to Bentham. This [267] doctrine, originally brought forward as an argument against the indefinite improvability of human affairs, we took up with great zeal in the contrary sense, as indicating the sole means of realizing that improvability, by securing full employment at high wages to the whole labouring population through a restriction [64v] of the increase of their numbers. The other leading characteristics of our creed, as mainly derived from my father, may be stated as follows.

In politics, an almost unbounded [268] confidence in the efficacy of two things: representative government, & complete freedom of discussion. So great was my father's reliance on the influence of reason upon the minds of mankind, whenever it was allowed to reach them, that he felt as if all would be gained if the people could be universally taught to read, if all sorts of opinions were allowed to be preached to them by word & writing, & if through the suffrage they could nominate a legislature to give effect to their opinion when formed. He thought that if the legislature no longer represented a class interest it would mostly aim at the general interest with adequate wisdom, as the people would be sufficiently under the guidance of educated intelligence to make in general a good choice of representatives & to leave a liberal dis-

---

[265] us.] us juniors.   [266] banner,] leading idea,   [267] important
[268] an almost unbounded] a most exaggerated

cretion to those whom they had chosen. Accordingly aristocratic government, the government of the Few in any of its shapes, was the object of his sternest disapprobation, [65r] & a democratic suffrage the principal article of his political creed, not on the ground of "rights of man," "liberty" or any of the phrases more or less significant by which up to that time democracy had usually been defended, but as the most essential of "securities for good government." In this too he held fast only to what he deemed essentials: he was comparatively indifferent to monarchical or republican forms, far more so than Bentham, to whom a king in the character of "corrupter general" appeared necessarily very noxious. Next to aristocracy, an established church, or corporation of priests, was the object of his strongest detestation; though he disliked no clergyman personally who did not [269] deserve it, & was on terms of sincere friendship with several. I have already spoken of his rejection of both Christianity & Deism, both of which he regarded not only as false but as morally mischievous. In ethics his standard was utility or the general happiness; & his moral feelings were energetic & rigid on all points which he deemed important to human well being, while he was supremely indifferent to all those doctrines of the common morality which he thought had no foundation but in asceticism & priestcraft. He looked forward for example to [65v] a great increase of freedom in the relations between the sexes; & he anticipated as one of the beneficial effects of that freedom, that the imagination would no longer dwell upon the physical relation & its adjuncts, & swell this into one of the principal objects of life, which perversion of the imagination & feelings he regarded as one of the deepest seated & most pervading evils in the human mind.[270] In psychology [271] his fundamental doctrine was the formation of all human character by circumstances, through the principle of association, & the consequent unlimited possibility of improving the moral & intellectual attributes of mankind by education. Of all his doctrines none was more valuable [272] than this, or needs more to be insisted on: unfortunately there is none which is more in contradiction to the prevailing tendency of speculation both in his time & at present.[273]

---

[269] personally who did not] who did not personally
[270] *Originally continued after a comma:* particularly in the modern form of it. *deleted first by HM*
[271] psychology] philosophy   [272] valuable] true
[273] both in his . . . present.] in his time & since. *HM wrote at left: "some-*

These various opinions were seized on with youthful fanaticism by the little knot of young men of whom I was one; & we threw into them a sectarian spirit from which, in intention at least, my father was free. What we (or rather a phantom substituted in the place of us) were by a ridiculous exaggeration called by others, namely a "school," we for some time really hoped & aspired to be. In the first two or three years of the [66r] Westminster Review, the French *philosophes* of the 18th century were the example we sought to imitate & we hoped to accomplish as much as they did. I even proposed to myself to chronicle our doings, from that early period, on the model of Grimm's Correspondence, & actually for some time kept a journal with that intention. Charles Austin had a [274] project of a Philosophical Dictionary, suggested by Voltaire's, in which everything was to be spoken out freely; I entered eagerly into it & sent three or four articles (the only ones, I believe, ever written) towards a commencement of it. My particular companions & Charles Austin's however did not much associate with one another: an attempt we made to bring them together periodically at his lodgings was soon given up, & he & I did not long travel in the same direction. The head quarters of me & my associates [275] was not my father's house but Grote's, which I very much frequented. Every new proselyte & every one whom I hoped to make a proselyte, I took there to be indoctrinated. Grote's opinions were at that time very much the same both in their strong & their weak points as those of us younger people, but he was of course very much more [66v] formed, & incomparably the superior of all of us in knowledge & present abilities.

All this however is properly the outside of our existence; or at least the intellectual part alone, & only one side of that. In attempting to penetrate inward, & to shew what we really were as human beings, I shall at present speak only of myself, of whom alone I can speak from sufficient knowledge.

I conceive, then, that for these two or three years of my life the description commonly given of a Benthamite, as a dry, hard logical machine, was as much applicable to me, as it can well be applicable to any one just entering into life; to whom the common objects of desire must in general have at least the attraction of

---

thing more decided than since" *and* "now"—*and then altered the text to its final form, Mill copying over her interlineations in ink*
     [274] a] an old   [275] associates] friends

novelty. Ambition [276] & desire [277] of distinction I had in abundance; & zeal for what I thought the good of mankind was my most predominant sentiment, mixing with & colouring all other wishes & feelings. But this zeal, at that period of my life, was as yet little else than zeal for speculative opinions. It did not proceed from genuine benevolence [67r] or sympathy with mankind; though those qualities held their due [278] place in my moral creed. Nor was it connected with any high enthusiasm for ideal nobleness. Yet of this feeling I was imaginatively very susceptible; but there was at that time an intermission in me of what is its natural source, poetical culture; while there was a superabundance of the discipline antagonistic to it, that of mere logic & analysis. Add to this that the tendency of my father's teachings was to the undervaluing of feeling. It was not that he was himself hard hearted or insensible; I believe it was rather from the contrary quality; he thought that feeling could take care of itself, & that there was sure to be enough of it if actions were properly cared about. Offended by the frequency with which in ethical & philosophical controversy, feeling is made the ultimate reason & justification of conduct, instead of being itself called on for a justification; while in practice, actions, the effect of which on human happiness is mischievous, are defended as being required by feeling, & the character of a person of feeling receives a credit for desert which he thought only due to actions, he had a real impatience [67v] of the attributing praise to feeling or of any but the most sparing reference to it either in the estimation of persons or in the discussion of things. In addition to the influence which this characteristic in him had on me & others, we found all our principal opinions constantly attacked on the ground of feeling. Utility was denounced as cold calculation; political economy as hard hearted; anti-population doctrines as repulsive to the natural feelings of mankind. We retorted by the word "sentimentality" which along with "declamation" & "vague generalities" served us as common terms of opprobrium. Although we were generally right as against those who were opposed to us, the effect was that the cultivation of feeling (except, indeed,

---

[276] Ambition] As for myself most of those common objects were quite sufficiently attractive to me. Money, indeed, having no expensive tastes, I only wished for as a means of independence & of promoting public objects; but ambition *all but the last word marked for deletion by HM*

[277] desire] love

[278] their due] a high

the feelings of public & private duty) had very little place in the thoughts of most of us, myself in particular.[279] All we thought of was to alter people's opinions; to make them believe according to evidence, & know what was their real interest, which if they knew, they would by "public [68r] opinion" enforce a regard to it from one another. While fully recognizing the superior excellence of unselfish benevolence & love of justice, we expected the regeneration of mankind not from any direct action on those sentiments but from educated intellect enlightening the selfish feelings. Although this last is an important means of improvement in the hands of those who are themselves impelled by nobler principles of action, I do not believe that any one person known to me now relies mainly upon it for the regeneration of human life.

From this neglect both in theory & practice of the cultivation of feeling, naturally resulted among other things an undervaluing of poetry, & of Imagination generally as an element of human nature. It is or was part of the common notion of Benthamites that they are enemies to poetry: this was partly true of Bentham; he used to say "all poetry is misrepresentation": but in the sense in which he meant it, the same thing might be said of all impressive speech, of all representation or inculcation more oratorical in its character than a sum in arithmetic. An article of Bingham's in the first number of the Westminster, [68v] in which he gave as an explanation of some things which he disliked in Moore that "Mr Moore *is* a poet & therefore is *not* a reasoner," did a good deal to attach the notion of hating poetry to the writers in the review. But the truth was that (to speak only of poetry in the narrowest, the purely literary sense) many of us & Bingham himself, were great readers of poetry, & as for myself, who at that time was not so, the correct statement would be (& the same thing might be said of my father) that I was speculatively indifferent to poetry, not hostile to it. I disliked any sentiments in poetry which I should have disliked in prose, & that included a great deal. And I was wholly blind to its place in human culture as a [280] means of educating the feelings. But [281] I was always personally very susceptible to some kinds of it. In the [282] most sectarian period of my Bentham-

---

[279] And therefore we had at this time no idea of real culture. In our schemes for improving human affairs we overlooked human beings.

[280] a] the great   [281] its effect on me when I did read it was always great.

[282] narrowest &

ism I happened to look into Pope's Essay on Man & though every opinion in it was contrary to mine I well remember how much I was struck with the poem.[283] I do not know whether at that time poetical composition of any higher type than eloquent discussion in verse, would have produced a similar effect on me.

[69r] This however was a mere passing state. Long before I out-grew the narrowness of my *taught* opinions, or [284] enlarged in any considerable degree the basis of my intellectual creed, I had ob-tained in the natural course of my mental progress, poetic culture of the most valuable kind, by means of reverential admiration for the lives & characters of heroic persons; especially the heroes of philosophy. The same animating effect which so many remark-able persons have left on record that they had experienced from Plutarch's Lives, was produced on me by Plato's pictures of Soc-rates, & by [285] some modern biographies, but chiefly by Condorcet's Life of Turgot; a book well calculated to excite the best sort of enthusiasm, since it contains one of the noblest & wisest of lives, described by one of the noblest & wisest of men. The heroic vir-tue of these admirable representatives of the opinions with which I sympathized deeply affected me, & I perpetually recurred to them as others do to a favourite poet, when needing to be carried up into the more elevated regions of feeling & thought. I may ob-serve by the way that this book also cured me of my sectarian tastes. The two or three pages beginning "Il regardait toute secte comme nuisible," & explaining why Turgot always kept himself distinct from the [69v] Encyclopedists, sank deeply into me.[286] I left off designating myself & others as Utilitarians, or by the pronoun "we," or any other collective denomination: I ceased to *afficher* [287] sectarianism: but my real, inward sectarianism I got rid of later & much more gradually.

About the end of 1824 or beginning of 1825, Mr Bentham having lately got back his papers on Evidence from M. Dumont (whose

---

[283] how much I . . . poem.] the strength of my admiration of it.

[284] outgrew the narrowness . . . or] had thrown off my sectarian narrow-nesses & (*in revising Mill first wrote "adopted opinions" for "taught opinions"*)

[285] Plato's pictures . . . by] *interlined*

[286] *Originally continued after a semicolon:* &, combined with passing remarks now & then thrown out by my father, made me feel how injurious it is to the progress of new opinions for the holders of them to band themselves together as a sect, call themselves by a name, & encourage the world to hold them jointly & severally responsible for one another.

[287] *afficher*] affect

Traité des Preuves Judiciaires, grounded on them, was then first completed & published) resolved to have them printed in the original & bethought himself of me as capable of preparing them for the press; in the same manner as his Book of Fallacies had been recently edited by Bingham. I undertook this task & it occupied nearly all my leisure for about a year, exclusive of the time afterwards spent in seeing the five large volumes through the press.[288] Bentham had begun the book [70r] three times, at considerable intervals, each time in a different manner, & each time without reference to the preceding: two of the three times he had gone over nearly the whole field. These three masses of papers I had to condense into a single treatise: adopting the one last written as the groundwork, and inserting into it[289] as much of the two others as it had not completely superseded. I had also to unroll such of Bentham's involved & parenthetical sentences as seemed to me to overpass in obscurity what readers were likely to take the pains to understand.[290] Further, it was Bentham's particular desire that I should endeavour to supply, from myself, any *lacunæ* which he had left: & I read at his instance Phillipps on the Law of Evidence & part of Starkie & wrote comments[291] on those few among the defective points in the English rules of evidence which had escaped Bentham's notice. I added replies to the objections which had been made to some of Bentham's doctrines by reviewers of the Traité des Preuves, & a few supplementary remarks on some of the more abstract parts of the subject, such as the theory of improbability & impossibility. The tone of these additions, or at least of the controversial part of them, was more assuming than became[292] one so young & inexperienced as I was: but indeed I had never [70v] contemplated coming forward in my own person; &, as an anonymous editor of Bentham, I fell into the tone of my author, not thinking that tone unsuitable to him or to the subject however it might be so to me. My name as editor was put to the book after it was printed, at Bentham's positive desire, which I in vain attempted to persuade him to forego.

The time occupied in this editorial work was extremely well employed for my own improvement. The "Rationale of Judicial Evi-

---

[288] The nature of the editorial work was this:
[289] inserting into it] interlarding it with
[290] I had also to unroll . . . understand.] *written at left*
[291] comments] such comments as I could
[292] more assuming than became] assuming, even to arrogance, & unbecoming

dence" is one of the richest in matter of all Bentham's writings. The theory of evidence being itself one of the most important of his subjects, and ramifying into most of the others, the book contains a great proportion of all his best thoughts: while, among more special things, it comprises the most elaborate exposure of the vices of English law which he ever made, including not the law of evidence only, but by way of illustrative episode, the whole procedure or practice of the courts of justice. The direct knowledge therefore, which I obtained from the book & which was imprinted on me [71*r*] much more thoroughly than it could have been by mere reading, was itself no inconsiderable acquisition. But this occupation [293] also did for me what might seem less to be expected: it gave a great start to my powers of composition. Everything which I wrote after this editorial work was markedly superior to anything I had written before it.[294] Bentham's later style as is well known, was heavy & cumbersome, from the excess of a good quality, the love of precision, which made him introduce clause within clause into the heart of every sentence that the reader might take into his mind all the qualifications simultaneously with the main proposition: & the habit grew on him until his sentences became, to those not accustomed to them, most laborious reading. But his earlier stile, that of the Fragment on Government, Plan of a Judicial Establishment, &c, is a model of liveliness & ease combined with fulness of matter scarcely ever surpassed: & of this earlier stile there were many striking specimens in the Manuscripts on Evidence, all of which I endeavoured to preserve. So long a course of this admirable writing had a great effect on my own; & I increased that effect by the assiduous reading of other styles, both French & English, which combined ease with force, such as Fielding, Goldsmith, Pascal, Voltaire, and Courier.[295] [71*v*] Through these influences my writing lost the jejuneness of my early compositions: the bones and cartilages began to clothe themselves with flesh & the stile became, at times, lively & almost light.

This improvement was first shewn in a new field. Mr Marshall,

---

[293] occupation] day's work *altered to read:* year's work

[294] This was the effect of the familiarity I gained with Bentham's style as a writer.

[295] and Courier.] Courier (whom as a writer my father [71*v*] placed almost at the head of modern literature) & others.

of Leeds, father of the present generation of Marshalls, an earnest [296] parliamentary reformer, & a man of large fortune of which he made a liberal use, had been much struck with Bentham's Book of Fallacies: & the thought occurred to him that it would be useful to publish annually the Parliamentary Debates, not in [297] chronological order as in Hansard, but classified according to subjects, & accompanied by a commentary pointing out the fallacies of the speakers. With this intention he very naturally addressed himself to the editor of the Book of Fallacies; & Bingham, with the assistance of Charles Austin, undertook the editorship. The work was called "Parliamentary History & Review". Its sale was not sufficient to keep it in existence, & it only lasted three years.[298] It excited however some attention among parliamentary & political people. The best strength of the party was put forth in it; & its execution did them much more credit [72r] than that of the Westminster had ever done. Bingham & Charles Austin wrote much in it; so did Strutt, Romilly & some other liberal lawyers.[299] My father wrote one very able article; the elder Austin another. Coulson wrote one of great merit. I myself was selected to lead off the first number by an article on the principal topic of the session (1825) the Catholic Association & the Catholic disabilities.[300] In the second number I wrote an elaborate essay on the Commercial Crisis of 1825 & the Currency Debates. In the third I wrote two articles, one on a minor subject, the other on the Reciprocity principle in commerce, a propos of a celebrated diplomatic correspondence between Canning & Gallatin.[301] [72v] These articles were no longer mere reproductions & applications of what I had been taught; they were original thinking, as far as that name can be applied to old ideas in new forms & relations: & there was a ma-

---

[296] an earnest] a strong   [297] mere

[298] *Originally continued after a semicolon:* in the third of which the Review appeared without any History.

[299] liberal lawyers.] of the legal friends of the editors.

[300] This article was much complimented in the Edinburgh Review by Brougham (who was attacked in it) although to my annoyance, Bingham had struck out, or obliged me to modify many of what I thought the most piquant passages, among which I remember was a piece of ridicule (which my father thought successful) of the Duke of York's famous declaration against Catholic Emancipation.

[301] *Originally continued without punctuation:* respecting the trade with the West India Colonies.

turity & a well-digested character about them which there had not been in any of my previous performances.[302] In execution therefore they were not at all juvenile; but their subjects have been so much better treated since, that they are entirely superseded, & should remain buried in the same oblivion with my contributions to the first dynasty of the Westminster Review.

During several years of this period of my life the social studies of myself & several of my companions assumed a shape which contributed very much to my mental development. The idea occurred to us of carrying on by reading & conversation, a joint [303] study of several of the branches of science which we wished to be masters of. We assembled to the number of a dozen or more. Grote lent a room of his house in Threadneedle Street for the purpose & his partner Prescott, one of [73r] the three original members of the Utilitarian Society, took an active part as one of our number. We met two mornings in every week, from half past eight till ten, at which time most of us were called off to our daily occupations. The subject we began with was Political Economy.[304] We chose some systematic treatise as our text-book; my father's "Elements" being our first choice. One of us (by turns) read aloud a chapter, or some smaller portion, of the book. The discussion was then opened, & any one who had an objection or other remark to make, made it.[305] Our rule was to discuss every point, great or small, which was raised, until all who took part were satisfied with the conclusion they had arrived at; & to follow up every topic of collateral speculation which the chapter or the discussion suggested, never leaving it till we had untied every knot which we found in it. We repeatedly kept up the discussion of some single point for several weeks, thinking intently on it during the intervals of our meetings & contriving solutions of the new difficulties which had risen up in the [73v] last morning's discussion. When we had finished in this way my father's Elements we went through in the same manner Ricardo's Principles of Political Economy; & afterwards, Bailey's Dissertation on Value. These discussions were not only instructive to those who took part in them, but brought out [306] new views of some topics of abstract Political Economy. The theory of

---

[302] there had not been . . . performances.] made them fully equal to the best things which had been written on the same class of subjects.
[303] joint] thorough   [304] Our plan was this.
[305] *Originally continued after a comma:* & it was thoroughly examined.
[306] entirely

International Values which I afterwards published [307] emanated
from these conversations, as did also the modified form of Ricardo's
theory of Profits, laid down in my essay on Profits & Interest. Those
among us from whom, generally speaking, any new speculations
originated, were Ellis, Graham & I: though others gave valuable aid
to the discussions, more especially Prescott & Roebuck; the one by
his knowledge, the other by his dialectical acuteness. The theories
of International Values & of Profits, were excogitated & worked out
in about equal proportions by myself & Graham, & we at one time
had thoughts [308] of [74r] publishing these theories, with some other
matters, in a volume of Essays bearing our joint names: but when
my expositions of them came to be written I found I had so much
overestimated my agreement with him, & he differed so much
from the most original of the two essays, that on International
Values, that I was obliged to consider the theory as now exclusively mine, & it came out as such when it was published many
years after.[309] I may mention that among the alterations made by
my father in revising his Elements for the third edition, several
were grounded on criticisms elicited by these Conversations,[310]
and in particular, he modified his opinions [311] (though not to the
extent of our new doctrines) on both the points which I have just
touched upon.

When we had enough of political economy we took up the scholastic logic in the same manner, Grote now joining us. Our first text
book was Aldrich, but being disgusted with its superficiality, we
[74v] reprinted by subscription one of the most finished among the
many manuals of the school logic, which my father, a great collector
of such books, possessed, the Manuductio ad Logicam of the
Jesuit Du Trieu. After finishing this we took up Whately's Logic
(then first republished from the Encyclopedia Metropolitana) &
finally, I think, the Computatio sive Logica of Hobbes. These books

---

[307] Values which I afterwards published] Values, afterwards explained in one
of my published Essays & in my larger treatise,

[308] Graham, & we at one time had thoughts] Graham. As the discussions
proceeded we got out of the depth of the others. [74r] Accordingly he & I
had at one time a project

[309] It remains true however that the speculation was partly his, though repudiated by him.

[310] among the alterations made by my father . . . Conversations,] my father,
in preparing the third edition of the Elements, made a considerable number of
alterations grounded . . . Conversations, which had reached him through me,

[311] opinions] original statements

gone through in our manner, afforded large scope for original metaphysical speculation: & most of what has been done in the First
Book of my "System of Logic" to rationalize & correct the principles
& distinctions of the school logic & to improve the theory of the
Import of Propositions, had its origin in these discussions; Graham
& I as before originating most of the novelties, while Grote & others
furnished an excellent tribunal or test. From this time I formed the
project of writing a book on Logic, though on a much humbler
scale than the one I ultimately executed.

Having done with Logic we launched into analytic psychology:
& having chosen Hartley for our text book, we raised Priestley's
edition to an extravagant price by searching through London to
furnish each of us with a [75r] copy. When we had finished Hartley
we suspended our meetings; but my father's Analysis being published soon after, we reassembled for the purpose of reading it.
With this our exercises ended. I have always dated from these conversations my own real inauguration as an original & independent
thinker. It was also through them that I acquired, or very much
strengthened, a mental habit to which I attribute all that I have
ever done, or ever shall do, in speculation; the habit of never receiving half-solutions of difficulties as complete; never abandoning
a puzzle, but returning again & again to it till it was resolved; never
allowing obscure corners of a subject to remain unexplored, because they did not seem important; nor ever thinking that I perfectly
understood any part of a subject until I understood every part. It
became a mental necessity with me, to require for my own complete conviction what Moliere calls "des clartés de tout," & this
qualified me to make things clear to others, which is probably what
I have best succeeded in as an expository writer.

Various other studies & exercises were carried on during this
period by some of the same people in the same social manner. [75v]
We formed a class of five or six to learn German in the Hamiltonian
manner; & we held weekly evening meetings for a considerable
time [312] to study the theory & practice of elocution. Roebuck here
stepped into the first rank; I contributed the rules I had learnt
from my father, & among us we thought out a set of principles on
the subject.

Our doings from 1825 to 1830 in the way of public speaking filled

---

[312] in chambers which Graham & Roebuck jointly occupied in Gray's Inn
(they then & for long after lived together)

a considerable place in my life during those years, & had important effects on my developement.[313]

There was for some time in existence a society of Owenites, under the name of the Cooperative Society, which held weekly public discussions. In the early part of 1825 accident brought Roebuck in contact with several of its members & led to his attending one or two of the meetings & taking part in the debate, in opposition to Owenism. Some one of us started the notion of going there in a body & having a general battle, and it fell out that Charles Austin & some of his friends entered into the project. [76r] It was carried into effect by concert with the principal members of the Society, themselves nothing loth, as they naturally preferred a controversy with opponents to a tame discussion among their own body. The question of population was proposed as the subject of debate: Charles Austin led the case on our side with a brilliant speech, & the fight was kept up by adjournment for five or six weekly meetings before crowded auditories, including along with the members of the Society & their friends, many hearers & some speakers from the Inns of Court.[314] When this debate was ended another was commenced on the general merits of Owen's system: & the contest altogether lasted about three months. It was a lutte corps à corps between Owenites & political economists, whom the Owenites regarded as their most inveterate opponents: but it was a perfectly friendly dispute. We who represented political economy had the same objects in view which they had, & took pains to shew it, & the principal champion on their side was a very estimable man with whom I was well acquainted, Mr William Thompson of Cork, author of a book on the Distribution of Wealth, & of an Appeal in behalf of women against the passage relating to them in my father's [76v] Essay on Government. I myself spoke oftener than any one else on our side, there being no rule against speaking several times in the same debate.[315] Ellis & Roebuck took a prominent part, & among those from the Inns of Court who joined in the debate I

---

[313] considerable place . . . important . . . developement.] sufficient place . . . sufficiently important . . . developement to require a rather full account of them. *This short paragraph was originally written as the last sentence of the preceding paragraph*

[314] *Originally continued after a comma:* whose curiosity had been excited through Austin.

[315] several times in the same debate.] twice: I believe I made two long & elaborate speeches on the first question & either one or two, I believe two, on the second.

remember Charles Villiers. The other side obtained also, on the
population question, very efficient support from without. The well
known Gale Jones, then an elderly man, made one of his florid
speeches; but the speaker by whom I was most impressed although
I dissented from every argument he used & from almost every
opinion he expressed,[316] was Thirlwall, the historian, since bishop
of St David's, then a Chancery Barrister unknown, except (as I
found on enquiry) by a reputation for eloquence acquired at the
Cambridge Union before the era of Austin & Macaulay. His speech
was in answer to one of mine. Before he had uttered ten sentences
I set him down as the best speaker I had ever heard, & I do not
think I have since heard a better. [77r] I made an elaborate reply
to him at the next meeting, but he was not there to hear it; &
except a few words interchanged between us as soon as he had
done speaking, of admiration on my side, & politeness on his, we
remained strangers to each other until I met him at dinner at
M. Guizot's in 1840.

During or about the time when these discussions were going
on, McCulloch the political economist who was then temporarily
in London to deliver the "Ricardo Lectures" on political economy,
threw out the idea one day to my father & me, that a society was
wanted in London similar to the Speculative Society of Edinburgh
in which Brougham, Horner & others first cultivated public speaking. The discussions at the Cooperative Society had put me in a
frame of mind to catch at the suggestion. I liked the kind of thing
in itself, & those debates seemed to give cause for being sanguine
as to the sort of men who might be brought together for such a
purpose in London. McCulloch mentioned the matter to several
young men of influence [317] to whom he was then giving private
lessons in political economy. Some of these entered warmly into
the project, [77v] particularly George Villiers (now Earl of Claren-
don).[318] He & his two brothers, Hyde & Charles; Romilly, Charles
Austin, & I, with some others, met & completed the plan; a larger
meeting was then held to constitute the Society. We determined to

---

[316] although I dissented from every . . . expressed,] & who although every
argument he used & almost every opinion he expressed appeared to me a
fallacy, struck me as almost the perfection of an orator,

[317] influence] note *altered to read:* consequence *altered to read:* importance
(*the last word deleted first by HM*)

[318] *Originally continued without punctuation:* with whom I was not then
acquainted.

meet once a fortnight from November to June, at the Freemason's Tavern, & we had soon a splendid list of members, containing, along with several members of parliament, nearly all the great speakers of the Cambridge Union & of the United Debating Society at Oxford.[319] It is curiously illustrative of the tendencies of the time that our principal difficulty in recruiting for the society was to find a sufficient number of Tory speakers. Almost all whom we could press into the service were Liberals, of different orders & degrees. We had Charles Austin, Macaulay, Thirlwall, Praed, Samuel Wilberforce (now Bishop of Oxford) Lord Howick, Charles Poulett Thomson (afterwards Lord Sydenham) Fonblanque,[320] Edward & Henry Lytton Bulwer, & many others whom I cannot now recollect, who made themselves afterwards more or less conspicuous in public life. Nothing could seem more promising. But when the time for action drew near & it was necessary to fix on a President & to [78r] find somebody to open the first debate none of our celebrities would consent to perform either office. Of the many who were pressed on the subject, the only one who could be prevailed on was a man of whom I knew very little but who had taken high honours at Oxford, & was said to have acquired a great oratorical reputation there; who some time after became a Tory member of parliament. He accordingly was fixed on both for filling the President's chair & for making the first speech. The important day arrived: the benches were crowded: all our great speakers were present to judge of but not to help our efforts. The Oxford orator's speech was an utter failure. This threw a damp on the whole concern: the speakers who followed were few & none of them did their best.[321] The affair was a complete fiasco: & the oratorical celebrities we had counted on went away never to return, giving to me at least a lesson in knowledge of the world. Not one of the notabilities whom I have just enumerated except Praed (& he only once or twice) ever opened their lips in the society. This unexpected breakdown completely altered my relation to the project. I had not anticipated taking personally a prominent part, or speaking much [78v] or often, especially at first; but I now saw that the success of the scheme depended on the new men, & I put my shoulder

---

[319] United Debating Society at Oxford.] Oxford Debating Society formed in imitation of it.

[320] *The names "Praed" and "Fonblanque" are interlined*

[321] *Originally continued after a colon:* a short sensible speech by Romilly was the only creditable performance.

to the wheel. I opened the second question & from that time spoke in nearly every debate. The three Villiers' & Romilly stuck to the scheme for some time longer, & took their part well in several debates. Robert Hildyard, a clever & vehement speaker from the Cambridge Union, then a violent radical Benthamite, since a Tory & Protectionist writer in the Morning Post & now a silent Derbyite member of Parliament, spoke two or three times well & some new men, among others Henry Taylor, Vernon Smith & his brother Leveson,[322] occasionally took part. But in the main the debates during the whole season rested on me and Roebuck: & very uphill work it was in the latter part of it, even the Villiers' & other founders of the society having ceased to attend. In the season following, 1826/27, we had acquired two excellent Tory speakers, Hayward, & Shee (now Serjeant Shee): the radical side was reinforced by Charles Buller, Cockburn, & others of the second generation of Cambridge Benthamites: & with such occasional aid & the two Tories as well as Roebuck & me for regular speakers, almost every debate was a bataille rangée between the philosophic radicals [323] [79r] & the Tory lawyers, until our conflicts came to be talked about, & many persons of note & consideration came to hear us. This happened still more in the subsequent seasons 1828 & 1829, when another set of speakers, of whom hereafter, had joined the society. Some of our debates were really worth hearing; not for oratory, but as good specimens of polemical discussion on the great questions of politics. Radicalism of the type of the Westminster and Parliamentary Reviews, was then a recognized power in politics & literature: it was the only attempt which had been made to give principles & philosophy to the Liberalism which was growing into importance, while the temporary vogue of political economy had so far encroached upon the ordinary English antipathy to theory, as to give a prestige to any pretension to treat politics scientifically. Now, some of our speeches were really better expositions than could be heard anywhere else, of our principal doctrines: & as the side of existing opinions & institutions was very ably defended by Shee with rhetoric, by Hayward with sophistry,[324] our doctrines were fairly pitted against their opposites. At least our debates were very different from those of common debating

---

[322] Vernon Smith . . . Leveson,] *interlined. After "Henry Taylor," Mill wrote and then deleted:* (with whom I then first became acquainted)

[323] (as we thought ourselves)   [324] the Society was the only arena where

[79v] societies, for they habitually consisted of the strongest arguments & most philosophic principles which either side was able to produce, thrown often into close & *serré* confutations of one another. For my own part, nothing I ever wrote was more carefully elaborated both in matter and expression than some of those speeches. My delivery was & remained bad; but I could make myself listened to; & I even acquired a certain readiness of extemporary speaking, on questions of pure argument, & could reply offhand, with some effect, to the speech of an opponent: but whenever I had an exposition to make in which from the feelings involved or from the nature of the ideas to be developed, expression seemed important, I always most carefully wrote the speech & committed it to memory, & I did this even with my replies, when an opportunity was afforded by an adjourned debate. Therefore many [325] of my speeches were of some worth as compositions, to be set against [326] a bad & ungraceful manner. I believe that this practice greatly increased my power of effective writing. The habit of composing speeches for delivery gave me not only an ear [80r] for smoothness & rhythm but a practical sense for *telling* sentences & an immediate criterion of their telling property, by their effect on a mixed audience.

The Society & the preparation for it, together with the preparation for the morning conversations [327] which were going on simultaneously, occupied the greater part of my leisure; & made me feel it personally a relief when, in the spring of 1828, I ceased to write for the Westminster Review. The review had fallen into difficulties. Though the sale of the first number had been encouraging, the permanent sale was never, I believe, sufficient to pay the expenses on the scale on which the review was carried on. Those expenses had been considerably, but not sufficiently reduced. One of the editors, Southern, had resigned; & some of the writers, including my father & me, who had been paid like other contributors for our earlier articles, had latterly written without payment. Nevertheless the original funds contributed by Bentham were nearly or quite exhausted, & if the review was to be continued some new arrangement for carrying it on became indispensable. My father & I had several [80v] conferences [328] with Bowring on the subject. We were willing to do our utmost for maintaining the review as an

---

[325] many] most   [326] be set against] make amends for   [327] at Grote's
[328] several conferences] frequent [80v] communications

organ of our opinions, but not under Bowring's editorship: while
the impossibility of its any longer supporting a paid editor, afforded a ground on which, without affront to him, we could propose
to dispense with his services. We & some of our friends were
prepared to carry on the review as unpaid writers, either finding
among ourselves an unpaid editor, or dividing the editorship
among us. But while this negociation was proceeding, with Bowring's apparent acquiescence, he was carrying on another, in a
different quarter (as it afterwards appeared, with Colonel Per-
ronet Thompson) [329] of which we received the first intimation in a
letter from Bowring as editor saying that an arrangement had been
made & proposing to us to write for the next number, with promise
of payment. We thought the concealment which he had practised
on us, while seemingly entering into our own [330] project, an affront; & even had we not thought so, we were indisposed to take
any further trouble for the review under his management. Accordingly my father excused himself from writing (though two
[81r] or three years later he did write one political article, being
strongly urged). As for me, I absolutely refused. And thus ended
my connexion with the original Westminster. The last article which
I wrote in it had cost me more time & trouble than any previous;
but it was a labour of love, being a defence of the early French
revolutionists against the Tory misrepresentations of Sir Walter
Scott in his Life of Napoleon. For this the number of books which
I read, making notes & extracts, even the number which I bought
(for in those days there was no public or subscription [331] Library
from which books of reference could be taken home) far exceeded
the worth of the immediate object; but I had a half formed intention of writing a History of the French Revolution: & though I
never executed it, my collections afterwards served Carlyle for a
similar purpose.

   For some years after this I wrote very little, & nothing regularly,
for publication: & great were the advantages I derived from the
intermission. It was of immense importance to me at this period,
to be able to digest & mature my thoughts with a view to my own
mind only, without any immediate call for [81v] giving them out
in print.[332] Had I gone on writing it would have much disturbed

---

   [329] of a kind more agreeable to him; &   [330] own] very different
   [331] public or subscription] institution like the London
   [332] A passage of Herder on this subject quoted in Coleridge's Biographia
Literaria, often occurred to me as applicable to my own case.

the important transformation in my opinions & character which took place during these years. The origin of this transformation, or at least the process by which I was prepared for it, can only be explained by turning some distance back.

From the winter of 1821, when I first read Bentham, & especially from the commencement of the Westminster Review, I had what might truly be called an object in life; to be a reformer of the world. My conception of happiness was entirely identified with this object: the personal sympathies I wished for were those of fellow labourers in this enterprise; I picked up as many flowers as I could by the way, but as a serious & permanent personal satisfaction to rest upon my whole reliance was placed on this; & I was accustomed to felicitate myself on the certainty of a happy life which I enjoyed by placing my happiness in something durable & distant, in which some progress might be always [82r] making, but which could never be exhausted by complete attainment. This did very well for several years, during which the general improvement going on in the world, & the idea of myself as engaged with others in struggling to promote it [333] seemed enough to fill up an interesting & animated existence. But the time came when I awakened from this as from a dream. It was in the autumn of 1826. I was [334] in a dull state of nerves, such as everybody is occasionally liable to, unsusceptible to enjoyment or pleasurable excitement: one of those moods in which what is pleasure at other times, becomes insipid & indifferent.[335] In this frame of mind it occurred to me to put the question distinctly to myself, "Suppose that all your objects in life were realized, that all the changes in institutions & opinions which you are looking forward to,[336] could be completely effected at this very instant; would this be a great joy & happiness to you?" & an irrepressible self-consciousness distinctly answered "No!" At this my heart sank [82v] within me; the whole foundation on which my life was constructed fell down. All my happiness was to have been found in the continual pursuit of this end. The end had ceased to charm, & how could there ever again be excitement in the means? I had nothing left to live for.

At first I hoped [337] that the cloud would pass away of itself:

---

[333] by spreading enlightened opinions & urging practical reforms,

[334] was] was, probably from physical causes (connected perhaps merely with the time of year)

[335] insipid & indifferent.] indifferent or disgusting.

[336] which you are looking forward to,] for which you are exerting yourself,

[337] hoped] cherished a hope *altered to read:* clung to a hope

but it did not. A night's sleep, the sovereign remedy for the smaller vexations of life, had no effect on it. I awoke to a renewed consciousness of the woful fact. I carried it with me into all companies, into all occupations. Hardly anything had power to cause me even a few minutes oblivion of it. For some months the [338] cloud seemed to grow thicker & thicker. The lines in Coleridge's poem "Dejection" exactly describe my case:

> "A grief without a pang, void, dark & drear
> A drowsy, stifled, unimpassioned grief
> Which finds no natural outlet or relief
> In word, or sigh, or tear." [339]

In vain I sought relief from my favourite books, those memorials of past nobleness & greatness from which I had always hitherto drawn strength & animation. I read them now without feeling, or with the accustomed feeling *minus* all its charm; & I became persuaded [340] that my love of mankind & of excellence for their own sake, had worn itself out. I sought no relief by speaking to others of what I felt. If I had loved any one sufficiently [341] to make the confiding to them of my griefs a necessity, I should not have been in the condition I was. [83r] I was conscious too that mine was not an interesting or in any way respectable distress. There was nothing in it to attract sympathy. Advice if I had known where to seek it would have been most precious. The words of Macbeth to the physician often recurred [342] to my thoughts. But there was no one on whom I could build the faintest hope of such assistance. My father, to whom I should most naturally have had recourse as an adviser in any practical difficulties, was the last person to whom in such a case as this I looked for help. Everything convinced me that he had no knowledge of any such mental state as I was suffering from, & that even if he could be made to understand it he was not the physician who could heal it. My education, which was wholly his work, had been conducted without any regard to the possibility of its ending in this result; & I saw no use in endeav-

---

[338] For some months the] This state continued for some months without any improvement. The

[339] The lines in Coleridge's poem . . . tear."] *written at left* (*Mill first wrote:* "The lines in Coleridge's poem 'Dejection' beginning 'A grief without a pang' exactly describe my case." *He later added the four verses in pencil, recopied them in ink, and deleted the shorter quotation from his original sentence*)

[340] became persuaded] said in my own mind,

[341] sufficiently] *underlined by HM*   [342] often recurred] recurred incessantly

ouring to prove to him that his plans had failed, when the failure was probably irremediable & at all events beyond the power of *his* remedies. Of other friends I had at that time none to whom I had any hope of making my condition intelligible. It was however abundantly intelligible to myself; & the more I dwelt upon it, the more hopeless it appeared.

[83v] My course of study had led me to believe [343] that all mental & moral feelings & qualities, whether of a good or a bad kind, were the results of association; that we love one thing & hate another, have pleasure in one sort of action or contemplation & pain in another sort, through the clinging of pleasurable & painful ideas to those things from the effect of education or of experience. As a consequence of this I had always heard it maintained by my father, & was myself [344] convinced, that the object of education should be to form the strongest possible associations of the salutary class; associations of pleasure with all things beneficial to the great whole, & of pain with all things hurtful to it. All this appeared inexpugnable, but it now seemed to me on retrospect, that my teachers had occupied themselves but superficially with the means of forming & keeping up these salutary associations. They seemed to have trusted altogether to the old familiar instruments praise & blame, reward & punishment. Now I did not doubt that by these means, begun early & applied vigilantly, intense associations of pain & pleasure might be raised up, especially of pain, and might produce desires and aversions capable of lasting undiminished [84r] to the end of life. But there must always be something artificial & casual in associations thus generated: the pains & pleasures thus forcibly associated with things, are not connected with them by any natural tie; & it is therefore, I thought, essential to the durability of these associations, that they should have become so intense & inveterate as to be practically indissoluble before the habitual exercise of the power of analysis had commenced. For I now saw, or thought I saw, what I had always before received with incredulity—that the habit of analysis has a tendency to wear away the feelings. This is a commonplace, but it is true, & only errs in being but a half-truth. The habit of analysis has really this

---

[343] My course of study . . . believe] I had been taught & was [83v] thoroughly persuaded

[344] consequence of this I had . . . myself] corollary from this I had been taught & had always been

tendency when no other mental habit is cultivated, & the analysing tendency remains without its natural complements & correctives. At this time I did not see what these complements & correctives are.[345] The very excellence of analysis (I argued) is that it tends to weaken & undermine whatever is prejudice; that it enables us mentally to separate ideas which have only casually clung together, & no associations whatever could ultimately resist its dissolving force, were it not that we owe to analysis our clearest knowledge of the permanent sequences in nature; the real connexions between things, quite independent of our will & feelings; natural laws by which in many cases, one thing is inseparable from another & which laws in proportion as they are clearly perceived & imaginatively realized, cause the ideas of things which always accompany one another [84v] in fact, to cohere more & more closely in conception. Analytic habits may thus even strengthen the associations between causes & effects but tend to weaken all those which are, to speak familiarly, a mere matter of feeling. They are, therefore (I thought) favourable to prudence & clearsightedness, but a perpetual worm at the root both of the passions & of the virtues: & above all, fearfully undermine all desires & all pleasures which are the result of association, that is, according to the theory I held, all except the purely physical & organic: of the entire insufficiency of which, to make life desirable, no one had a stronger conviction than I had. These were the laws of human nature by which, as it seemed to me, I had been brought to my present state. All those to whom I looked up, were of opinion [346] that the pleasures of sympathy with human beings, & the feelings which made the good of others & especially of mankind on a large scale the object of existence, were the greatest & surest source of happiness. I was well convinced of this, but to know that a feeling would make me happy if I had it, did not create the feeling. My education had failed, as I thought, to give me these feelings in sufficient strength to resist the dissolving influence of analysis, while the whole course of my intellectual [85r] cultivation had made precocious & premature analysis the inveterate habit of my mind. I was thus, as I said to myself, left stranded at the commencement of my voyage, with a well equipped ship & a rudder but no sail; without any real desire for the ends which I had been so carefully

---

[345] This is a commonplace, but it is true . . . are.] *written at left*
[346] All those to whom . . . opinion] I had been taught

fitted to labour for: no delight in virtue or the general good, but also just as little in anything else. The sources [347] of vanity & ambition seemed to have dried up within me, as completely as those of benevolence. I had had (as I reflected) some gratification of vanity at too early an age; I had obtained some distinction & felt myself to be of some importance before the desire of distinction & of importance had grown into a passion; & little as it was which I had attained, yet having been attained so early, like all pleasures enjoyed too soon, it had made me *blasé* & indifferent to the pursuit. Thus neither selfish nor unselfish pleasures were pleasures to me. And there seemed no power in nature sufficient to begin the formation of my character afresh & create in a mind now irrevocably analytic, fresh associations of pleasure with any of the objects of human desire.

These were the thoughts which mingled with the dry heavy dejection of the melancholy winter of 1826–7.[348] During this time [85v] I was not incapable of my usual occupations; I went on with them mechanically, by the mere force of habit. I had been so drilled in a certain sort of mental exercise that I could carry it on when all the spirit had gone out of it. I even composed & spoke several speeches at the debating society; how, or with what degree of worth I know not. Of four years continual speaking at that society, this is the only year of which I remember next to nothing. Two lines of Coleridge, in whom alone of all writers [349] I have found a true description of what I felt, were often in my thoughts, not at this time, but in a later period of the same mental malady.

"Work without hope draws nectar in a sieve
"And hope without an object cannot live."

I often asked myself, if I could, or was bound, to live on, when life must be passed in this manner. I generally answered to myself, that I did not think I could possibly bear it beyond a year. When however not more than half that length of time had passed, a small ray of light broke in upon my gloom. I was reading, accidentally, Marmontel's Memoirs, & came to the passage where he relates his father's death, the distressed position of his family, & how he, then a mere boy, by a sudden inspiration, felt & made them feel that he would be everything, would supply the place of everything to them. A vivid conception of [86r] this scene [350] came over me, & I was

---

[347] sources] pleasures   [348] 1826–7.] 1846–7.   [349] writers] poets
[350] this scene] his & [86r] their feelings

moved to tears. From this moment my burthen grew lighter. The oppression of the thought that all feeling was dead within me, was gone. I was no longer hopeless. I was not a stock or a stone. I had still, it seemed, some of the material out of which all worth of character & all capacity of happiness are made. Relieved from my ever present sense of wretchedness, I gradually found that the ordinary incidents of life could again give some pleasure; that I could again find enjoyment in sunshine & sky, in books, in conversation, in public affairs, not intense, but sufficient for cheerfulness; & that there was once more, excitement though but of a moderate kind, in exerting myself for my opinions & for the public good. Thus the cloud gradually drew off, & I again enjoyed life; & though before the gloom entirely passed away [351] I had several relapses, some of which lasted many months, I never again was as miserable as I had been.

The experiences of this period had two very decided effects on my opinions & character. In the first place, they led me to adopt a theory of life very unlike that on which I had before acted, & having much in common with what at that time I had never heard of, the anti-self-consciousness theory of Carlyle. I never indeed varied in the conviction that happiness is the test of all rules of conduct, & the end of life. But I now thought that this end was only to be attained by not making it the direct aim. Those only are happy (I thought) [86v] who have their attention fixed on something other than their own happiness: on the happiness of others, either individually or collectively; on the improvement of mankind, even on some art or favorite pursuit followed not as a means but as an ideal end. Aiming thus at something else, they find happiness by the way. The enjoyments of life (such was now my theory) are sufficient to make life pleasant when they are taken en passant, without being made a principal object. Once make them so however & they are immediately felt to be insufficient. They will not bear a scrutinizing examination: ask yourself if you are happy, & you cease to be so. The only chance is to treat not happiness but some end external to it, as the object of life. Let your self consciousness, your scrutiny, your self interrogation exhaust themselves on that, & if otherwise fortunately circumstanced you will inhale happiness with the air you breathe, without dwelling on it or thinking about it, without either forestalling it in im-

---

[351] before the gloom . . . away] during the next few years

agination or putting it to flight by fatal self questioning. This theory now became the basis of my philosophy of life. And I still hold to it as the best theory for those who have but a moderate degree of sensibility & of capacity for enjoyment, that is, for the great majority of mankind.

The other great change which my opinions at this time underwent, was that I now for the first time [87r] gave its proper place among the prime necessities of human well being, to the internal culture of the individual. I ceased to attach almost exclusive importance to the ordering of outward circumstances, & to the training of the human being for knowledge & for action. I now knew by experience that the passive susceptibilities needed to be cultivated as well as the active capacities, & required to be nourished & enriched as well as guided. I never for an instant lost sight of or undervalued, that part of the truth which I saw before: I never turned recreant to intellectual culture, or ceased to value the power & habit of analysis as essential both to individual & to social improvement. But I thought that it had consequences which required to be corrected by joining other sorts of cultivation with it: & the maintenance of a due balance among the faculties, now seemed to me of primary importance.[352] The cultivation of the feelings now became one of the cardinal points in my ethical & philosophical creed. And my thoughts & inclinations turned more & more towards whatever I thought capable of being instrumental to that object.

I now [353] began to find meaning in the things which I had read or heard said about the importance of poetry & art as instruments of culture. But it was some time longer before I began to know this by personal experience. The only one of the imaginative arts in which I had from childhood taken great pleasure was music: the best effect of which (& in this it surpasses perhaps every other art) consists in exciting enthusiasm; in winding up to a high pitch those feelings of an elevated kind which are already *in* the character [87v] but to which this excitement gives a glow & a fervour which though transitory in its utmost height, is precious for sustaining them at other times. This effect of music I had often experienced: but like all my better susceptibilities it was suspended during my gloomy period. I had sought relief again & again from this quarter

---

[352] I never for an instant . . . importance.] *written at left*
[353] I now] It was a natural consequence of this, that I

but found none. After the tide had turned, indeed, & I was in process of recovery, I had been helped forward by music, but in a much less elevated [354] manner. I at this time first became acquainted with Weber's Oberon, & the extreme pleasure which I drew from its delicious melodies did me good by shewing me a source of pleasure to which I was as susceptible as ever: this good however being much impaired by the thought that the pleasure of music (as is quite true of such pleasure as this was, that of mere tune) fades with familiarity, & requires to be fed by continual novelty. And it is very characteristic both of my then state & of my general mental character at that time, that I was seriously tormented by the thought of the exhaustibility of musical combinations. The five tones & two semitones of the octave can be put together only in a limited number of ways; of these only a small proportion are beautiful; most of these must have been already discovered & there could not be room for a long succession of [88*r*] Mozarts & Webers to strike out as they had done entirely new & surpassingly rich veins of musical beauty. This source of anxiety may appear perhaps to resemble [355] that of the philosophers of Laputa who feared lest the sun should be burnt out. It was however connected with the best point of my character, the only good point indeed to be found in my very unromantic & in no way honorable distress. For though my dejection honestly looked at, cannot be called other than egotistical, produced by the ruin as I thought of my fabric of happiness; yet the condition of mankind in general was ever in my thoughts, & could not be separated from my own; I felt that the evil in my life must be an evil in life itself; that the question was whether if the reformers of society & government could succeed in their objects & every person living were free & in physical comfort the pleasures of life, being no longer kept up by privation & struggle would cease to be pleasures: & I felt that unless I could see my way to some better hope than this for the general happiness of mankind, my dejection must continue; but that if I could, I should then look on the world with pleasure, content with any fair share [356] of the general lot.

This state of my thoughts & feelings made the fact of my [88*v*] first reading Wordsworth (in the autumn [357] of 1828) an important

---

[354] less elevated] more vulgar   [355] to resemble] as ridiculous as
[356] fair share] share which might happen to fall to me
[357] (in the autumn] (at the end of the summer

event of my life. I took up the collection of his poems from curiosity, with no expectation of mental relief from it, though I had before resorted to poetry with that hope. In the worst period of my mental depression I had read through the whole of Byron (then new to me) to try whether a poet whose peculiar department was supposed to be that of the intenser feelings, could rouse any feeling in me. As might be expected, I got no good from this reading but the reverse. The poet's state of mind was too like my own. His was the lament of a man who had worn out all pleasures & who seemed to think that life to all who possessed the good things of it, must necessarily be the vapid uninteresting [358] thing which I found it. His Harold & Manfred had the same burthen on them which I had; & I was not in a frame of mind to derive any comfort from the vehement sensual passion of his Giaours or the sulkiness of his Laras. But while Byron was exactly what did not suit my condition, Wordsworth was exactly what did. I had looked into the Excursion two or three years before & found little or nothing in it; & should probably have found as little [89r] had I read it now. But the miscellaneous poems, in the two-volume edition of 1815, (to which little valuable was added in any of the subsequent editions) [359] proved to be the precise thing for my mental wants at that particular time.

In the first place, these poems addressed themselves powerfully to one of the strongest of my pleasurable susceptibilities, the love of rural objects & of natural scenery; to which I had been indebted not only for much of the pleasure of my life, but quite recently for relief from one of my longest relapses into depression.[360] In this power of rural beauty over me there was a foundation laid for taking pleasure in Wordsworth's poetry; the more so, as his scenery is mostly among mountains, which owing to my early Pyrenean

---

[358] uninteresting] *Mill interlined and deleted* joyless *above this word*

[359] (to which little valuable . . . editions)] comprising nearly everything good which he ever wrote, *deleted by HM*

[360] About Midsummer of that same year 1828 I set out on a short walking tour: for months before I had been in my old state of gloomy dejection though as I have already mentioned not so intense as at first; this continued the greater part of the first day, but the walk by the side of the Thames from Reading to Pangbourne, in one of the loveliest of summer evenings with the western sky in its most splendid colouring before me, & the calm river, rich meadows & wooded hills encompassing me, insensibly changed my state, & except a short interval two days later I had no return of depression during that excursion nor for several months afterwards.

excursion were my ideal of natural beauty. [89*v*] But Wordsworth would never have had any great effect on me if he had merely placed before me beautiful pictures of natural scenery. A collection of very second rate landscapes does this more effectually than any books. What made Wordsworth's poems a [361] medicine for my state of mind was that they expressed, not outward beauty but states of feeling, & of thought coloured by feeling, under the excitement of [362] beauty. They seemed to be the very culture of the feelings which I was in quest of. By their means I seemed to draw from a source of inward joy, of sympathetic & imaginative pleasure, which could be shared in by all human beings, which had no connexion with struggle or imperfection, but would be made richer by every improvement in the physical or social condition of [363] mankind. I seemed to learn from them what would be the perennial sources of happiness when all the greater evils of life should be removed. And I felt myself at once better & happier as I came under their influence. At present my estimate of Wordsworth as a poet is very far indeed below that which I then formed; but poetry of deeper & loftier feeling could not have done for me at that time what this did. I wanted to be made to feel that there was happiness in tranquil contemplation. Wordsworth taught me this and [90*r*] not only without turning away from, but with a greatly increased interest in, the common feelings & common destiny of human beings. And the [364] delight which these poems gave me, proved to me that with culture of this sort there was nothing to dread from the most confirmed habit of analysis. At the end of the poems came the famous Ode, falsely called Platonic; in which, along with more than his usual sweetness of rhythm & melody, & along with the two passages of fine description but bad philosophy so often quoted, I found [365] that he too had had similar experience to mine; that he had felt that the first freshness of youthful enjoyment of life was not lasting; but that he had sought for compensation, & found it, in the way in which he was now teaching me to find it.[366] The consequence of all these things was that I gradually but completely emerged from my habitual depression & was never again subject to it. I long continued to value Wordsworth less according to his

---

[361] a] so exactly the   [362] natural   [363] the mass of
[364] unfading, or rather the increasing
[365] what was much more to my purpose, namely
[366] This moral of the whole, so different from Byron's, was valuable to me, but I did not need it, as I had already drawn the same from the previous poems.

intrinsic merits than [90v] to what he had done for me.[367] My present judgment of him is, that he is the poet of unpoetical natures, when accompanied by quiet & contemplative tastes. But it must be remembered that unpoetical natures are precisely those which require poetic cultivation. This cultivation Wordsworth is more fitted to give them, than poets incomparably his superiors.

It so happened that the merits of Wordsworth were the occasion of my first public declaration of my new way of thinking, &[368] separation from those of my habitual companions who had not undergone a similar change. The person with whom at that time I was most in the habit of comparing notes[369] was Roebuck; & I induced him to read Wordsworth, in whom he also at first seemed to find much to admire: but I like most Wordsworthians threw myself into strong antagonism to Byron, both as a poet & in respect to his effect on the character.[370] Roebuck, all whose instincts were those of action & struggle,[371] had on the contrary a strong relish & admiration of Byron whose writings he regarded as the poetry of real life while Wordsworth's according to him were that of flowers & butterflies. We agreed to have the fight out at our Debating Society, where we accordingly discussed for [91r] two evenings the comparative merits of Byron & Wordsworth, propounding, & illustrating by long recitations,[372] our respective theories of poetry. This was the first debate on any weighty subject on which Roebuck & I were on opposite sides. The schism between us widened more & more from this time & though for some years we continued to be companions our differences of opinion on life & philosophy became so strongly pronounced that we ceased to be allies either in opinion or in action except as to the immediate objects of radicalism.[373]

I suppose that of the set of young men with whom I had associated, Roebuck would have been & was generally regarded as the most complete type of what was considered narrow Benthamism. This however is only an example of the extreme inaccuracy of

---

[367] I long continued to value . . . me.] All these things being considered it is not strange that I rated very high the merit [90v] & value of Wordsworth.

[368] apparent [369] as to matters of opinion, [370] character.] mind.

[371] action & struggle,] passion & of action,

[372] propounding, & . . . recitations,] each bringing forward the merits of the poet he preferred, vehemently attacking the other, & propounding

[373] be allies either . . . radicalism.] consider ourselves as allies in opinion, further than as we were both of us radicals & democrats. *marked with a line in the margin by HM*

that common conception. Roebuck was in many things totally opposite to the vulgar notion of a Benthamite. He was a lover of
poetry & of almost all the fine arts. He took great pleasure in
music, in dramatic performances, especially in painting, & himself
drew & designed landscapes with great facility & beauty. Instead
of being, as Benthamites are supposed to be, unfeeling, he had
[91*v*] very quick & susceptible feelings: & his feelings towards persons, favourable & hostile, have greatly influenced his course all
through life. No description of a class would exactly fit [374] Roebuck;
he had a decided character of his own, & took only that portion of
any creed which was in harmony with his character. Of this,
pugnacity was one of the principal elements. Nine years of his
boyhood & youth had been passed in the back woods of Canada;
& his character had a great tinge of the backwoodsman: formed
to self help, to self assertion, & to be ever ready for conflict; with
the reservation, that as the small & weakly brother among a family
of giants, mental & not bodily weapons were those with which his
battles had been fought & his victories gained. These early circumstances gave him the audacity & self reliance which most distinguished him from the common run of Englishmen, in whom
those qualities become every day more rare. On the other hand,
his mother (a daughter of Tickell, & of the sister of the first Mrs
Sheridan) by whom chiefly he was educated & of whom he always
spoke with great admiration & affection, had cultivated in him a
polish of manners not at all American which he always manifested
towards friends, though not always towards opponents.[375] [92*r*]
Roebuck was a Radical in Canadian politics though his stepfather,
on whom at that time he was entirely dependent, was a placeman.
He came to England to qualify for the bar, & finding that he could
maintain himself by writing, remained there. On his arrival he
almost immediately fell in with me & my set, & had Bentham's &
my father's writings presented to him as the philosophy of radicalism. He seized on this political creed with great & sincere zeal.
Naturally quick of perception & comprehension, though not inven-
tive or original, he was qualified to become a reasoner rather than
a thinker; & his intellectual type, in all matters of speculation, continued to be one of ratiocination rather than of insight, as Carlyle

---

[374] No description . . . fit] Roebuck was not one who could be classed; he
was, above all, *marked with a line in the margin by HM*

[375] An ambitious young man with his fortune to make is naturally a Radical:

calls it, or (to describe it more precisely) [376] induction & analysis. He arrived at his conclusions by deduction from the principles of his creed, never anxious to enlarge the basis of the creed itself by perpetual examination of the specialities of the questions to which he was called on to apply it. This deficiency I used to account for to myself,[377] by the deep rooted pugnacity of his character. When any proposition [92v] came before him as that of an opponent, he rushed eagerly to demonstrate its falsity, without taking any pains to discover & appropriate the portion of truth which there might be in it. This mental type, very natural to persons of impetuosity of character & which I saw in a less extreme degree [378] in my father, became more & more alien to my tastes & feelings. I had now taken a most decided bent in the opposite direction, that of eclecticism; looking out for the truth which is generally to be found in errors when they are anything more than mere paralogisms, or logical blunders. My disputes with Roebuck in the early part of our discussions turned mainly on the culture of the feelings; & in these he who had certainly the quickest feelings took the unfeeling side. But this, instead of a paradox, is the explanation of the whole matter. Like most Englishmen who have feelings, he found his feelings stand very much in his way: he was much more susceptible to the painful sympathies than to the pleasurable, & looking for his happiness elsewhere, wished that his feelings should be deadened rather than quickened. And in truth the English character & English social circumstances make it so seldom possible to derive happiness from the exercise of the sympathies that [93r] it is not wonderful they should count for very little in an Englishman's scheme of life. In all other countries the paramount importance of the sympathies as a constituent of happiness is an axiom, taken for granted rather than needing any formal statement; but most English thinkers seem to regard them as necessary evils, required to keep men's actions benevolent & compassionate. Roebuck was this sort of Englishman, or seemed to be so; he saw little good in the cultivation of the feelings, & none in their cultivation through the imagination, which he thought was only cultivating illusions. It was in

---

[376] (to describe it more precisely)] as I at this time called it, *marked with an X in the margin by HM*

[377] probably truly,

[378] less extreme degree] much milder form *altered to read:* less aggravated form

vain I urged on him that the imaginative emotion which an idea
when vividly conceived excites in us, is not an illusion but a fact,
as real as any of the other qualities of objects; and far from imply-
ing anything erroneous & delusive in our [379] mental apprehension
of the object, is quite consistent with the most accurate knowledge
& practical recognition of all its physical & intellectual laws &
relations. The intensest feeling of the beauty of a cloud lighted by
the setting sun, is no hindrance to my knowing that the cloud is
the vapour of water, subject to all the laws of vapours in a state
of suspension; & I am just as [93v] likely to allow for, & act on,
these physical laws whenever there is occasion to do so, as if I
were incapable of perceiving any distinction between beauty &
ugliness. To conclude here my notice of Roebuck; when three years
afterwards he under almost every disadvantage of fortune & position took his seat in the House of Commons,[380] he fulfilled [381] my
expectation & prediction at the time, viz. that he would fail, apparently irretrievably, half a dozen times & succeed at last. He
escaped the imputation which almost all persons in his position are
subject to, of being an adventurer. Nobody ever suspected him of
wishing to be bought off. His ambition was not of this low kind:
& his very faults, his asperity & the needless offensiveness of his
attacks, protected him from the suspicion. Notwithstanding his
many defects of judgment, he succeeded by perseverance & by
really having something to say, in acquiring the ear of the house.
He conquered all external obstacles, & if he ceased rising it was
because he had got to the end of his tether. He made considerable
exertions for radicalism during some years in the H. of Commons,
& was the vigorous champion of two great [94r] questions; national
education, which he reoriginated in parliament (the first unsuccessful move had been made by Mr Brougham twelve years before) & responsible government in the colonies, of which Roebuck
was in this country altogether the originator, both in the press &
in parliament, & remained up to the period of Lord Durham's mis-
sion the principal pillar. It ought to be recorded among the most
honorable points in his career, that he braved his own supporters
& lost his seat at Bath by his vigorous opposition to the bills for
the puritanical observance of Sunday. But he did not labour to
master the special questions of legislation which were brought or

---

[379] anything erroneous . . . our] any perversion of the
[380] as a radical member of parliament,   [381] exactly

which he might usefully have brought before parliament; & his voice, at last, was heard almost solely on personal questions, or on such as he was able to make personal. He made no progress in general principles; like the Parliamentary Radicals generally, made no addition to his original stock of ideas; [382] & when the mental movement of Europe outstripped him even in politics, as was manifested in February 1848, he turned against the movement of Europe.[383] Even on English matters, when he had succeeded in being somebody, & above all when he had married & become involved in the petty vanities & entanglements of what is called society, he gradually ceased to be the champion of [94v] any important progress; he became a panegyrist of England & things English, a conformist to the Church,[384] & in short merged in the common herd of Conservative Liberals.

But to return to the point of separation between his course & mine. I have mentioned that the difference of our philosophy first declared itself in the debate on Wordsworth, at the Society we had founded & in which, in addition to the Tory party with whom we had hitherto been combating, we were now face to face with another set of adversaries of far greater intrinsic worth, the Coleridgians, represented in the society by Frederick Maurice & John Sterling: both subsequently well known, the former by his writings, the latter through the two biographies by Hare & Carlyle. Of these two [385] friends, Maurice was the thinker, Sterling the orator, & impassioned expositor of thoughts which were, at this time, almost entirely formed for him by Maurice. With Maurice I had been for some time acquainted through Eyton Tooke, who had known him at Cambridge, & although my discussions with him were almost always disputes, I had [95r] carried away from them much that helped to build up my new fabric of thought; in the same way as I was deriving much [386] from Coleridge, & from writings of Goethe & other Germans which I read during these years.[387] I have always thought that there was more intellectual

---

[382] made no addition to . . . ideas;] his ideas did not advance with events;
[383] turned against the . . . Europe.] was found [*altered to read:* became] a reactionary.
[384] *At this point Mill wrote* (*but did not complete the clause before deleting*): & is now no longer worth counting as an element in
[385] intimate   [386] valuable thought
[387] *Originally continued without punctuation:* either in the original or in translations.

power misapplied & wasted in Maurice than in any other of my cotemporaries. Great power of generalization, rare ingenuity & subtlety & a wide perception of important & unobvious truth, served him not for putting something better into the place of the worthless heap of received opinions in spiritual matters but for proving that the Church of England had known everything from the first, & that all the truths on the ground of which the Church & orthodoxy have been attacked, are not only consistent with the 39 articles but are better understood & expressed in those articles than by any one who rejects them. Such was the perverting effect on what would otherwise have been a fine intellect, of the combination of a timid character & conscience with an originally [95*v*] highly sensitive temperament. In this he resembled Coleridge, to whom, in merely intellectual powers, apart from poetical genius, I think him decidedly superior. At this time however he might be described as a disciple of Coleridge, & Sterling as a disciple of Coleridge & of him. In our Debating Society they made their appearance as a second Liberal & even Radical party, on totally different grounds from Benthamism & vehemently opposed to it; & they brought into their discussions the general doctrines & modes of thought of the European reaction against the philosophy of the 18th century: thus adding a third & very important belligerent party to our discussions, which were now no bad exponent of the movement of opinion among the most cultivated of the new generation. The modifications which were taking place in my old opinions naturally gave me some [388] points of contact with them; & both Maurice & Sterling were of considerable use to my developement. In after conversations with Sterling he told me how he & others had been accustomed to look upon me as a "made" or manufactured man, having had a certain impress of opinion stamped upon me which I could only [389] [96*r*] reproduce; & what a change took place in his feelings when he found, in the discussion on Wordsworth & Byron (in which as might be expected he made a brilliant speech) that Wordsworth & all that is implied in Wordsworth [390] "belonged to" me as much as to him & his friends. But if I agreed with them much more than with Bentham on poetry & general culture, I was as much opposed to them as ever on religion, political philosophy, ethics & metaphysics, & as long as we con-

---

[388] some] more   [389] I could only] my sole [96*r*] function was to
[390] all that is implied in Wordsworth] much else of a kindred nature

tinued our debating practice we were almost always on contrary sides. One vehement encounter between Sterling & me, he making what I thought a violent & unfair attack on the political philosophy I professed, to which I responded as sharply, fixed itself particularly in my memory because it was immediately followed by two things: one was, Sterling's withdrawing from the society; the other, that he & I sought one another privately much more than before, & became very intimate. His frank, cordial, affectionate & expansive character made him very attractive to me as he was to every one who knew him. The failure of his health soon [96v] scattered all his plans of life & compelled him to live at a distance from London, & I living almost constantly in it, we after the first year or two of our acquaintance only saw each other at distant intervals. He never became, in the proper sense of the word, a thinker; but his open mind & heart, & the moral courage in which he was greatly superior to Maurice, made him soon outgrow the dominion over his intellect of Maurice & of Coleridge. Except in that short & passing phasis of his life, during which he made the [391] mistake of becoming a clergyman, his mind was ever progressive; the advance he always seemed to have made when I saw him again after an interval, made me apply to him what Goethe said of Schiller's "fürchtliche Fortschreitung." He & I started from intellectual points almost as wide apart as the poles, but the distance between us was always growing less: if I made [392] steps towards some of his opinions, he, during his short life, was constantly approximating more & more to mine: & if he had lived & had health & vigour to prosecute his ever assiduous self culture I have little doubt that his mental emancipation on all [97r] the leading points of opinion would have become complete.

After 1829 I withdrew from attendance on the Debating Society. I had had enough of speech making, & was glad to carry on my private studies & meditations without any immediate call for outward assertion of their results. I found the fabric of my old & taught opinions giving way in many fresh places, & I never allowed it to fall to pieces, but was incessantly occupied in weaving it anew: I never, in the course of my transition, suffered myself to remain confused & unsettled. When I had taken in any new idea I could not rest till I had adjusted its relation to all my old opinions,

---

[391] great   [392] many

& ascertained exactly how far its effect ought to extend in modifying or superseding them.[393]

The conflicts which I had so often had to carry on in defence of the theory of government laid down in Bentham's & my father's writings, & the acquaintance I had obtained with other modes of political thinking, had made me [394] aware of many things which that doctrine, professing to be a theory of government in general, [97v] ought to have made room for, & did not. But these things as yet remained with me rather as corrections to be made in applying the theory to practice, than as defects in the theory. I felt that politics could not be a science of specific experience; that the accusations against the Benthamic theory of *being* a theory, of proceeding *a priori*, by way of general reasoning instead of Baconian experiment, shewed complete ignorance of Bacon's principles, & of the necessary conditions of political investigation. At this juncture appeared Macaulay's famous attack, in the Edinburgh Review, on my father's Essay on Government. This gave me much to think about. I saw that Macaulay's conception of political reasoning was [395] wrong; that he stood up for the empirical mode of treating political phenomena against the philosophical. At the same time I could not help feeling that there was truth in several of his strictures on my father's treatment of the subject; that my father's premises were really too narrow, & included but a small part of the general truths on which, in politics, the important consequences depend. Identity of interest, in any practical sense which can be attached to the term, between the governing body & the community at large, [98r] is not the only thing on which good government depends; neither can this identity of interest be secured by the mere conditions of election: I was not at all satisfied with the mode in which my father met the criticisms of Macaulay. He did not, as I thought he ought to have done, justify himself by saying "I was not writing a scientific treatise on politics. I was writing an argument for parliamentary reform." He treated Macaulay's argument as simply irrational; as an attack on the reasoning faculty; an example of the remark of Hobbes that when reason is against a man a man will be against reason. This made me think that there was really something more fundamentally erroneous in my father's conception of philosophical Method, as

---

[393] In this part of my life at least, whatever may have been the case at others, I had a really active mind. *marked with a question mark by HM*

[394] fully   [395] thoroughly

applicable to politics, than I had hitherto supposed there was. But I did not at first see clearly what the error might be. At last however it flashed upon me all at once in the course of my reflexions on another subject. I had begun in the early part of 1830 to put on paper the ideas on Logic (chiefly on the distinctions among Terms, & the import of Propositions) which had been suggested & in part worked out in the morning conversations already spoken of.[396] Having secured these thoughts by putting them into writing, I pushed on into the other parts [98v] of the subject, to try whether I could do anything further to clear up the theory of Logic generally. I attempted at once to grapple with the problem of Induction, postponing that of Reasoning on the ground that it is necessary to obtain premisses before we can reason from them. Now Induction is mainly finding the causes of effects; & in endeavouring to give an account of the manner of tracing causes & effects in the physical sciences, I soon saw that in the more perfect of those sciences we ascend, by generalization from particular instances to the tendencies of causes considered singly, & then reason downward from those separate tendencies, to determine the action of the same causes when combined. I then asked myself, what is the ultimate analysis of this deductive process? the common theory of the syllogism evidently throwing no light upon it. My [397] practice being to study abstract principles in the best concrete instances I could find, the Composition of Forces, in dynamics, occurred to me as the most complete example of the logical process I was investigating. On examining what the mind does when it applies the principle of the Composition of Forces, I found that it performs a simple act of addition. It adds the separate effect of the one cause [99r] to the separate effect of the other, & puts down the sum of the separate effects as the joint effect. But is this a legitimate process? In dynamics & in the other branches of mathematical physics it is; but in some other cases, as in chemistry it is not; & I then recollected that this was pointed out as one of the distinctions between chemical phenomena & those of natural philosophy, in the introduction to that favorite book of my boyhood, Thomson's Chemistry. This distinction cleared up what [398] was perplexing me in respect to the philosophy of politics. I saw that a science is deductive or experimental according as the effects of

---

[396] already spoken of.] at Grote's.   [397] constant
[398] distinction cleared up what] threw a flash of light upon all that

its causes when conjoined are or are not the sums of the effects of the same causes when separate; which, in the moral & political sciences, they may on the whole be said to be. Hence it appeared that both Macaulay & my father were wrong; the one in assimilating the method of philosophizing in politics to the purely experimental method of chemistry; while the other though right in adopting an a priori method, had made a wrong selection of one, having taken, not the appropriate [99v] method, that of the deductive branches of natural philosophy, but the inappropriate method of pure geometry, which not being a science of causation at all, did not require or admit of the summation of effects. A foundation was thus laid in my thoughts for the principal chapters of what I afterwards published on the "Logic of the Moral Sciences"; & my position in respect to my old political creed was now to my own mind quite cleared up.[399]

[100r] If I am asked what other system of political philosophy I substituted for that which, as a philosophy, I had abandoned, my answer is, no system: merely a conviction, that the true system was something much more complex & many sided than I had hitherto had any idea of, & that its office was to supply, not a set of model institutions, but principles from which the institutions suitable to any given circumstances[400] might be deduced. The influences of European, that is to say, Continental thought, & especially those of the reaction of the nineteenth century against the eighteenth, were now showering in upon me. They came from various quarters; partly from the writings of Coleridge, which I had begun to read with interest even before the change in my opinions; partly from[401] the Coleridgians with whom I was in

---

[399] I did not at this time push my logical speculations any further. *Mill then began a new paragraph:* This was not the only modification which was taking place in my old opinions in the political department of things. The early writings of the St Simonian school, with which I had now become acquainted, were gradually opening my eyes to the very limited & temporary value of the old political economy, which assumes individual hereditary property as a necessary fact, and freedom of production & exchange as the dernier mot of social improvement. *The paragraph continues with three sentences substantially the same as the third and fourth sentences and part of the fifth sentence of the second paragraph below ("They were then only in . . . even this length"— pp. 137–138). For the rest of this earlier version, continued on R105–106, see pp. 187–189*

[400] circumstances] state of civilization

[401] opinions; partly from] opinions, & of which I was now a frequent reader: partly from Sterling, Maurice, &

personal contact: partly from what I had read of Goethe; [402] partly from Carlyle's early articles in the Edinburgh & Foreign Reviews, though for a long time I saw nothing in these, (as my father saw nothing in them to the last) but insane rhapsodies. From all these, & from the acquaintance I kept up with the French writers of the time, I derived, among other [403] ideas, which the general turning upside down of the opinions of European thinkers had brought uppermost, these in particular: that the human mind [100v] has a certain order of possible progress in which some things must precede others, an order which governments & public instructors can alter to some extent, but not to an unlimited extent: that all questions of institutions are relative, not absolute, & that different stages of human progress not only *will* have (which must always have been evident) but *ought* to have, different institutions; that government is always either in the hands, or passing into the hands, of whatever is the strongest power in society, & that what this power is, does not depend on institutions, but institutions on it: that any general theory or philosophy of politics supposes a previous theory of human progress, in other words a philosophy of history. These opinions, true in the main, were held in an exaggerated & violent manner by the thinkers with whom I was now becoming acquainted, & [404] who, in the true spirit of a reaction, ignored that half of the truth which the thinkers of the eighteenth century saw. I never went along with them in this but kept as firm a hold of one side of the truth as I took of the other. The fight between the nineteenth century & the eighteenth always reminded me of the battle about the shield one side of which was black & the other white. I marvelled at the blind rage with which the combatants rushed against one another. I applied to them, & to Coleridge among the rest, many of the sayings of Coleridge himself about [101r] half truths; & Goethe's device "manysidedness" was much [405] in my thoughts.

The writers by whom more than by any others a new mode of political thinking was brought home to me, were those of the St Simonian school in France. In 1829 & 1830 I became acquainted with some of their writings. They were then only in the earlier stages of their speculations: they had not yet dressed up their philosophy as a religion, nor had they organized their scheme of

---

[402] partly from what I had read of Goethe;] *interlined*   [403] valuable
[404] the thinkers with whom . . . &] my new instructors,
[405] much] continually

Socialism. They were just beginning to question the principle of hereditary property. I was by no means prepared to go with them even this length; but I was greatly struck with the connected view which they for the first time presented to me, of the natural order of human progress; & especially with their division of history into organic periods & critical periods. During the organic periods (they said) mankind accept with firm conviction some positive creed, containing more or less of truth & of adaptation to the needs of humanity. Under its influence they first make all the progress compatible with that creed, & then finally outgrow it: & a period follows of criticism & negation, in which mankind lose their old convictions without acquiring any new ones except the conviction that the old are false. The period of Greek & Roman polytheism, so long as really believed in by [406] instructed Greeks & Romans, was an organic period, followed by the critical or sceptical period of the Greek philosophers. [101*v*] Another organic period came in with Christianity; the corresponding critical period began with the Reformation, has lasted ever since, & cannot altogether cease until a new organic period has been inaugurated by the triumph of a still more advanced creed. These ideas, I knew, were nowise peculiar to the St Simonians; they were the general property of Europe, or at least [407] of Germany & France; but they had never to my knowledge been so completely systematized as by these writers, nor the distinguishing characters of a critical period so powerfully set forth. In Carlyle indeed I found bitter denunciations of the evils of an "age of unbelief" & of the present age as such, which I & [408] most other people at that time supposed to be intended as passionate protests in favour of the old belief. But all that was true in these denunciations I thought that I found more calmly & philosophically stated by the St Simonians. Among their publications [409] too there was one which seemed to me far superior to the rest, & in which the general idea was matured into something much more definite & instructive. This was an early writing of Auguste Comte, who then called himself, & even announced himself in the title page as, an élève of Saint-Simon. In this tract M. Comte first enunciated the doctrine which he afterwards so copiously illustrated, of the natural succession of three stages in every department of inquiry; first [102*r*]

---

[406] the most   [407] or at least] especially   [408] (I believe)
[409] publications] early writings

the theological, second the metaphysical, & third, the positive stage; & contended that social science must be subject to the same law; that the feudal & Catholic system was the last phasis of the theological state of the social science, Protestantism the commencement & the doctrines of the French Revolution the consummation of its metaphysical, & that its positive state was yet to come. This doctrine harmonized very well with my existing notions. I already regarded the methods of physical science as the proper models for political. But the chief service which I received at this time from the trains of thought suggested by the St Simonians & by Comte, was that I obtained a much clearer conception than before of the peculiarities of an age of transition in opinion, & ceased to mistake the moral & intellectual characteristics of such an age, for the normal attributes of humanity. I looked forward, through the present age of loud disputes but generally weak convictions, to a future which will unite the best qualities of the critical with the best of the organic periods; unchecked liberty of thought, perfect freedom of individual action in things not hurtful to others; [102v] but along with this, firm convictions as to right & wrong, useful & pernicious, deeply engraven on the feelings by early education & general unanimity of sentiment, & so well grounded in reason & in the real exigencies of life, that they shall not, like all former & present creeds, religious, ethical & political, require to be periodically thrown off & replaced by others.

[103r] M. Comte soon left the St Simonians, & I lost sight of him & his writings for a number of years. But the Saint Simonians I continued cultivating. I was kept *au courant* of their progress by one of their most enthusiastic disciples, Gustave d'Eichthal, who about that time passed a considerable period in England. I was introduced to their chiefs, Bazard & Enfantin, in 1830; & as long as their public teachings & proselytism continued, I read nearly everything they wrote. Their criticisms on the common doctrines of liberalism seemed to me full of important truth; & it was partly by their writings that my eyes were opened to the very limited & temporary value of the old political economy, which assumes private property & inheritance as indefeasible facts, & freedom of production & exchange as the dernier mot of social improvement. The scheme gradually unfolded by the St Simonians, by which the labour & capital of the community would be managed for the general account, every individual being required to take a share of

labour either as thinker, teacher, artist or producer, & all being classed according to their capacity & rewarded according to their works, appeared to me a far superior kind of Socialism to Owen's; their aim [103*v*] seemed to me perfectly rational, however their means might be inefficacious; & though I neither believed in the practicability nor in the beneficial operation of their social machinery, I felt that [410] the proclamation of such an ideal of human society could not but be calculated to give a beneficial direction to the efforts of others to bring society, as at present constituted, nearer to that ideal standard. I honoured them above all for the boldness & freedom from prejudice with which they treated the subject of family, the most important of any, & needing more fundamental alterations than any other, but which scarcely any reformer has the courage to touch. In proclaiming the perfect equality of men & women, & an entirely new order of things in regard to their relations with one another, the St Simonians in common with Owen & Fourier have entitled themselves to the grateful remembrance of all future generations.[411]

In giving an account of this period of my life, I have only specified such of my new impressions as appeared to me both at the time & since to be a kind of turning points, marking a definite progress in my modes [104*r*] of thought: But these few selected points give a very insufficient idea of the quantity of thinking which I carried on respecting a host of subjects during these years of transition. It is true much of the thinking consisted in rediscovering things known to all the world, which I had previously disbelieved, or disregarded. But even then the rediscovery usually placed these [412] truths in some new light by which they were reconciled with, & served to confirm even while they modified, the truths *not* generally known which were contained in my early opinions [413] & in no essential part of which I at any time wavered. All my thinking only rendered the foundation of these deeper & stronger, while it often removed misunderstandings & confusion of ideas which had

---

[410] I neither believed in the . . . that] their social machinery could not possibly be worked, & if worked, would produce, I thought, very different effects from what they expected,

[411] This however is anticipating; for at the time of which I am now writing the St Simonians had not yet developed the practical parts of their system. The effect they had on me at this time was solely by their philosophy of history.

[412] old & well known

[413] were contained in my early opinions] I had had the good fortune to be taught

perverted their effect. For example; during the later returns of my dejection, the doctrine of what is called Philosophical Necessity weighed like an incubus on my existence. I felt as if I was the helpless slave of antecedent circumstances; as if the character of all persons had been formed for them by agencies beyond their control, & was wholly out of their [414] power. I often said to myself what a relief it would be if I could disbelieve the doctrine of the formation of character by circumstances; & remembering the wish of Fox respecting the doctrine of resistance to governments, [104v] that it might never be forgotten by kings, nor remembered by subjects, I said in like manner that it would be a blessing if the doctrine of necessity could be believed by all in respect to the characters of others & disbelieved in respect of their own. I pondered on the subject till gradually I saw light through it; I saw that the word necessity as a name for the doctrine of cause & effect applied to human action, carries with it a misleading association; & that this association is the main cause of the depressing & paralysing influence which I had experienced. I perceived that though character is [415] formed by circumstances, our own desires can influence those circumstances; & that what is really inspiriting & ennobling in the doctrine of free will, is the conviction that our will has real power over the formation of our character; that our will, by influencing some of our circumstances, can modify our future habits or capacities of willing. This was perfectly consistent with the doctrine of circumstances or rather was that doctrine itself properly understood. From that time I drew in my own mind a clear [416] distinction between [105r] the doctrine of circumstances & fatalism, discarding altogether the misleading term necessity. The theory, which I now for the first time rightly apprehended, ceased to be discouraging: & I no longer suffered under the burthen, so heavy to one who aims at being a reformer in [417] opinions, of thinking one doctrine true & the contrary doctrine morally beneficial. The train of thought which had extricated me from this dilemma seemed to me fitted to render a similar service to others, & it now forms the chapter on Liberty & Necessity in the concluding book of my "System of Logic."

In like manner in politics though I no longer accepted the doc-

---

[414] the character of all persons . . . their] my character had been formed for me by agencies beyond my control, & was now out of my
[415] entirely   [416] a clear] the clearest   [417] in] of the world's

trine of the Essay on Government as a scientific theory; though I ceased to consider representative democracy as an absolute principle & regarded it as a question of time, place, & circumstance; though I now looked on the choice of political institutions as a moral & educational question rather than a question of material interest, & thought it should be decided mainly by considering what great improvement in life & culture stood next in order for the people concerned, as the condition of their further progress, & what institutions were most likely to promote that; nevertheless [105*v*] this change in the premises of my political philosophy did not alter my practical political creed as to the requirements of my own time & country. I was as much as ever a radical and democrat for Europe & especially for England. I thought the predominance of the aristocracy & the rich in the English Constitution an evil worth any struggle to get rid of: not on account of taxes or any such comparatively trifling inconvenience but as the great demoralizing influence in the country. Demoralizing, first, because it made the conduct of the government an example of a gross public immorality—the predominance of private over public interest—the abuse of the powers of legislation for the advantage of separate classes.[418] Secondly, & above all, because the respect of the multitude always attaches itself principally to that which is the principal passport to power; for which reason under the English institutions where riches, hereditary or acquired, were the almost exclusive source of political importance, riches & the signs of riches were almost the only things really respected, [106*r*] and to the pursuit of these the life of the people was mainly devoted. Further, I thought that while the higher & richer classes held the power of government, the instruction & improvement of the mass of the people was contrary to the self interest of those classes, because necessarily tending to raise up dissatisfaction with their monopoly: but if the democracy obtained a share in the supreme power, & still more if they obtained the predominant share, it would become the interest of the opulent classes to promote their education, in order to guard them from really mischievous errors & especially to ward off unjust violations of property. For these reasons I was not only as ardent as ever for democratic institutions but earnestly hoped that Owenite, St Simonian & all other anti-property opinions

---

[418] separate classes.] a whole host of separate small classes at the expense of the community.

might spread widely among the poorer classes, not that I thought those doctrines true but in order that the higher classes might be led to see that they had more to fear from the poor when uneducated, than from the poor when educated.

In this frame of mind the French Revolution of July found me. It roused my utmost [106v] enthusiasm, & gave me as it were a new existence. I went at once to Paris,[419] was introduced to Lafayette, & got acquainted with several of the active chiefs of the popular party.[420] After my return I entered warmly, as a writer, into the [421] politics of the time, which soon became still more exciting by the coming in of Lord Grey's ministry, & the proposing of the Reform Bill. For the next few years I wrote largely in newspapers. It was just about this time that Fonblanque, who had for some time previous written the political articles in the Examiner, became the proprietor & editor of the paper. It is not forgotten with what verve & talent he carried it on, during the whole period of Lord Grey's ministry, & what importance it assumed as the principal representative of radical opinions in the newspaper press. At least three fourths of the original writing in the paper was his own; but of the remaining fourth [422] I contributed during the first years a considerable share. [107r] I wrote nearly all the articles on French subjects, including a weekly summary of French politics often extending to considerable length. I also wrote many leading articles on general politics, on commercial & financial legislation, & any miscellaneous subjects suitable to the paper in which I felt interested, besides occasional reviews of books. In mere newspaper articles on the occurrences & questions of the moment there was little room for the developement of any general mode of thought; but I attempted in the beginning of 1831, to embody in a series of articles, under the heading of "The Spirit of the Age" some of my new opinions & especially to point out in the character of the present age the anomalies & evils characteristic of the transition from one system of opinions which had worn out, to another only in process of formation. These articles were I believe lumbering in style, & not lively & striking enough to be acceptable to newspaper readers at any time; but had they been much more attrac-

---

[419] (with Charles Buller, Roebuck & others)

[420] *Originally continued after a comma:* an acquaintance which I afterwards extended to others of their number.

[421] exciting

[422] At least three fourths of . . . fourth] Nine parts in ten of . . . tenth

tive, still at that particular time [107*v*] when great political changes
were impending, & occupied all minds, these discussions were ill-
timed, & missed fire altogether.* The only effect which I know to

---

* Note.[423] This was an error I frequently committed: for example,
in the summer of 1832, when the country was preparing for the
first elections after the passing of the Reform Bill, I wrote several articles in the Examiner in strong opposition to the exaction
of pledges from representatives. The doctrine of these articles was
right in itself, & very suitable to democratic institutions when firmly
established & rooted in the habits of the people: then no doubt
it would be wise in the electors to look out for the most honest
& most instructed men whom they could induce to undertake the
office of legislators, & refrain from binding them beforehand to
any definite measures: but I did not sufficiently consider that the
transition from bad to good institutions was only commencing.
Like many other persons at the time, I thought that we had had
our revolution; that the way was now smooth for the advance of
democracy, that precautions [108*r*] were henceforth chiefly required against the evils which might come from the popular side;
and I little anticipated that the coming years would require a long
continuance of struggle to give democracy even its due influence.
End of Note.

---

have been produced by them is [424] that Carlyle, then living in a
secluded [425] part of Scotland, read them in his solitude, & saying
to himself (as he afterwards told me) "here is a new Mystic" en-
quired on coming to London that autumn, concerning their authorship, an enquiry which was the immediate cause of our becoming personally acquainted.

I have mentioned Carlyle's earlier writings as one of the channels through which the influences reached me, which had en-

---

[423] *This note was originally a part of the main text. Mill subsequently marked
it off with lines and added "Note." and "End of Note." at left*
[424] The only effect which I . . . is] *interlined to replace the following, which
was originally a continuation of the text now in Mill's note:* If my advice had
been taken the democracy would have laid down its weapons after a mere
partial success. The Examiner, I believe, lost near two hundred of its subscribers by those articles & I much doubt whether it ever gained as many by
everything else that I wrote for it. The papers called "the Spirit of the Age"
did no similar damage, nor had any effect at all that I know of; except
[425] & desolate

larged my early narrow creed: [108v] but I do not think that those writings by themselves would ever have had any effect on my opinions. What truths they contained were presented in a form & vesture less suited than any other to give them access to a mind trained as mine had been. They seemed a haze of poetry & German metaphysics, in which the only clear thing was a strong animosity to most of the opinions which were the basis of my mode of thought, religious scepticism, utilitarianism, the doctrine of circumstances, & the attaching any importance to democracy or logic or political economy. Instead of being taught anything in the first instance by Carlyle it was only in proportion as I came to see the same truths through media more suited to my mental constitution that I recognized them in his writings. Even afterwards the chief good they did me was not as philosophy to instruct but as poetry to animate. In this respect they ultimately became, & long continued, very valuable & delightful to me. Even at the time when our acquaintance began I was not sufficiently advanced in my new modes of thought to appreciate him fully: a proof of which is that when he shewed me [109r] the manuscript of Sartor Resartus, his best & greatest work, which he had then just finished,[426] it made hardly any impression on me: though I read his article on Johnson, published a few months later in Fraser's Magazine, with enthusiastic admiration,[427] & when Sartor came out in the same periodical in 1833 or 1834, I read that with equal enthusiasm.[428] I did not seek & cultivate Carlyle less on account of the fundamental differences in our philosophy. He soon found out that I was not "another mystic," & when I wrote to him for the sake of my own integrity a distinct profession of all those of my opinions which I knew he most disliked, he replied that the chief difference between us was that I "was as yet consciously nothing of a mystic": but he continued for a long time to think that I was destined to become one. I need hardly say that in this expectation he was disappointed, &

---

[426] & had come to town to find a publisher for, *R113r* (*see p. 189*), *deleted*

[427] enthusiastic admiration,] an enthusiastic admiration I had seldom felt for any cotemporary writing, *R113r, subsequently altered to final form*

[428] In this part of my life I was in such a state of reaction against sectarianism of thought or feeling, that those in whom I recognized any kind of superiority I did not judge or criticize at all; I estimated them by that side of their qualities or achievements by which they were admirable & valuable to me, while whatever I saw that seemed criticizable was not a *per contra* to be deducted, but was simply uncounted & disregarded. Therefore *R113r, marked for deletion by HM*

that although both his & my opinions underwent in subsequent
years various changes, we never approached much [429] nearer to
each other's modes of thought than we were in the first years of
our acquaintance.[430] But I did not consider myself a competent
judge of Carlyle. I felt that he was a poet & that I was not, that he
was a man of intuition, which I was not; & that as such he not
only saw many things long before me [109*v*] which I could
only, when they were pointed out to me, hobble after & prove, but
that it was possible [431] he could see many things which were not
visible to me even when pointed out. I knew that I could not see
round him, & could never be quite sure that I saw over him; &
I never formed [432] a definitive judgment of him until he was interpreted to me by one far the superior of us both—who was more
a poet than he, & more a thinker than I—whose own mind & nature included all his & infinitely more.[433]

Among [434] the persons of intellect whom I had known of old,
the one with whom I had now most points of agreement was the
elder Austin. I have mentioned that he always set himself in opposition to our early sectarianism; & latterly he had, like myself,
come under new influences. Having been appointed Professor of
Jurisprudence in the London University (now University College)
then just founded, he had lived for some time at Bonn to study
for his lectures, & the influences of German literature & of the German character & state of society had made a very perceptible
change in his views of life. His personal disposition was much
softened; he was less militant & polemic; his tastes were greatly
turned to the poetic & contemplative. He now attached much less
importance than formerly to outward changes, unless accompanied

---

[429] much] *deleted in R113v by HM*

[430] acquaintance.] intimacy. *R113v, altered to final reading first by HM. In
R113v the next two and a half sentences—through "formed a definitive judgment"—are marked with a line in the margin by HM; Mill struck through
them and the rest of the paragraph, and wrote a condensed version at left:*
But I never felt sure that I was a competent judge of Carlyle; & I never formed
a definitive judgment . . . *etc. as in fol. 109v*

[431] possible] probable *R113v (deleted first version), R109v*

[432] formed] presumed to form *R113v (deleted first version), altered to final
reading by HM*

[433] I never formed a definitive . . . more.] *deleted in R109v, and replaced at
left by:* of those with whom this was the case, I never had the presumption to
think that I was yet capable of forming a final judgment.

[434] *Originally this and the next paragraph on the Austins followed the third
paragraph below (see p. 189)*

by higher cultivation of the inward nature. [110r] He had a strong distaste for the meanness of English life, the absence of enlarged thoughts & unselfish desires, the low objects on which the faculties of all classes of the English are intent. Even the kind of public interests which Englishmen care for he held in very little estimation. He thought that there was more practical good government, & infinitely more care for the education & improvement of the people of all ranks under the Prussian monarchy than under the English representative government: & he held, with the French Economistes, that the real security for good government is not popular institutions but "un peuple éclairé". Though he approved the Reform Bill he predicted what in fact occurred, that it would not produce the great immediate improvements in government which many expected from it. The men, he said, do not exist in the country. There were many points of sympathy between him & me both in the new opinions he had adopted & in the old ones he retained. Like me he never ceased to be a utilitarian & with all his love of the Germans, never became in the smallest degree reconciled to the innate-principle metaphysics. He however cultivated more & more a kind of German religion, more comfortable though assuredly less virtuous than the bitter opposition to the order of the universe which had formerly distinguished him; & in politics he acquired an indifference, bordering on contempt, for the progress of popular institutions, though he rejoiced in that of socialism as the most effectual means of compelling the powerful classes to educate the people & to point out to them the real road to an improvement of their material condition, that of a limitation of their numbers. Neither was he fundamentally [110v] opposed to socialism in itself, as an ultimate result of improvement. He professed great disrespect for the "universal principles of human nature of the political economists" & insisted on the evidence which history & daily experience afford, of the "extraordinary pliability of human nature."

His wife, who was then first beginning to be known by her translations, took the principal conduct of the active & practical part of their life: for he, though he always felt like a gentleman & judged like a man of the world, in the good sense of both those terms, retired as far as he could from all business or contact with worldly affairs. She laid herself out for drawing round her as many persons of consideration or promise of consideration, as she could

get, & succeeded in getting many foreigners, some literary men &
a good many young men of various descriptions, & many who came
for her remained for him. Having known me from a boy, she made
great profession of a kind of maternal interest in me. But I never
for an instant supposed that she really cared for me; nor perhaps for anybody beyond the [111r] surface; [435] I mean as to real
feeling, not that she was not quite ready to be friendly or serv-
iceable.[436] She professed Benthamic opinions when Mr Austin
professed the same, & German opinions when he turned in that direction; but in truth, though she had considerable reading & acquirements, she never appeared to me to have anything [437] deserving
the name of opinions. If at that time she had anything capable of
being so called, & coming from her own mind, it consisted of pru-
dential maxims for the conduct of life. Under the influence of these
she slid into the opinions agreeable to the well-to-do classes, as
soon as she saw a possibility of making any way for herself among
a few people of consequence. She cultivated blandness of manner
& the ways which put people at their ease; & [438] while she was quite
ready to listen, she had always plenty to say, though chiefly in
the form of narrative & that mainly of what had been said to her
by other people. She made herself agreeable to young men by encouraging them with professions of sympathy to talk about themselves; but I do not think the impression thus made lasted long
with them, though she often succeeded in retaining that [111v]
degree of good will which is obtained by an appearance of good
nature. The good nature, in the sense in which that quality can
be ascribed to a person of so little feeling, was I dare say, to a
certain extent genuine; but it was not inconsistent with her having,
at times, a very mischievous tongue, which sowed *médisance* far
& wide by expressions so guarded as almost to elude responsibility
for any distinct statement.[439]

---

[435] nor perhaps for anybody beyond the surface;] indeed the idea of her
caring for anybody beyond the [111r] surface was not one which naturally
suggested itself;

[436] *Originally continued without punctuation:* on occasion.

[437] never appeared to me to have anything] had nothing

[438] I think one of her secrets was that

[439] *The remainder of fol. 111v contains the beginning three and a half sentences of the second paragraph below, which Mill canceled here and recopied
(with minor revisions) at left on fol. 113r when he changed the order of paragraphs (see p. 189). The next paragraph, on fol. 112r, originally began:* At the
time of which I am now speaking there was no one with whom I was in any
complete or even general sympathy of opinion. My father's tone . . .

[112r] My father's tone of thought & feeling I now felt myself at a great distance from: much greater than a full & calm explanation & reconsideration on both sides, would have shewn to exist in reality. But my father was not one with whom calm & full explanations on fundamental points of doctrine, could be expected, at least [440] by one whom he might consider a deserter from his standard. Fortunately we were almost always in strong agreement on the political questions of the day, which engrossed a large part of his interest & of his conversation. On those matters of opinion on which we differed, we talked little. He knew that the habit of thinking for myself, which he had given me, sometimes led me to opinions different from his, & he perceived from time to time that I did not always tell him *how* different. I expected no good, but only pain to both of us, from discussing our differences, & I never expressed them but when he gave utterance to some opinion or feeling very repugnant to mine, in a manner which would have made it [112v] disingenuousness on my part to remain silent. At such times we used to have a short sharp contest, never leading to any result.[441]

[113r] During the years of which I am now speaking, I did a not inconsiderable quantity of writing over & above my contributions to newspapers. In 1830 & 1831 I wrote the five Essays since published as "Essays on Some Unsettled Questions of Political Economy" almost as they now stand, except that in 1833 I partially rewrote the fifth essay. I wrote them with no immediate purpose of publication, & only sent them to press in 1844 in consequence of the success of the Logic. I also resumed my speculations on this last subject, & puzzled myself (like others before me, but with, I hope, more of useful result) with the great paradox of the discovery of new truth by general reasoning. As to the fact there could be no doubt; as little could it be doubted, that all reasoning was resolvable into syllogisms & that in every syllogism the conclusion is actually contained & implied in the premisses. How being so contained & implied, it could be new truth, & how the theorems of geometry so different to all appearance from the definitions & axioms could be all contained in them, was a difficulty which no one, I thought, had sufficiently felt, & which at all events

---

[440] at least] especially
[441] *The remainder of fol. 112v contains the first seven and a half sentences of the paragraph on Austin (pp. 146–147), which Mill canceled here and rewrote in fols. 109v–110r (see p. 189)*

no one had succeeded in clearing up. The attempts at explanation
by Whately & others seemed rather explainings away; & though
they might give a temporary satisfaction always left a mist still
hanging over the subject. At last, when [442] reading for the second
or third [443] time the chapters on Reasoning in the second volume
of Dugald Stewart, interrogating myself on every point & following
out the various topics of thought which the book suggested, I came
to an idea of his about the use of axioms in ratiocination, which I
did not remember to have noticed before, but which now in meditat-
ing on it seemed to me to be not only true of axioms but of all general propositions whatever, & [113*v*] to lead to the true solution
of my perplexity. From this germ grew the theory of the syllogism
propounded in the second book of the Logic; which I immediately
made safe by writing it out. And now with greatly increased hope
of being able to produce a book of some originality on Logic, I proceeded to write the First Book, from the rough & imperfect draft I
had previously made. What I now wrote became the basis of that
part of the subsequent Treatise; except that it did not contain the
theory of Kinds, which was a much later addition. At this point I
made a halt, which lasted five years. I had come to the end of my
tether; I could make nothing satisfactory of Induction at this time.
I continued to read any book which promised light on the subject,[444]
& to appropriate as well as I could the results, but for a long time
I found nothing which opened to me any very instructive vein of
meditation.

In 1832 I wrote several papers for the first series of Tait's Magazine, & one for a quarterly periodical called the Jurist, which had
been founded & was for a short time carried on by a set of reform-
ing lawyers with several of whom I was acquainted. This [114*r*]
paper, entitled "on Corporation & Church Property", I still think a
very complete discussion of the rights of the state over Foundations.
It shewed both sides of my opinions; asserting as firmly as I should
ever have done, the doctrine that endowments are national property
which the government may & ought to control, but not, as I should
formerly have done, condemning endowments in themselves & proposing that they should be taken to pay off the national debt. On
the contrary I urged strongly the importance of having a provision
for education, not dependent on the mere demand of the market,

---

[442] sitting in the garden at Mickleham   [443] second or third] third or fourth
[444] when it fell in my way,

that is, on the knowledge & discernment of ordinary parents, but calculated to establish & keep up a higher standard of instruction than is likely to be spontaneously demanded by the buyers of the article. This essay which was little read would be better worth reprinting than most of the short things I have written.[445]

[115r] It was at the period of my mental progress which I have now reached, that I formed the friendship which has been the honour & blessing of my existence, as well as the source of a great part of all that I have attempted to do, or hope to effect hereafter for human improvement. My first introduction to the lady who, after a friendship of twenty years, consented to become my wife, was in 1830, when I was in my twenty fifth & she in her twenty third year. With her husband's family it was a renewal of an old acquaintanceship. His grandfather lived in the next house to my father's in Newington Green & I had sometimes when a boy been invited to play in the old gentleman's garden. He was a fine specimen of the old Scotch puritan; stern, severe & powerful, but very kind to children, on whom such men make a lasting impression. Although it was years after my introduction to Mrs Taylor before my acquaintance with her became at all intimate or confidential, I very soon felt her to be the most admirable person I had ever known. It is not to be [115v] supposed that she was, or that any one, at the age at which I first saw her, could be all that she afterwards became. Least of all could this be true of her, with whom self-improvement, progress in the highest & in all senses, was a law of her nature; a necessity equally from the ardour with which she sought it, & from the spontaneous tendency of faculties which could not receive an impression or an experience without making it the source or the occasion of an accession of wisdom. Up to the time when I knew her, her rich & powerful nature had chiefly unfolded itself according to the received type of feminine genius. To her outer circle she was a beauty & a wit, with an air of natural distinction, felt by all who approached her: to the inner, a woman of deep & strong feeling, of penetrating & intuitive intelligence, & of a most

---

[445] *Following this paragraph, on the rest of fol. 114 and R119–121 Mill originally wrote the two paragraphs on the Parliament of 1832 and his writings of 1832–34, and part of the next paragraph on the founding of the* London and Westminster Review (*pp. 154–157*), *with which he brought to a close Part I of the early draft (see n. 460 and p. 190). A variant from the canceled text of fol. 114v is given in n. 449 below. Fols. 115 and following represent a rewritten form of the original Part II (see pp. 190–200)*

meditative & poetic nature. Married at a very early age, to a most upright, brave, & honorable man, of liberal opinions & good education, but without the intellectual or artistic tastes which would have made him a companion for her—though a steady & affectionate friend, for whom she had true esteem & the strongest affection through life & whom she most deeply lamented [116r] when dead; shut out by the social disabilities of women from any adequate exercise of her highest faculties in action on the world without; her life was one of inward meditation, varied by familiar intercourse with a small circle of friends, of whom one only was a person of genius, or of capacities of feeling or intellect kindred with her own, but all had more or less of alliance with her in sentiments & opinions. Into this circle I had the good fortune to be admitted, & I soon perceived that she possessed in combination the qualities which in all other persons whom I had known I had been only too happy to find singly. In her, complete emancipation from every kind of superstition, & an earnest protest both against society as at present constituted & against the pretended perfection of the order of nature & the universe, resulted not from the hard intellect but from strength of noble & elevated feeling, & coexisted with a highly reverential nature. In general spiritual characteristics as well as in temperament & organization I have often compared her, as she was at this time, to Shelley, but in thought & intellect Shelley, so far as his powers were developed in his short life, was but a child to her. [116v] Alike in the highest regions of philosophy & in the smallest practical concerns of daily life, her mind is the same perfect instrument, going down to the very heart & marrow of the matter—always seizing the essential idea or principle. The same exactness & rapidity of operation pervading her sensitive as well as her mental faculties, would with her gifts of feeling & imagination have fitted her to be a consummate artist, as her fiery & tender soul & her vigorous eloquence might have made her a great orator, & her profound knowledge of human nature & discernment & sagacity in practical life would in the times when such a *carrière* was open to women, have made her eminent among the rulers of mankind.[446] Her intellectual gifts did but minister to a moral character at once the noblest & the best balanced which I have ever met with in life. Her unselfishness was not that of a

---

[446] the rulers of mankind.] statesmen. *altered currently in the course of first writing*

taught system of duties but of a heart which thoroughly identified itself with the feelings of others & even imaginatively invested them with the intensity of its own. The passion of justice might have been thought to be her strongest feeling but for her boundless generosity & a lovingness ever ready to pour itself forth upon any or all human beings who were capable of giving the smallest feeling in return. All the rest of her moral characteristics were such as naturally accompany these [117r] qualities of mind & heart: the most genuine modesty combined with the loftiest pride; a simplicity & sincerity which was absolute towards all who were fit to receive it; the utmost scorn of everything mean & cowardly, & indignation at everything brutal or tyrannical, faithless or dishonorable in conduct & character; while making the broadest distinction between *mala in se* & mere *mala prohibita*—between acts giving evidence of intrinsic badness of feeling & character, & those which are only violations of conventions either good or bad, & which whether in themselves right or wrong, are capable of being done by persons otherwise loveable or admirable.

To be admitted into any degree of personal intercourse with a being of these qualities, could not but have a most beneficial influence on my development. The benefit I received was far greater than any which I could hope to give; except that, to her, who had reached her opinions by the moral intuition of a character of strong feeling, there was doubtless help as well as encouragement to be derived from one who had arrived at many of the same results by study & reasoning: & in the rapidity of her intellectual growth, her mental activity which converted everything into knowledge, doubtless drew from me, as well as from other sources, many of its materials. What I owe to her intellectually, is that without [117v] which all I possessed before is of little value. With those who, like all the wisest & best of mankind, are dissatisfied with human life as it is & whose feelings are wholly identified with its radical amendment, there are two main regions of thought: one is the region of ultimate aims; the constituents of the highest realizable ideal of human life; the other is that of the immediately useful & practically attainable. In both of these departments I have learnt more from her than from all other persons taken together.[447] And to say truth, it is in these two extremes that the only real cer-

---

[447] I have learnt more . . . together.] she has been my main instructor.

tainty lies. My own strength lay wholly in the uncertain & slippery intermediate region, that of theory, or moral & political science: respecting the conclusions of which in any of the forms in which I have received or originated them, whether as political economy, analytic psychology, logic, philosophy of history, or anything else, it is not the least of my intellectual obligations to her that I have derived from her a wise scepticism; which while it has not hindered me from following out the honest exercise of my thinking faculties to whatever conclusions might result from it, has prevented me, I hope, from holding or announcing those conclusions with a confidence which the nature of such speculations does not warrant, [118r] & has kept my mind always open to admit clearer perceptions & better evidence.[448]

During the first years of our acquaintance the principal effect of her nature upon mine was to enlarge & exalt my conceptions of the highest worth of a human being. The poetic elements of her character, which were at that time the most ripened, were naturally those which impressed me first, & those years were, in respect of my own development, mainly years of poetic culture. My faculties became more attuned to the beautiful & elevated, in all kinds, & especially in human feeling & character, & more capable of vibrating in unison with it; & I required, in all those in whom I could take interest, a strong taste for elevated & poetic feeling, if not the feeling itself. This however did not check, but gave additional animation to my activity in all the modes of exertion for public objects to which I had been accustomed. I retained unabated interest in radical politics, kept up my connexion with such of the rising or promising politicians on the radical side, as I was previously acquainted with, & even became more involved than before in political as well as literary relations.

[118v] In the autumn of 1832 occurred the election of the first Reformed Parliament, which included several of the most notable of my Radical friends & acquaintances; Grote, Roebuck, Charles Buller, Sir William Molesworth (with whom through Buller I had lately become acquainted) John & Edward Romilly & several others; besides Strutt & others who were in parliament already. Those who thought themselves, & were called by their friends, the philo-

---

[448] *The next paragraph originally began:* These effects, however, on my mental development, were produced gradually, & proceeded *pari passu* with her own intellectual growth. During the first years . . .

sophic radicals, had now a fair opportunity, in a more advantageous position than they had ever before occupied, of shewing what was in them; & I as well as my father founded great hopes on them. Those hopes were destined to be disappointed. The men were honest, & faithful to their opinions, as far as votes were concerned; often in spite of much discouragement. But they did very little to promote any opinions. One or two of the youngest did as much, perhaps, as could reasonably have been expected from them individually. What Roebuck did has already been mentioned: Buller & Molesworth also by degrees did something. But those from whom most was expected did least. They had no enterprise, no activity; they left the lead of the radical portion of the House to the old hands, to Hume & O'Connell. Nobody disappointed my father & me more than Grote [119r] because no one else had so much in his power. We had long known him fainthearted, ever despairing of success, thinking all obstacles gigantic; but [449] the Reform Bill excitement seemed for a time to make a new man of him: he had grown hopeful, & seemed as if he could almost become energetic. When brought face to face however with an audience opposed to his opinions, when called on to beat up against the stream, he was found wanting.[450] The years which he withdrew from his History & spent in the House of Commons were almost wasted.[451] Except an annual motion for the ballot (to which he continued to stick after the change of times had made it no longer desirable) and an honorable stand made now & then against a bad measure, such as the Irish & Canada Coercion Bills, Mr Grote was almost an inactive member of parliament. If his courage & energy had been equal to the circumstances, or [452] to his knowledge & abilities, the history of those ten years of relapse into Toryism might have been very [453] different. His standing & social position would have enabled him to create a real Radical party, for which the materials then existed; he could [119v] have put heart into the many younger men who would have been ready to join him—could have

---

[449] gigantic; but] gigantic, & seldom able to summon up energy & spirit to carry him into & through any real contest for his opinions. But *fol. 114v* (*see n. 445 above*)

[450] was found wanting.] proved that he was one of those who can see what is good but cannot do it. *R119r* (*see p. 190*)

[451] wasted.] entirely wasted. *R119r*

[452] even *R119r, underlined by HM and deleted by Mill*

[453] very] totally *R119r*

made them available to the extent of their talents in bringing advanced ideas before the public—could have used the House of Commons as a rostra or a teacher's chair for instructing & impelling the public mind, & would either have forced the Whigs to take their measures from him, or taken the lead of the Reform party out of their hands. All this would probably [454] have happened if my father had been in Parliament. For want of such a man the instructed Radicals sank into a mere *côté gauche* of the Whig party. With a keen sense of the great [455] possibilities which were open to the Radicals if they made even ordinary exertion for their opinions, I laboured from this time till 1839 both by personal influence with some of them, & by writings, to put ideas into their heads & purpose into their hearts. I did some good with Charles Buller, & some with Sir W. Molesworth; [456] but on the whole the attempt was vain. To have had a chance of succeeding in it, required a different position from mine. It was a task only for one who being himself in parliament, could have mixed with the radical members in daily consultation, & instead of saying to others "Lead," could himself have led, & incited them to follow.

[120r] During the year 1833 I continued working in the Examiner with Fonblanque, who at that time was zealous in keeping up the fight for radicalism against the Whigs, though after 1834 he sank into little better than their supporter & panegyrist. During the session of 1834 I wrote comments on passing events, under the title "Notes on the Newspapers," in the "Monthly Repository," a magazine conducted by Mr Fox (with whom I had lately become acquainted) & which I wrote for, chiefly on his account. I contributed several other articles to this periodical, some of them (especially two on the theory of poetry) containing a considerable amount of thought. Altogether, the writings (independently of those in newspapers) which I published from 1832 to 1834, amount to a large [457] volume. This however includes abstracts of several of Plato's Dialogues, with introductory remarks, which though not published until 1834, had been written several years earlier; & which I afterwards on various occasions found to have been read,

---

[454] probably] infallibly *R119v, subsequently altered to final reading*
[455] great] glorious *R119v; altered to final reading in fol. 119v*
[456] I did some good . . . Molesworth;] *not in R119v, in which HM penciled at left opposite the preceding sentence: "mention Buller & your efforts with him"*
[457] octavo *R120r; deleted in fol. 120r*

& their authorship known, by more people than were aware of anything else which I had written up to that time. To complete the tale of my writings I may add that in 1833, at the request of Bulwer, who was just then completing his [120v] "England & the English" I wrote for him a critical account of Bentham's philosophy, a small part of which he incorporated in his text, & printed the rest as an Appendix. In this, along with the favorable, a part also of the unfavourable side of my estimation of Bentham's doctrines, considered as a complete philosophy, was for the first time put into print.

As the "philosophic radical" party fell off my endeavours to put life into it were redoubled. Among the possibilities which had been much talked of between my father & me, & some of the parliamentary & other radicals who frequented his house,[458] was the foundation of a periodical organ of philosophic radicalism, to take the place which the Westminster had been intended to fill; & the scheme went so far as to bring under discussion the pecuniary contributions which could be looked for, & even the choice of an editor. The project however seemed to have fallen to the ground, when in the summer of 1834 Sir W. Molesworth, himself a laborious student, & one of the most zealous at that time [459] of the Parliamentary Radicals, of himself proposed to establish a Review, provided I would consent to be the real, if not the nominal, editor. Such an offer was not to be refused; & the review was founded, [121r] under my direction, though under the ostensible editorship of Roebuck's brother in law, Falconer.[460] In the years between 1834 & 1840 the conduct of this review occupied the greater part of my spare time. It came out in April 1835 under the name of the London Review, & four numbers were published with that title, after which Molesworth bought the Westminster Review from its proprietor Colonel Thompson & the two were united under the name of the London & Westminster Review. In the beginning the review did not, as a whole, by any means represent my opinions. I was under the necessity of conceding much to my inevitable associates. The review was established to be the representative of the "philosophic radicals" with most of whom I was at

---

[458] in the years 1833 & 1834, one *R120v; deleted in fol. 120v*

[459] zealous at that time] sincere & convinced *R120v, marked with a question mark by HM*

[460] *For the ending of the original Part I, following this sentence, see p. 190*

issue on many essential points & among whom I could not even claim to be the most important individual.[461] My father's cooperation as a writer we all deemed indispensable, & he wrote largely in it until prevented by illness. The subjects of his articles & the strength & decision with which his opinions were expressed in them, made the review at first derive its colour & tone from him much more than from [462] any of the other writers. I could not exercise editorial control over his articles & I was even obliged to sacrifice to him portions of mine. The old Westminster Review opinions, little modified, thus formed the staple of the review, but I hoped by the side of these to introduce other ideas & another tone, & to give to my opinions a fair representation in the review along with those of other members of the party. For this [121v] purpose chiefly I made it one of the peculiarities of the review that every article should bear an initial or some other signature & be held to express only the opinions of the writer, the editor being only responsible for its being worth publishing, & not conflicting with the objects for which the review was set on foot. I had an opportunity of putting in practice my scheme of conciliation between the old & the new "philosophic radicalism" by the choice of a subject for my own first contribution. Mr Sedgwick had then lately published his Discourse on the Studies of Cambridge, a tract of which the most prominent feature was an abusive assault on analytic psychology & on utilitarian ethics, in the form of an attack on Locke & Paley. This had excited great indignation in my father & others, which I thought was fully deserved. And here, I conceived, was an opportunity of at the same time repelling an unjust attack & inserting into my defence of Hartleianism & utilitarianism, a number of the opinions which constituted my view of those subjects as distinguished from that of my old associates. In this I partially succeeded, though I could not speak out my whole mind at this time without coming into conflict with my father.[463] [122r] There are things however which incline me to believe that my father was not so much opposed as he seemed,

---

[461] *Originally continued after a comma:* especially while my father lived.

[462] me or

[463] could not speak out my . . . father.] was obliged to omit two or three pages of comment on what I thought the mistakes of utilitarian moralists, which my father considered as an attack on Bentham & on him. I certainly thought both of them in some degree open to it but far less so than [122r] some of their followers.

to the modes of thought in which I supposed myself to differ from him; that he did injustice to his own opinions by [464] the unconscious exaggerations of a pugnacious & polemical intellect, & that when thinking without an adversary *en présence* he was ready to make room for a great portion of the truths he seemed to deny. His "Fragment on Mackintosh" which he wrote & published about this time, although I greatly admired some parts of it, was as a whole very repulsive to me; yet on reading it again, long after,[465] I found very little in the opinions it contains but what I think in the main just; & I can even sympathize in his disgust at the verbiage of Mackintosh though his asperity went beyond not only what was judicious but what was even fair. One thing which I thought at the time of good augury, was the very favourable reception he gave to Tocqueville's "Democracy in America." It is true he said & thought much more about what Tocqueville said in favour of Democracy than about what he said against it. Still, his high appreciation of a book which was at any rate an example of [122v] a mode of treating the question of government almost the reverse of his—wholly inductive & analytical instead of purely ratiocinative—gave me great encouragement. He also approved of an article which I published in the first number following the junction of the two reviews, under the heading "Civilization," into which I threw many of my new opinions & criticized rather emphatically the mental tendencies of the time on grounds & in a manner which I certainly had not learnt from him.

All speculation however on the possible future developments of my father's opinions & on the probabilities of successful cooperation between him & me in the promulgation of our thoughts, was doomed to be cut short. During the whole of 1835 his health had been declining; his symptoms became unequivocally those of pulmonary consumption & after lingering to the last stage of debility he died on the 23d of June 1836. Until the last few days of his life there was no apparent abatement of intellectual vigour; his interest in all things & persons that had interested him through life, was unabated; nor did the approach of death cause the smallest wavering (as in so strong a mind it was impossible that it should)

---

[464] he did injustice . . . by] the lengths to which he allowed himself to go in his denunciations of opinions, which I regarded as merely the other half of the truths one half alone was seen by him were in a great measure

[465] again, long after,] again lately

in his anti-religious convictions. His chief satisfaction, after he knew that his end was near, seemed to be the thought of what he had done to make the world better than he found it; & his chief regret in not living longer, that he had not had time to do more.

His place is an eminent one in the literary & even the political history of this country; & it is far from honorable [123r] to the generation which has [466] benefitted by his worth, that he is so seldom mentioned & so little remembered. Probably the chief cause of the neglect of his memory, is that, notwithstanding the great number of his opinions which have now been generally adopted, there was a marked opposition between his spirit & that of the present time. As Brutus was the last of the Romans, so was he the last of the eighteenth century: he continued its tone of thought & sentiment into the nineteenth (though with great additions & improvements) partaking neither in the good nor in the bad influences of the reaction against the eighteenth century which is the great characteristic of the first half of the nineteenth. The eighteenth century was a great age, an age of stronger & braver men than the nineteenth, & he was [467] a fit companion for its strongest & bravest. By his writings & his personal influence, he was a great centre of light to his generation. During the latter years of his life he was quite as much the head & leader of the intellectual radicals in England as ever Voltaire was of the *philosophes* of France. It is only one of his minor merits that he was the originator of all sound statesmanship in regard to the subject of his largest work, India. He wrote on no subject which he did [123v] not enrich with valuable thought: & if we except the Political Economy, very useful when written but which has now for some time [468] finished its work, it will be long before any of his books will be wholly superseded, or will cease to be instructive reading to students of their subjects. In the power [469] of influencing by mere force of mind & character, the convictions & purposes of others, & in the strenuous exertion of that power to promote freedom & progress, he has left no equal among men—& but one among women.

Though acutely sensible of my own inferiority in the qualities by which he acquired his personal ascendancy, I had now to try

---

[466] so much   [467] both in thought & action
[468] now for some time] long since
[469] power] capacity (*HM marked the first twelve words of this sentence with a line in the margin*)

what it might be possible for me to accomplish without him; [470] &
the review was the instrument on which I built my chief hopes of
establishing a useful influence over the liberal & democratic portion of the public mind. Deprived now of my father's aid, I was
also exempted from the restraints & retinences by which that aid
was purchased: I did not feel that there was any other radical
writer or politician to whom I was bound to defer further than
consisted with my own opinions: & having the complete confidence of Molesworth I resolved from henceforth to give full scope
to my own opinions & modes of thought & to open the review
widely to all writers [124r] who were in sympathy with Progress
as I understood it, even though I should lose by it the support of
my former associates. Carlyle from this time became a frequent
writer in the review; Sterling, soon after, an occasional one; &
though each individual article continued to be the expression of
the private sentiments of its writer, the general tone conformed in
some tolerable degree to my opinions. This was not effected without parting company with the nominal editor, Falconer, who, after
holding on for some time in spite of [471] differences of opinion, at
last resigned.[472] I supplied his place by a young Scotchman of the
name of Robertson, who had some ability & information, much
industry, & an active scheming head, full of devices for making
the review more saleable, & on whose capacity in that particular
I founded a good deal of hope: insomuch that when Molesworth,
in the beginning of 1837, became tired of carrying on the review
at a loss, & desirous of getting rid of it, I, very imprudently for
my own pecuniary interest, & very much from reliance on Robertson's devices, determined to continue it at my own risk until his
plans should have had a fair trial. The devices were good in their
way, but I do not believe that any devices would have made a
radical & democratic review pay its expenses [124v] including a
liberal payment to writers. I myself & several frequent contributors
gave our labour gratuitously,[473] as we had done for Molesworth,
but the paid contributors continued to be paid at the usual rate of

---

[470] what it might be possible . . . him;] how far I might be capable of
supplying his place;

[471] many

[472] *Originally continued without punctuation:* rather on account of an article
of Carlyle's.

[473] gave our labour gratuitously,] wrote without pay,

the Edinburgh & Quarterly Reviews: & this could not be done from the proceeds of the sale.

In the same year, 1837, & in the midst of these occupations, I resumed the Logic. I had now done nothing to it for five years, having been stopped, & brought to a pause, on the threshold of Induction. I had gradually discovered that what was mainly wanting to overcome the difficulties of that subject was a comprehensive & at the same time accurate view of the whole circle [474] of physical science, which I feared it would take a long course of study to acquire, since I knew not of any book or other guide that would display before me the generalities & processes & believed that I should have no choice but to extract them for myself, if I could, from the details of the sciences. Happily for me, Dr Whewell, early in this year, published his History of the Inductive Sciences. I read it with eagerness & found in it a considerable approximation to what I wanted. Much if not most of his philosophy appeared [125r] to me erroneous; but the materials were there, for my own thoughts to work upon, & the author had given to those materials that first degree of elaboration which so greatly abridges & facilitates the subsequent labour. I felt that I had now got what I had been waiting for.[475] Under the impulse given me by the thoughts excited by Whewell I read again Herschel's Discourse on the Study of Natural Philosophy, which I had read (& even reviewed) several [476] years before, but had found little help in it. I now found much. I then set vigorously to work out the subject in thought & in writing. I had just two months to spare in the intervals of writing for the review. In those two months I wrote (in the first draft) about a third, the most difficult third, of the book. What I had before written I estimated at another third, so that only a third remained. What I wrote at this time consisted of the remainder of the doctrine of Reasoning (the theory of Trains of Reasoning, & Deductive Science) & the greater part of the Third Book, on Induction. I had now, as it seemed to me, untied all the really hard knots & the completion of the book had become only a question of time. When I had got thus far I had to leave off in order to write two articles for the next number of the review.

---

[474] circle] field

[475] felt that I had now . . . for.] now felt for the first time that I could write a book on logic.

[476] reviewed) several] reviewed in the Examiner) five

When these were written I returned to the subject & now for the first time fell in with Comte's Cours [125v] de Philosophie Positive or rather with the two volumes of it which were then all that had been published. My theory of Induction was substantially completed before I knew of Comte's book & it is perhaps well that I came to it by a [477] different road from his, since the consequence has been that my treatise contains what his certainly does not, a reduction of the inductive process to strict rules & to a scientific test, such as the Syllogism is for ratiocination. Comte is always profound on the methods of investigation but he does not even attempt any exact definition of the conditions of proof: & his own writings shew that he has no just conception of them. This however was specifically the problem which, in treating of Induction, I had proposed to myself. Nevertheless I gained much from Comte with which to enrich my chapters in the subsequent rewriting, & his book was of essential service to me in the parts which still remained to be thought out. After completing the study of his two volumes I wrote three more chapters in the autumn of 1837 after which I did not return to the subject until the middle of the next year: the review engrossing all the time I could devote to authorship, or to thinking with authorship in view.

In the conduct of the review I had two principal objects. One was to free radical opinions from the reproach of narrow Benthamism. I desired, while retaining the [126r] precision of expression, the definiteness of meaning, the aversion to declamatory phrases & vague generalities which were so honorably characteristic of Bentham, & my father, to give a wider basis & a freer & more genial character to radical speculations; to shew that there was a radical philosophy better & more complete than Bentham's, though recognizing & incorporating all of Bentham's which is permanently valuable. In this first object I to a certain extent succeeded. The other thing I attempted was to stir up the educated radicals in & out of parliament to exertion, & induce them to make themselves what I thought they might by taking the proper means have become, a powerful party, capable of taking the government of the country, or at least of dictating the terms on which they should share it with the Whigs. This attempt totally failed, partly because the time was unfavourable; the Reform fervour being then in its period of ebb, & the old Tory influences powerfully rallying;

---

[477] totally

but far more, because, as Austin so truly said, "the country did not contain the men." Among the Radicals in Parliament there were two or three qualified to be useful members of an enlightened Radical party, but none capable of forming or leading such a party.[478] [126*v*] The exhortations of the review found no response. One occasion did present itself when there seemed to be room for a bold & successful stroke for radicalism. Lord Durham had left the ministry, as was thought, because they were not sufficiently liberal: he afterwards accepted from them the task of removing the causes of rebellion in Canada: he had shewn a disposition to surround himself at his outset with radical advisers; one of his earliest measures, a good measure both in intention & in effect, having been disapproved & reversed by the government at home, he had resigned his post & placed himself openly in a position of quarrel with the ministers. Here was a possible chief for a radical party, in the person of a man of importance who was hated by the Tories, and had just been injured by the Whigs. It was an opportunity to be seized.[479] Lord Durham was bitterly attacked from all sides; he appeared to be returning a defeated & discredited man, & those who would willingly have defended him did not know what to say. I had followed the course of Canadian events from the beginning; I had been one of the prompters of his prompters; his policy was almost exactly what mine would have been, & I was in a position to defend it. I wrote & published a manifesto in the form of a review article in which I claimed for him not mere acquittal but praise & honour. I believe that [127*r*] there was a portion of truth in what Lord Durham afterwards with polite exaggeration said to me, that to this article might be attributed the almost triumphal reception which he met with on his arrival in England. I believe it to have been the word in season which at a critical moment decides the result; the touch which determines whether a stone set in motion at the top of a hill shall roll down on the north or on the south side. All hopes connected with Lord Durham as a politician soon vanished; but with regard to Canadian & generally to colonial policy, the cause was gained: Lord Durham's report, written by Charles Buller under the inspiration of

---

[478] *Originally continued after a comma:* & not one who [126*v*] was fit to go forward by his single strength & fight to any great purpose for advanced opinions. *The next sentence is interlined*

[479] *Originally continued after a semicolon:* & I seized it.

Wakefield, began a new era; its recommendations extending to complete internal self government were in full operation in Canada within two or three years, & are becoming rapidly extended to all the other colonies which have as yet any existence as considerable communities: & I may say that in successfully upholding the reputation of Lord Durham & of his advisers at the most important moment, I contributed materially [480] to this result.

There was one other case during my conduct of the review which similarly illustrated [127*v*] the effect of taking a decided initiative. I believe that the early success & reputation of Carlyle's French Revolution were very materially promoted by what I wrote about it in the review. Immediately after its publication, & before the commonplace critics, all whose rules & modes of judgment it set at defiance, had time to preoccupy the public with their disapproval of it,[481] I wrote & published a review of the book [482] hailing it as one of those productions of genius which are above all rules & are a law to themselves. Neither in this case nor in Lord Durham's do I ascribe the impression which I think was produced by what I wrote, to any particular merit of execution; & indeed, in at least one of the two cases (Carlyle's) I do not think the execution was good. I believe that anybody in a position to be read, who had expressed the same opinion at the same precise time & had made any tolerable statement of the just grounds for it, would have produced exactly the same effect. But after the complete failure of my plans for putting a new life into radical politics by means of the review I am glad to look back on these [128*r*] two instances of success in an honest attempt to do immediate service to things & persons that deserved it.

After the last hope of the formation of a Radical party had disappeared, it was time for me to stop the heavy expenditure of time & money which the review cost me. It had to some extent answered my purpose as a vehicle for my opinions: It had enabled me to express in print much of my then present mode of thought & to distinguish it in a marked manner from the narrower Benthamism of my early writings. This was done by the general tone of all I wrote, including various literary articles (among which the one which contained most thought was on Alfred de Vigny)

---

[480] materially] not a little
[481] their disapproval of it,] a notion that they ought not to admire it,
[482] displaying its merits &

but especially by two articles which attempted a philosophical estimate of Bentham & of Coleridge. In the first of these, while doing full justice to the merits of Bentham, I pointed out what I thought the errors & deficiencies of his philosophy. The substance of this criticism I still think just, but I have much doubted since whether it was right to publish it. I have often felt that Bentham's philosophy as an instrument of progress has been in a great measure discredited before it had half done its work & that lending a hand [128*v*] to pull down its reputation was doing more harm than service to improvement. In the article on Coleridge I attempted to characterize the European reaction against the negative philosophy of the 18th century: & here I erred by giving undue prominence to the favourable side, as I had done in the case of Bentham to the unfavourable. In both cases, the impetus with which I had detached myself from what was untenable in the doctrines of Bentham & of the 18th century carried me too far to the opposite side; but so far as relates to the article on Coleridge the excuse may be made for me that I was writing for radicals & liberals & had therefore an inducement to dwell most on that in writers of a different school, from the knowledge of which they might derive most benefit.

The number of the review which contained the article on Coleridge was the last which was published under my proprietorship. In the spring of 1840 I made over the review to Mr Hickson, who had been a very useful unpaid contributor to the London & Westminster, only stipulating that the change should be marked by a resumption of the old name, the Westminster Review. Under this name he carried it on for ten [129*r*] years, on the plan of dividing among contributors only the net proceeds of the review (giving his own labour as a writer & editor gratuitously). Under the difficulty in obtaining writers which arose from this low scale of remuneration it is highly creditable to him that he was able to maintain in some tolerable degree the character of the review as an organ of radicalism & progress. For my own part, though I still occasionally wrote in newspapers & in the Westminster & Edinburgh Reviews when I had anything to say for which they appeared to be suitable vehicles, I henceforth employed my writing faculties mainly on things of a less temporary nature.

The first use which I made of the leisure I gained by disconnecting myself with the review, was to finish the Logic.[483] In July & August 1838 I had found an interval in which to complete the first draft of the third book. In working out the logical theory of those laws of nature which are not laws of causation, or corollaries from such laws, I was led to recognize Kinds as realities & not mere distinctions for convenience, a light which I had not yet obtained when the first Book was originally written & in consequence of which I now modified & enlarged [129v] the corresponding portion of that Book. The book on Language & Classification, & the Chapter on the Classification of Fallacies, were drafted in the autumn of the same year; the remainder of the work in the summer & autumn of 1840. From April following to the end of 1841 my spare time was devoted to a complete rewriting of the book from its commencement. During this operation Dr Whewell's Philosophy of the Inductive Sciences made its appearance; a fortunate circumstance for me, as it gave me what I very much needed, an antagonist, & enabled me to present my ideas with greater clearness & emphasis as well as fuller & more various development, in defending them against definite objections, & confronting them distinctly with an opposite theory. The controversies with Whewell as well as much matter derived from Comte were first introduced into the book in the present rewriting.

At the end of 1841, the book being ready for press, I offered it to Murray, who kept it until too late for publication that season & then refused it for reasons which could just as well have been given at first. I next offered it to Parker, & in the spring of 1843 it was published. My expectations of success were extremely moderate. A book on such a subject could [130r] not be popular; it could only be a book for students, & students on such subjects in England are not only few, but are mostly in the present generation addicted to the opposite school of metaphysics, the ontological & "innate principle" school. I therefore did not expect that the book would have many readers, or approvers; & would gladly have compounded for a sale sufficient to prevent the publisher from losing by it. What hopes I had of its exciting attention were mainly grounded on the polemical propensities of Dr Whewell; who I thought would have replied, & that promptly, to the attack on his opinions. He did reply, but not till 1850, just in time for me to

---

[483] After what I had done in 1837 its completion was only a question of time.

answer him in the third edition. How the book came to have, for a work of the kind, so much success & what sort of persons compose the bulk of those who have bought, I will not venture to say read it, I have never thoroughly understood; & I have never indulged the illusion that it had made any considerable impression [484] on philosophic opinion. The German, or ontological view of human knowledge & of the knowing faculties, still predominates & will probably long predominate (though it may be hoped in a diminishing degree) among those who occupy themselves with such enquiries either here or on the Continent. But the "System of Logic" supplies what was much wanted, a text book of the opposite doctrine, that which derives all knowledge from experience, & all moral & intellectual qualities principally from the direction given to the associations. And in [130v] this consists, I think, the chief worth of the book as a contribution to human improvement. I make as humble an estimate as anybody of what either an analysis of logical processes, or any possible canons of evidence, can do, taken by themselves, to guide or rectify the operations of the understanding. But whether the direct practical use of a true philosophy on these matters be great or little, it is difficult to exaggerate the mischief of a false one. The doctrine that truths external to the mind may be known by intuition or consciousness, independently of observation & experiment, is, I am persuaded, in these times the great intellectual support for false doctrines and bad institutions. By the aid of this philosophy every inveterate belief & every strong feeling, of which the artificial origin is not remembered, is dispensed from the obligation of justifying itself by evidence or reason, & is erected into its own sufficient justification. There never was such an instrument devised for consecrating all deepseated prejudices. It is the main doctrinal pillar of all the errors which impede human improvement. And the chief strength of this false philosophy in the departments of morals & religion lies in the appeal which it is accustomed to make to the evidence of mathematics & of the cognate branches of physical science. To expel it from these is to attack it in its stronghold: & [131r] because this had not been effectually done, the intuition school, even after what my father had written in his "Analysis", had, at least in appearance, & as far as published writings were concerned, on the whole the best

---

[484] have never indulged the illusion . . . impression] see no signs of its having had at all a proportional influence

of the argument. In attempting to clear up the real nature of the evidence of mathematical & physical truths, the "System of Logic" met the intuition doctrine as it had never before been met; & gave its own explanation, from experience & association, of that peculiar character of what are called necessary truths which is adduced as proof that they cannot be derived from experience. Whether this has been done effectually, is still *sub judice;* & even if so, merely to deprive a mode of thought so strongly rooted in human prejudices & partialities of its speculative support, goes but a little way towards conquering it: but though this is but one step, that step is indispensable; for since, after all, prejudice can only be successfully [131v] combated by philosophy, no way can be effectually made against it until it has been shewn not to have philosophy on its side.[485]

[132r] Being now released from any active concern in temporary politics & from any literary occupation involving personal communication with contributors and others, I was enabled to indulge the inclination, natural to thinking persons when the age of boyish

---

[485] though this is but one step, that step is indispensable . . . side.] *an earlier version, written and canceled in the upper half of fol. 131r, reads:* however little the refutation may amount to, nothing could be done to weaken the roots of the greatest existing mischiefs without it. *The remainder of fol. 131v, now canceled, contains the beginning of a new paragraph, which is continued in RII.20r (see p. 191):* The success of the Logic led to the publication in 1844 of the Political Economy Essays, written as I have already mentioned in 1830 & 1831. With this terminates what may be termed the second period of my writings; reckoning the old Westminster Review period as the first. The "Principles of Political Economy" & all subsequent writings belong to a third & different stage of my mental progress, [*the rest of the paragraph is marked with a line in the margin by HM*] which was essentially characterized by the predominating influence of my wife's intellect & character. Up to this time I have spoken of my writings & opinions in the first person singular because the writings though (after we became intimate) mostly revised by her, & freed by her judgment from much that was faulty, as well as enriched by her suggestions, were not, like the subsequent ones, largely & in their most important features the direct product of her own mind: & the opinions though in a state of continued growth, were not generically different from those which I had gradually wrought out on emerging from the narrowness of my original Benthamism. But in the great advance which I have since made in opinion I was wholly her pupil. Her bolder & more powerful [RII.20r] mind arrived before mine at every conclusion which was derived from a more thorough comprehension of the present and insight into the future; & but for her intellect & her high moral feelings leading me on it is doubtful if I should ever have advanced much further than the point I had now reached. (*RII.20r then continues with a new paragraph, which begins with what is now the second sentence of the paragraph beginning on p. 171:* At this period of her life she lived mostly . . .)

vanity is once past, for limiting my own society to a very few persons. General society as now carried on, at least in England, is so thoroughly insipid an affair, even to the very persons who make it what it is, that it is kept up for any reason rather than the pleasure it affords. All serious discussion on matters on which opinions differ, being considered ill bred, & the national deficiency in liveliness & sociability having prevented the cultivation of the art of talking agreeably on trifles, in which the French of the last century so much excelled, the sole attraction of what is called society to those who are not at the top of the tree, is the hope of climbing a little higher on it, while to those who are already at the top it is chiefly a compliance with custom & with the supposed requirements of their station. To a person of any but the commonest order in thought or feeling, such society must unless he has personal objects to serve by means of it, be supremely unattractive: & most people, in the present day, of any really high class of intellect, make their contact with it so slight & at such long intervals as to be almost considered as retiring from it altogether. Those persons of [132*v*] any real mental superiority who act otherwise, are almost without exception, greatly deteriorated by it. Not to mention loss of time, the tone of their feelings is always lowered: they become less in earnest about those of their opinions about which they feel that they must remain silent in the society they frequent; [486] they come to think their more elevated objects unpractical, or at least too remote from realization to be more than a vision or a theory; or even if, more fortunate than most, they retain their higher principles unimpaired, yet with regard to the persons & affairs of the present they insensibly adopt the modes of feeling & judgment of the company they keep. A person of high intellect should never go into unintellectual society unless he can enter it as an apostle. And all persons of even intellectual aspirations had much better, if they can, make their habitual associates of at least their equals, & as far as possible, their superiors in knowledge, intellect, & elevation of sentiment.[487] Further, if their character is formed & their minds made up on the few cardinal points in human opinion, agreement of opinion & feeling on those, has been felt in all times to be an essential requisite of anything

---

[486] about which they feel . . . frequent;] with which the society they frequent does not & will not or cannot sympathize;

[487] This became more & more my practice.

worthy the name of friendship, in a really earnest mind. All these circumstances united made necessarily, in England [133r] (it might not have been so much so in some countries of the Continent) the number very small of those whose society, & still more whose intimacy, I ever voluntarily sought.

Among these, by far the principal was the incomparable friend of whom I have already spoken. At this period of her life she lived mostly, with one young daughter, in a quiet part of the country,[488] & only occasionally in town, with her first husband, Mr Taylor. I visited her equally in both places, & was greatly indebted to the strength of character which enabled her to disregard the false interpretations liable to be put on the frequency of my visits to her while living generally [489] apart from Mr Taylor, & on our occasionally travelling together, though in all other respects our conduct, during these years, gave not the slightest ground for any other supposition than the true one, that our relation to each other was one of strong affection & confidential intimacy only.[490] For though we did not consider the ordinances of society binding on a subject so entirely personal, we did feel bound that our conduct should be such as in no degree to bring discredit on her husband, nor therefore on herself; & [491] we disdained, as every person not a slave of his animal appetites must do, the abject notion that the strongest & tenderest friendship cannot exist [133v] between a man & a woman without a sensual relation, or that any impulses of that lower character [492] cannot be put aside when regard for the feelings of others, or even when only prudence & personal dignity require it.[493]

---

[488] though at no great distance from London; *RII.20r, deleted*

[489] generally] habitually *RII.20r; altered currently to final reading in fol. 133r*

[490] intimacy only.] intimacy, entirely apart from sensuality. *RII.20r, altered to final reading by HM*

[491] binding on a subject so entirely personal . . . &] on a subject so entirely personal, in the smallest degree binding on us in conscience, *RII.20r, altered and expanded to final form by HM*

[492] relation, or that any . . . character] tie; or that sensuality *RII.20r, altered by HM to read:* relation; or that the feelings alluded to

[493] Certain it is that our life, during those years, would have borne the strictest scrutiny, & though for the sake of others we not only made this sacrifice but the much greater one of not living together, we did not feel under an obligation of sacrificing that intimate friendship & frequent companionship which was the chief good of life & the principal object in it, to me, &, conscious as I am how little worthy I was of such regard, I may say also to her. *RII.20v*

In this (as it may be termed) third period of my mental progress, which still continues & which now went hand in hand with hers,[494] my opinions gained equally in breadth & depth. I understood more things, & those which I had understood before I understood more thoroughly. I had many new opinions, & the old which I retained I now saw much more deeply into the grounds of. One of the earliest changes which occurred in this stage of my progress was that I turned back from what there had been of excess in my reaction against Benthamism. I had, at the height of that reaction, certainly become much more indulgent to the common opinions of society & the world, & more willing to be content with seconding the superficial improvement which had begun to take place in those common opinions, than became one whose own convictions differed fundamentally from them. [134r] I was much more inclined, than I can now approve, to put in abeyance the most decidedly heretical part of my opinions, which I now look upon as almost the only ones the assertion of which tends in any way to regenerate society. But in addition to this, our opinions were now far *more* heretical than mine had been in the days of my most extreme Benthamism. In those days I had seen little further than the old school of political economists into the possibilities of future improvement in social arrangements. Private property as at present understood, & inheritance, appeared to me as to them, the *dernier mot* of legislation: & I looked no further than to mitigating the inequalities consequent on these institutions, by abolishing primogeniture & entails. The notion that it was possible to get rid in any considerable degree of the flagrant injustice involved in the fact that some are born to riches & the vast majority to poverty, I reckoned chimerical; & only hoped that by universal education, leading to voluntary restraint on population, the portion of the poor might be made more tolerable. In short, I was a democrat but not the least of a Socialist. We were now less democrats than I had formerly been, because we dreaded more the ignorance & especially the selfishness & brutality of the mass: but our ideal [134v] of future improvement was such as would class us decidedly under the general designation of Socialists. While we repudiated with the greatest energy the tyranny of society over the individual, we yet looked forward to a time when society should no longer

---

[494] which still continues & . . . hers,] in which I moved forward hand in hand with her, *RII.20v, deleted by HM*

be divided into the idle & the industrious,[495] when the rule that they who do not work shall not eat, should be applied not to the pauper merely, but impartially to all; when the division of the produce of labour, instead of being dependent as in so great a degree it is, on the accident of birth, should be made by concert, on an acknowledged principle of justice, & when it should no longer either be, or be thought to be, impossible for human beings to exert themselves strenuously for benefits which were not to be exclusively their own, but to be shared with the society they belong to. The social problem of the future we considered to be, how to unite the greatest individual liberty of action with an equal ownership of all in the raw material of the globe & an equal participation of all in the benefits of combined labour. We knew that to render any such social transformation practicable an equivalent change of character must take place both in the [135r] uncultivated herd who now compose the labouring masses, & in the immense [496] majority of their employers. Both these classes must learn by practice to labour & contrive for generous, or at all events for public & social purposes, & not as hitherto solely for self interested ones. But the capacity for this has always existed in mankind, and is not, nor is ever likely to be, extinct. Education & habit will make a common man dig or weave for the public as well as fight for the public. Interest in the common good is at present so weak a motive in the generality, only because the mind is not accustomed to dwell on it as it dwells from morning to night on things which tend only to personal good. When called into activity as only self interest now is, by the daily course of life, & spurred from behind by the love of distinction & the fear of shame, it is adequate to produce even in common men the most strenuous exertions as well as the most heroic sacrifices. Doubtless it requires a long course of training to alter the deeprooted selfishness which the whole course of existing institutions tends to generate; & modern institutions still more than ancient, since the occasions on which the individual is called on to act for the public without receiving its pay, are far less frequent in modern life, than in the smaller commonwealths

---

[495] looked forward to a time when . . . industrious,] *opposite these words HM penciled at left: "The voice of Society on the great fundamental questions of social & political morals should be the voice of all"*

[496] in the immense] even in the grasping, money getting (*all but "in the" deleted by HM*)

of antiquity. But in this direction lies assuredly the course of future progress.[497]

[135*v*] In The "Principles of Political Economy" these opinions are promulgated; less clearly & fully in the first edition, rather more so in the second, & quite unequivocally in the third. The difference arose partly from the change of times, the first edition having been written & sent to press before the French Revolution of 1848 when the public mind was far less open to the reception of novelties in opinion, especially those of a socialistic character, than it became after that great event.[498] In the first edition the difficulties of Socialism were stated so strongly [499] that the tone was on the whole that of opposition to it. In the [136*r*] year or two which followed, much time was given to the study of the best Socialist writers on the Continent, & to meditation & discussion [500] on the whole range of topics involved in the controversy: & the result was that most of what had been written on the subject in the first edition was cancelled, & replaced by arguments & reflexions of a decidedly socialistic tendency.

The Political Economy was far more rapidly executed than the Logic, or indeed than anything of importance which I had yet written. It was commenced in the autumn of 1845 & completed before the end of 1847. In this period of little more than two years there was an interval of six months during which it was suspended, in order to write articles in the Morning Chronicle (which unexpectedly entered warmly into my purpose) urging the formation of peasant properties on the waste lands of Ireland. This was during the winter of 1846/47, the period of the famine, when the stern necessities of the time seemed to afford a chance of attracting attention to what appeared to me the only mode of combining relief to the immediate destitution with a permanent

---

[497] But in this direction lies . . . progress.] The remedy for this is [135*v*] voluntary association for cooperative industry; which, commenced as it naturally is by those among the industrious classes who are morally the best prepared for it, tends at every step to strengthen where they exist & create where they do not exist, the habits & dispositions requisite for its own success. *marked with an X and a line in the margin by HM*

[498] But it would be a mistake to imagine that we kept back in the first edition opinions as decided as those which appear in the third. Our own opinions had made a great advance in the interval between the two publications. *marked with a line in the margin by HM*

[499] & its advantages so weakly, *deleted first by HM*

[500] between ourselves *marked with a question mark by HM*

improvement of the social & economical condition of the Irish people. But the novelty & strangeness, in England, of the idea of peasant proprietors, one of the striking examples of the extreme ignorance of English politicians & the English public concerning all social phenomena not generally [136v] met with in England (however common elsewhere) made these efforts ineffectual. Instead of a great operation on the waste lands & the conversion of cottiers into proprietors, Parliament passed a Poor Law for maintaining them as paupers: & if the English Govt has not since found itself in inextricable difficulties from the joint operation of the old evils & the quackish remedy, it has to thank not its own foresight, but [501] that most unexpected & surprising fact, the depopulation of Ireland, commenced by famine & continued by voluntary emigration.

The rapid success of the Political Economy shews that the public wanted & were prepared for such a book. Published early in 1848, an edition of a thousand copies was sold in less than a year. Another similar edition [502] was published in the spring of 1849: & a third of 1250 copies early in 1852. It was from the first continually cited & referred to as an authority: because like the "Wealth of Nations" it was not a book merely of abstract science, but of application. It treated Political Economy not as a thing by itself, but [503] as a fragment of a greater whole, a mere department of Social Philosophy, & so interlinked with all the other branches [137r] that its conclusions, even in its own peculiar province, that of Wealth, are only true conditionally, subject to interference & counteraction from causes not directly within its domain: while to the character of a practical guide it has no [504] pretension, apart from other classes of considerations.[505] Political Economy has never, in reality, pretended to advise with no lights but its own, though some persons who knew nothing but political economy (& therefore knew that ill) may have done so. But the numerous sentimental enemies of political economy, & its still more numerous

---

[501] not its own foresight, but] *marked for deletion by HM*
[502] similar edition] edition of the same number of copies
[503] in the only way in which it can rationally be treated,
[504] no] not the slightest RII.24r (*see p. 191*), *altered to final reading by HM*
[505] *In RII.24r, the original Part II ended at this point with a sentence deleted by HM:* It is but the minister & servant of a larger & higher philosophy collecting & handing up to its master the materials which lie near it, to be wrought up with others into a fabric fit for use.

interested enemies in sentimental guise, have been very successful in gaining belief for this among other unmerited imputations upon it. The "Principles" having, in spite of the freedom of many of its opinions on social matters, become for the present the most popular exposition of the subject, has helped to disarm these enemies of so important a study, while I venture to think that it has both widened the basis of the science itself & made many useful applications of its truths in conjunction with others, [137*v*] to the [506] improvement of human practice, moral, political, & social.

Since this time I have published no work of magnitude, though I have written or commenced much, for publication at some future time. I have not to relate any further changes in my opinions, though I hope there has been a continued progress in my mental development. I have seen, in the last twenty years, many of the opinions of my youth obtain general recognition, & many of the reforms in institutions, for which I had through life contended, either effected or in course of being so. But these changes have been attended with much less benefit to human well being than I should formerly have anticipated, because they have produced very little improvement in that on which depends all real amelioration in the lot of mankind, their intellectual & moral state: it may even be questioned whether the causes of deterioration which have been at work in the meanwhile, have not more than counterbalanced the tendencies to improvement. I have learnt from experience that many false opinions may be exchanged for true ones, without in the least altering the habits of mind of which false opinions are the result. The English mind, for example, is quite as raw & undiscerning on subjects of political economy since the nation was converted to free trade, as it was before; although [138*r*] whoever really understands the theory of free trade, must necessarily understand much else, the grounds of that doctrine going very deep into the foundations of the whole philosophy of the production & distribution of wealth. Still further is the public mind from having acquired better habits of thought & feeling or being in any way better fortified against error on subjects of a more elevated nature. I am now convinced that no great improvements in the lot of mankind are possible until a [507] change takes place in the fundamental constitution of their modes of thought. The old opinions in reli-

_____

[506] great   [507] radical

gion, morals, & politics are so much discredited in the more intellectual minds as to have lost the greater part of their efficacy for good, while they have still vitality enough left to be an effectual obstacle to the rising up of better opinions on the same subjects. When the philosophic minds of the world can no longer believe its religion, a transitional period of weak convictions, paralysed intellects & growing laxity of principle commences, which can never cease but when a [508] renovation has been effected in the bases of [138*v*] belief, leading to the evolution of another faith, whether religious or not, which they *can* believe. Therefore I hold that all thinking or writing, which does not directly tend towards this renovation, is at present of very little value beyond the moment.

The last considerable event in my own life, & the latest of which I shall make mention here, is my marriage, in April 1851, to the lady whose incomparable worth had made her friendship the greatest source to me both of happiness & of improvement, during many years in which we never expected to be in any closer relation to one another. Ardently as I should have aspired to this complete union of our lives at any time in the course of my existence at which it had been practicable, I, no less than even my wife, would far rather have foregone that blessing for ever, than have owed it to the premature death of one for whom I had the sincerest respect, & she the strongest affection. That event however having taken place in July 1849, it was granted to me to derive my own greatest good from that [509] evil, by adding to the partnership of thought, feeling, & even writing which had long existed, a partnership of our entire existence. Before as well as [139*r*] since, I have owed the best part of what I was & did to her inspirations & often to her direct assistance: & so long as any of my writings subsequent to the Logic are read or remembered, I hope it will be borne in mind that to her intellect & character they are mainly indebted for whatever in them deserves remembrance.

---

[508] fundamental   [509] great

$$3$$

REJECTED LEAVES

R23–25, 24²–25², 19/20

R23–25 represent the first draft of the text between the present fols. 23, 25 (originally foliated 22, 26). In an intermediate stage of revision Mill rewrote R24 and part of R25 on two new leaves, R24², 25², and finally, sometime after the introduction of the present fol. 1, when the original fols. 1–22 were renumbered 2–23, reduced the whole sequence (R23, 24²–25², and a part of R25v) to a single new leaf, the present fol. 24, which he headed "24—25". The two paragraphs given here, from R23v–25v, originally followed the text of the paragraph ending on p. 57. In addition to the usual information concerning deleted text and HM's alterations, the notes here provide variants from the leaves of the intermediate stage, R24²–25². For variants from the paragraphs preceding and following this extract, see nn. 108, 109, 111 (p. 57).

My father thus took effectual precautions against some, & those very serious dangers, to which his plan of education was liable. There were others to which he was either not so much alive, or against which he did not guard with equal success.

Not, I am persuaded, by any necessity inherent [1] in my education, but certainly by some omission in it,[2] I grew up with great inaptness in [3] the common affairs of every day life.[4] I was far

---

[1] necessity inherent] inherent defect *marked with an exclamation mark in the margin by HM*

[2] certainly by some omission in it,] by some effect resulting jointly from my education & my circumstances

[3] great inaptness in] extraordinary inaptness & even incapacity in all *altered*

longer than children generally are before I could put on my clothes. I know not how many years passed before I could tie a knot. My articulation was long imperfect; one letter, *r*, I could not pronounce until I was nearly sixteen.[5] I never could, nor can I now, do anything [R24r] requiring the smallest manual dexterity, but I never put even a common share of the exercise of understanding into practical things.[6] I was continually acquiring odd or disagreeable [7] tricks which I very slowly & imperfectly got rid of. I was, besides, utterly [8] inobservant: I was, as my father continually told me, like a person who had not the organs of sense: my eyes & ears seemed of no use to me, so little did I see or hear what was before me, & so little, even of what I did see or hear, did I observe & remember. My father was the extreme opposite in all these particulars: his senses & his mental faculties were always on the alert; he carried decision & energy of character in his whole manner & into every action of life: & this, as much as his talents, contributed to the great impression which he always made upon those with whom he came in personal contact. The education he gave me was, however, considered in itself, much more fitted for training me to *know* than to *do*. Not that he was unaware of my defects; both as a boy & as a youth I was incessantly smarting under his [R24v] severe admonitions on the subject. He could not endure stupidity, nor

---

to final form (*except for the deletion of "all"*) *first by HM, who marked the next seven sentences for deletion and rewrote Mill's text to read:* I grew up with great inaptness for everything requiring manual dexterity. The education he gave me. . . . *Subsequently she canceled all the text of the paragraph on R24r–25v*

[4] I had hardly any use of my hands.

[5] *In the intermediate stage of revision, Mill deleted the next nine words, to the end of R23v, and continued with two new sentences on R24ᵉr:* I continued long, & in some degree always, inexpert in anything which required the smallest manual dexterity; & not only my hands, but my mind never did its work properly when it was applied, or rather when it ought to have been applied, to the practical details which, though singly unimportant, are in the aggregate essential to the conduct of daily life. I was, as my father continually told me, as inobservant as if I had no organs of sight or hearing, or no capacity of remembering what I saw & heard. *R24ᵉr then follows the text of R24r:* My father was the extreme opposite . . .

[6] but I never put even a common . . . things.] *written at left to replace:* but all the common things which everybody does, I did not only in an ungainly & awkward but in a thoroughly ineffective & bungling manner like a person without the most ordinary share of understanding. *The next sentence, originally marked for insertion after this canceled passage, is also written at left*

[7] or disagreeable] *deleted by HM*

[8] utterly] *altered by HM to read:* very

feeble & lax habits, in whatever manner displayed, & I was perpetually exciting his anger by manifestations of them. From the earliest time I can remember he used to reproach me, & most truly, with a general habit of inattention; owing to which, he said, I was constantly acquiring bad habits, & never breaking myself of them; was constantly forgetting what I ought to remember, & judging & acting like a person devoid of common sense;[9] & which would make me, he said, grow up a mere[10] oddity, looked down upon by everybody, & unfit for all the common purposes of life. It was not therefore, from any insensibility or tolerance on his part towards such faults, that my education, considered in this particular, must be regarded as a failure. Neither do I see any necessary tendency in his plan of education to produce those defects.[11] No doubt, they may have had some connexion with the fact, otherwise[12] most salutary, of my being educated at home, & not in a school, among other boys, & having no encouragement to practise bodily exercises, from which boys in general derive their earliest lessons of practical skill & contrivance.[13] [R25r] It must not however be supposed that play, or time for it, was refused me. Though no holidays were allowed, lest the habit of work should be broken, & taste for idleness acquired, I had abundant[14] leisure

---

[9] was constantly forgetting what I ought . . . sense;] *written at left. This and the preceding sentence are omitted from R24ᵃr*

[10] a mere] *altered by HM to read:* an

[11] Neither do I see . . . defects.] *marked for deletion by HM, who wrote at left: "To escape the contagion of boys society   Probably he purposely prevented the intercourse with other boys wh wd have prevented this defect & he was too much occupied himself to share a boys healthful exercises"*

[12] otherwise] *altered by HM to read:* morally

[13] otherwise most salutary, of my being . . . contrivance.] which was partly intentional on his part, of my having no playfellows or associates among other boys; since if I had, the bodily exercises I should have been led to cultivate & the activity of some sort, & adaptation of means to ends which might [R25r] have been called forth, would probably have made a difference for the better. In R24ᵃv (*in which HM interlined "dexterity & agility" above "practical skill & contrivance"*), Mill *added at this point:* Some sacrifice in this respect he was no doubt willing to make, as the price of my escaping the contagion of boys' society. But while he saved me from the demoralizing effects of school life he made no effort to provide me with any substitute for its practicalizing influences. Whatever qualities he, probably, had acquired without difficulty or special instruction, he seems to have supposed that I ought to acquire as easily: & bitter reproaches for being deficient in them, were nearly all the help he ever gave me towards acquiring them.

[14] abundant] *circled by HM; R25ᵃr reads:* ample

in every day to amuse myself: [15] but my amusements being solitary or with children younger than myself, gave little [16] stimulus to either bodily or mental activity. There [17] were wanting, in addition to the book-lessons which were the staple of my instruction, well devised practical lessons, exercising the hands, & the head in directing the hands, & necessitating careful observation, & adaptation of means to ends. I had also [18] the great [19] misfortune of having, in domestic matters, everything done for me. Circumstanced as I was, nothing but being thrown as much as possible, in daily matters, upon my [R25v] own powers of contriving & of executing could have given [20] me the proper use of my faculties for the occasions of life. This discipline, I presume my father did not see the necessity of; & it would never have occurred to my mother, who without misgivings of any sort worked from morning till night for her children.

R19/20, a leaf headed "between 19 & 20", is a rewritten, expanded version of the present fol. 21 (originally foliated 20). After Mill wrote the passage on manual dexterity in R23–25, rewrote and condensed it in R24²–25², and finally omitted it entirely in writing the present fol. 24, he inserted parts of it into an earlier summary paragraph on his education by rewriting fol. 21 as R19/20. Possibly the new version did not meet HM's approval, for Mill

----

[15] *For the rest of this sentence and the next sentence, R25²r reads:* but as I had no boy companions, & the animal need of physical activity being satisfied by walking, my amusements, which were mostly solitary, were almost all of a quiet, if not a bookish turn, & gave little stimulus to any kind of even mental activity other than that which was already called forth by my studies.

[16] little] no (*at left, opposite the ending of this sentence, HM penciled an exclamation mark and a question mark, and commented:* "It is always the eldest son of a large family who is especially the active & acting spirit")

[17] There] The deficiency in my education as regards this most vital point consisted I think in two things, first; that there

[18] I had also] This requisite my father did not provide. And, what was still more fatal, I had

[19] great] *deleted in R25²r*

[20] *For the rest of the paragraph, R25²r reads:* my practical faculties their fair share of developement. Along with this, I required, in addition to the book-lessons which were the staple of my instruction, well devised practical lessons, exercising the hands, & the head in directing the hands, & necessitating careful observation, & adaptation of means to ends. But my father had not bestowed the same amount of thought & attention on this, as on most other branches of education; & (as in some other points of my tuition) he seems to have expected effects without causes.

returned to fol. 21 (which he subsequently further revised) for his final text of the early draft. (After her death he introduced into his later draft the passage ending Chapter I—Columbia edition, pp. 24–26—which, of the three versions in the early draft, is most nearly like that of R24²–25².) The extract given here represents text that was to have come between the penultimate and last sentences of the paragraph ending on p. 54. Two other variants from R19/20 are given in nn. 91, 92 (p. 54).

Indeed, my deficiency in these qualities caused the results of my education to appear, in some respects, less advantageous than they really were, since it made my acquisition of those active & practical capacities which my father's discipline did not in the same degree provide for, slow & imperfect. The education he gave me was, considered in itself, much more fitted for training me to *know* than to *do*. Most boys acquire whatever they do acquire of bodily dexterity or practical skill & contrivance, by their own spontaneous activity when left to themselves, or by competition & conflict with other boys. [R19/20v] It was a main point with my father to save me from the contagion of boys' society; & though I had ample leisure in every day to amuse myself, my voluntary amusements were almost all of a quiet, & generally of a bookish turn, & gave little stimulus to any kind of even mental activity other than that which was already called forth by my studies. Whatever deficiencies these causes had a tendency to produce, would in the case of a naturally quick, or a naturally energetic youth, have rapidly disappeared on the first contact with the world. But with me, the discipline of life in this respect was long & severe, & even at last, was but imperfectly effectual. This, however, was not owing to the mode of my education but to natural slowness & to a certain mental & moral indolence which, but for the immense amount of mental cultivation which my father gave me, would probably have prevented me from either being or doing anything worthy of note.

R31–37

R31–37, containing the first draft of the text between the present fols. 30, 35 (which was then foliated 38), were rewritten and condensed in the present fols. 31–34. (It is not known whether this rewriting was done before or after the revisions already described: the substitution of fol. 24 for R23–25 shortened the draft by two leaves, but the addition of fol. 1, the original heading of fol. 24 as

"24—25", and then the introduction of fol. 28 made up the difference so far as the subsequent foliation is concerned.) Of the extract given here, from R31v–34r, the first three paragraphs were condensed into the single paragraph beginning on p. 65, and the remaining sentences (which do not represent a complete paragraph) were replaced by the first two sentences of the paragraph beginning on p. 66. Following the extract, the text of R34r continues as in fol. 33r, "I was a more frequent visitor. . . ." Other variants from R31, 34–37 are given in nn. 143–148, 156–167 (pp. 64–65, 67–70).

Personally I believe my father to have had much greater capacities of feeling than were ever developed in him. He resembled almost all Englishmen in being ashamed of the signs of feeling, & by the absence of demonstration, starving the feelings themselves. In an atmosphere of tenderness & affection he would have been tender & affectionate; but his ill assorted marriage & his asperities of temper disabled him from making such an atmosphere. I once heard him say, that there was always the greatest sympathy between him & his children until the time of lessons began but that the lessons always [R32r] destroyed it. Certainly his children till six or seven years old always liked him & were happy in his presence, & he liked them & had pleasure in talking to them & in interesting & amusing them; & it is equally true that after the lessons began, fear of his severity sooner or later swallowed up all other feelings towards him.[21] This is true only of the elder children: with the younger [22] he followed an entirely different system, to the great comfort of the later years of his life. But in respect to what I am here concerned with, the moral agencies which acted on myself, it must be mentioned as a most baneful one, that my father's children neither loved him, nor, with any warmth of affection, any one else.[23] I do not mean that things were

---

[21] At left, opposite the ending of this sentence and the next two sentences, HM commented: "I do not believe it is possible for a parent to teach their own children effectually without the exercise of a degree of severity & authority which will make it impossible that the children should love them. It is easier for a young person to like a schoolmaster—partly because many other youths go thro the same discipline, the severity therefore does not seem so personal   besides however some youth may respect & even like a schoolmaster they do not tenderly love him   the personal suffering voluntarily inflicted is probably incompatible with tender love on either side"

[22] younger] three youngest

[23] children neither loved him . . . else.] altered by HM to read: elder

worse in this respect than they are in most English families; in
which genuine affection is altogether exceptional; what is usually
found being more or less of an attachment of mere habit, like
that to inanimate objects, & a few conventional proprieties of
phrase & demonstration. I believe there [R32v] [24] is less personal
affection in England than in any other country of which I know
anything,[25] & I give my father's family not as peculiar in this respect but only as a too faithful exemplification of the ordinary fact.
That rarity in England, a really warm hearted mother, would in
the first place have made my father a totally different being, &
in the second would have made the children grow up loving &
being loved. But my mother with the very best intentions, only
knew how to pass her life in drudging for them. Whatever she
could do for them she did, & they liked her, because she was
kind to them, but to make herself loved, looked up to, or even
obeyed, required qualities which she unfortunately did not possess.

I thus grew up in the absence of love & in the presence of fear:
& many & indelible are the effects of this bringing-up, in the stunting of my moral growth. One of these, which it would have required a quick sensibility & impulsiveness of natural temperament
to counteract, was habitual reserve. Without knowing or believing that I was reserved, I grew up with an instinct of closeness.
I had no one to whom I desired to express everything which I
felt; & [26] the only person I was in [R33r] communication with, to
whom I looked up, I had too much fear of, to make the communication to him of any act or feeling ever a matter of frank impulse
or spontaneous inclination. Instead of a character whose instinct
& habit are openness, but who can command reserve when duty
or prudence require it,[27] my circumstances tended to form a character, close & reserved from habit & want of impulse, not from
will, & therefore, while destitute of the frank communicativeness
which wins & deserves sympathy, yet continually failing in reti-
nence where it is suitable & desirable.

Another evil I shared with many of the sons of energetic fathers.

children neither loved him, nor any one else. *At this point Mill originally continued (but did not complete the sentence before deleting)*: Things would have
been very different if under the influence of a mother of strong good sense &

[24] *The rest of this paragraph and the first sentence of the next are marked
with a line in the margin by* HM

[25] of which I know anything,] in the world,

[26] I had no one to whom . . . &] *deleted by* HM

[27] Instead of a character whose instinct . . . it,] The only character fit to
cultivate is that whose instinct . . . it;

To have been, through childhood, under the constant rule of a strong will, certainly is not favourable to strength of will.[28] I was so much accustomed to expect to be told what to do, either in the form of direct command or of rebuke for not doing it, that I acquired a habit of leaving my responsibility as a moral agent to rest on my father, my conscience never speaking to me except by his voice. The things I ought *not* to do were mostly provided for by his precepts, rigorously enforced whenever violated, but the [R33v] [29] things which I *ought* to do I hardly ever did of my own mere motion, but waited till he told me to do them; & if he forbore or forgot to tell me, they were generally left undone. I thus acquired a habit of backwardness, of waiting to follow the lead of others, an absence of moral spontaneity, an inactivity of the moral sense & even to a large extent, of the intellect,[30] unless roused by the appeal of some one else,—for which a large [31] abatement must be made from the benefits, either moral or intellectual, which flowed from any other part of my education.

Before taking leave of this first period of my life it may seem that something ought to be said of the persons with whom my father habitually associated & to some of whom it may be supposed, I was not a stranger. But I cannot trace to them any other influence on my development,[32] than what was due to such of my father's conversations with them as I had an opportunity of listening to. My father's narrow income, previous to his appointment from the East India Company, & his unwillingness to invite any persons to his house whom he could not, as he said, [R34r] make as comfortable as they were at home, caused the habitual frequenters of his house to be [33] limited to a very few persons, mostly little known,

---

[28] To have been, through childhood . . . will.] *marked with a line in the margin by HM; at left, opposite the last eight words of the sentence, she penciled two X's and a question mark*

[29] *The rest of the paragraph is marked with a line in the margin by HM*

[30] & even to a large . . . intellect,] *interlined*   [31] large] *terrible*

[32] But I cannot trace . . . development,] *at left HM penciled a question mark and queried:* "how shd *you?" In rewriting this paragraph in fol. 32v, Mill copied the first sentence verbatim, and for the whole of the second wrote:* But I cannot trace to any of them, considered individually, any influence on my developement. *After HM marked the passage there, he condensed it to its final form (see p. 66)*

[33] My father's narrow income, previous . . . be] *all but the last eight words are deleted by HM, who underlined and penciled a question mark opposite* "narrow", *wrote* "revisal" *and* "mesquin" *at left on R33v, penciled a large X and the direction* "omit or remark upon" *at the top of R34r, and then rewrote the sentence to read, up to this point:* The habitual frequenters of my fathers house were

but whom personal worth, & more or less of congeniality with his opinions (then not so frequently to be met with as since) disposed him to cultivate. His other friends he saw at their own houses; saving an occasional call which as they knew how important his time was to him they rarely made [34] except for some special purpose.[35] Such occasional calls (from my being an habitual inmate of my father's study) made me acquainted with the most intimate & congenial of his friends, David Ricardo, who by his benevolent countenance & kindliness of manner was very attractive to young persons,[36] & who after I became a student of political economy sometimes had [37] me to breakfast & walk with him in order to discuss or (as a more correct description of the relation which could exist between him & me) to examine me in [38] political economy.

R105–106

R105–106 were rewritten and expanded in the present fols. 103, 101, 102. As first numbered, 103, 104, they provided the text between the present fols. 99, 104 (originally foliated 102, 105). In an intermediate stage of revision, Mill introduced the present fols. 100, 101, 103 (then foliated 103, 104, 107), and deleted half of fol. 99v and most of R105. He subsequently took out R105–106 entirely, rewriting parts of the two leaves in the present fol. 102 (originally headed "105—106"). The following table gives the order of leaves in each stage, with the present folio numbers in square brackets. As the numbers indicate, the final revised form was arrived at before R31–37 were replaced by fols. 31–34.

Original	*Intermediate*	*Revised*
102 [99]	*102* [99]	*102* [99]
103 [R105]	*103* [100]	*103* [100]
104 [R106]	*104* [101]	*104* [101]
105 [104]	*105* [R105]	*105—106* [102]
	106 [R106]	*107* [103]
	107 [103]	*108* [104]
	108 [104]	

[34] His other friends he saw . . . made] *altered by HM to read:* His other friends he saw occasionally but as they knew how important . . . rarely came (*she then apparently marked the entire sentence for deletion*)

[35] I therefore saw little of most of them, & some not at all.

[36] young persons,] me,

[37] sometimes had] *altered by HM to read:* often invited

[38] or (as a more correct . . . in] *deleted and altered by HM to read:* questions of

*The text transcribed here, all but the first word ("length.") and
the last five lines of R105–106, originally continued the paragraph
begun and deleted in the present fol. 99v, which is described in
n. 399 (p. 136). The canceled last five lines of R106v contain most
of the first sentence of the paragraph beginning on p. 140.*

But I was struck with the ability, knowledge & large views of the
men. I was kept *au courant* of their progress by one of their most
enthusiastic disciples, Gustave d'Eichthal, who about that time
passed a considerable period in England: & from this time forward [39] I read nearly everything they wrote. The scheme gradually
unfolded by them, the management of the labour & capital of
the community for the national account, classing all persons according to their capacity & rewarding them according to their works,
appeared to me a far superior kind of Socialism to Owen's: their
aim seemed to me perfectly rational, & though the machinery for
attaining it could not possibly be worked, the proclamation (I
thought) of such an ideal of human society could not but be calculated to give a very beneficial direction to the efforts of others
for the improvement of society as already constituted. I honoured
them above all for the boldness & freedom from prejudice with
which they proclaimed the perfect equality of men & women &
an entirely new order of things [40] in regard to the relations between
the sexes: a merit which the other great French socialist [R105v]
Fourier possesses in a still greater degree.

This however is an anticipation. At the time of which I am now
speaking the only very strong impression which I received from
anything connected with St Simonism was derived from an early
writing of August Comte, who then called himself in the title page
an élève of Saint Simon. In this tract M. Comte announced the
doctrine which he has since so copiously illustrated of the natural
succession of three states in every branch of knowledge, first,[41] the
theological, second, the metaphysical, & third, the positive stage;
& contended that social science must be subject to the same law;
that the feudal & Catholic system was the last phasis of the theological state of the social science, Protestantism the commencement
& the doctrines of the French Revolution the consummation of its
metaphysical, & that its positive state was yet to come. This doc-

---

[39] & from this time forward] as long as they remained a school
[40] an entirely new order of things] a regime of freedom
[41] *The text up to this point was canceled when, in the intermediate stage of
revision, Mill added the present fols. 100, 101*

trine harmonized very well with my existing notions; I already regarded the methods of physical science as the proper models for
political: but one important point in the parallelism much insisted
on by M. Comte, had not before occurred to me. In mathematics
[R106r] & physics what is called the liberty of conscience or the
right of private judgment, is merely nominal: though in no way restrained by law, the liberty is not exercised: those who have studied
the subject are all of the same opinion; if any one rejected what
has been proved by demonstration or experiment he would be
thought to be asserting no right but the right of being a fool:
those who have not studied these sciences take their conclusions
on trust from those who have, & the practical world goes on incessantly applying laws of nature & conclusions of reasoning which
it receives on the faith not of its own reason but of the authority
of the instructed. Hitherto it had not occurred to me that the case
would be the same in the moral, social, & political branches of
speculation if they were equally advanced with the physical.[42] I
had always identified deference to authority with mental slavery
& the repression of individual thought. I now perceived that these
indeed are the means by which adherence is enforced to opinions
from which at least a minority of thinking & instructed persons dis-
sent; but that when all such persons are as nearly unanimous, as
they are in the more advanced of the physical Sciences, their authority will have an ascendancy which will be increased, not di-
minished, by the intellectual & scientific [R106v] cultivation of the
multitude, who, after learning all which their circumstances per-
mit, can do nothing wiser than rely for all beyond on the knowledge of the more highly instructed. I did not become one atom

---

[42] *The next four sentences ("I had always . . . their united authority.")
are written at left, replacing the following earlier text:* My hopes of improvement in these respects had hitherto rested upon the reason of the multitude,
improved as I hoped it might be by education. I henceforth saw that this was
not the best, & not even a reasonable, hope. Without becoming in the smallest
degree less zealous for every practicable increase [R106v] of the knowledge
& improvement of the understanding of the many, I saw that they were never
likely to be qualified for judges in the last resort of political any more than of
physical truths; that what was wanted was such an improvement in the methods
of political & social philosophy, as should enable all thinking & instructed persons, who have no sinister interest, to be of one mind on these subjects, as
they are on subjects of physical science: after which the more the intelligence
of the general multitude became improved, the more they would appreciate
the greater knowledge & more exercised judgment of the instructed & the more
disposed they would be to defer to their opinion.

less zealous for increasing the knowledge & improving the understanding of the man; but I no longer believed that the fate of mankind depended on the possibility of making all of them competent
judges of questions of government & legislation. From this time my
hopes of improvement rested less on the reason of the multitude,
than on the possibility of effecting such an improvement in the
methods of political & social philosophy, as should enable all thinking & instructed persons who have no sinister interest to be so
nearly of one mind on these subjects, as to carry the multitude with
them by their united authority. This was a view of matters which
as it seemed to me, had been overlooked, or its importance not
seen, by my first instructors: & it served still further to widen the
distance between my present mode of thinking, & that which I
had learnt from Bentham & my father.

R113, 109

*R113 represents the first draft of the present fol. 109 (to the end
of the paragraph on p. 146). It originally provided the text between the present fols. 108, 112 (then foliated 112, 114). In a subsequent rearrangement of the text, by which the paragraph on
doctrinal differences with his father (p. 149) was removed from
its original position before the two paragraphs on the Austins
(pp. 146–148) to its present position after them, Mill rewrote only
this leaf—in R109 (then foliated 113)—making the rest of the
alteration by reordering leaves, deleting parts of the text on some
pages and recopying them at left on others. The following table
gives the original and revised order of leaves, with the present
folio numbers in square brackets.*

Original	Revised
112 [108]	*112 [108]*
113 [R113]	*113 [R109]*
114 [112]	*114 [110]*
115 [110]	*115 [111]*
116 [111]	*116 [112]*
117 [113]	*117 [113]*

*After the leaves in this series received their final numbering, 108–
113, Mill recopied R109 as the present fol. 109—for no apparent
reason, since R109 has all the appearance of a fair copy, and his
principal alteration in recopying (he restored the original text of*

part of a sentence intermediately revised) could easily have been made at left. Variants from R113, 109 are given in nn. 426–433 (pp. 145–146).

R119–121

Although R119–121 were rewritten in the present fols. 119–121, the correspondence of folio numbers is merely coincidental. After the paragraph ending on p. 151—in the draft near the bottom of the present fol. 114r—Mill continued on fol. 114 (then foliated 118) and then on R119–121 with what were originally the last three paragraphs of Part I of the draft. In rearranging the materials of Part II (see the discussion below) he removed the first two of these paragraphs and part of the third to a later position in the text (pp. 154–157), and recopied them in fols. 118v–121r. Variants from the canceled text of fol. 114 and from R119–121 are given in nn. 449–459 (pp. 155–157). The original conclusion of Part I, which followed the fourth sentence of the paragraph beginning on p. 157, is transcribed here.

From this time to 1840, first in association with Molesworth, afterwards by myself, I was the conductor of a political review. But this new phasis in my literary existence belongs to a [43] different period in my personal history, for which all that preceded was of no value except as a preparation—that in which I enjoyed the friendship & was under the ennobling influence of one to whom I owe all that is best, either in me or in what I have written, & compared with whom I am in myself scarcely worthy of a passing thought.

RII.1–8, 20, 24

"Part II." originally consisted of twenty-four numbered leaves, the present RII.1–8, fols. 121–131 (originally numbered 9–19, the text of pp. 157–169 plus text now deleted), RII.20, fols. 134–136 (originally numbered 21–23, the text of pp. 172–175), RII.24. In revising (to an extent following HM's directions), Mill rewrote and compressed RII.1–8—sixteen manuscript pages on his relationship with Harriet—into the seven pages of the present fols. 115–118r, and then copied into fols. 118v–120 (adding eleven lines at left on fol. 121r) the paragraphs from fol. 114 and R119–121, as

---

[43] a] an entirely

described above. He kept fols. 121–131, his original II.9–19, deleting most of the text on the verso of fol. 131. The canceled text of fol. 131 with that of RII.20 he rewrote on two new leaves, fols. 132–133; he retained the old II.21–23 (fols. 134–136), and then wrote three new leaves (fols. 137–139) to replace the original abrupt conclusion on RII.24. Even though about a third of it was used verbatim in the final version of the early draft, I have given here the complete text of RII.1–8 (all but the last eight lines, which begin a new paragraph substantially the same as the fifth and following sentences of the paragraph beginning on p. 157, "In the years between 1834 & 1840 . . ."). Variants from RII.20, 24 are given in nn. 485, 488–494, 504–505 (pp. 169, 171–172, 175).

Part II.

My first introduction to the lady whose friendship has been the honour & blessing of my existence, & who after many years of confidential intimacy, deigned to be [44] my wife, dates from as early as 1830.[45] Its origin or rather occasion was the accident of a common acquaintance; but I have always been convinced that sooner or later, & rather sooner than later, we should have found each other out: for [46] both of us were at this time ardent seekers for persons of similar opinions & of any intellectual gifts. Had our acquaintance commenced later; had her judgment of me been first formed in maturer years it would probably have been far less favourable; but I, at whatever period of life I had known her, must always have felt her to be the most admirable person I had ever known, & must have made her approbation the guiding light & her sympathy the chief object of my life, though to appreciate the greatness [47] [RII.1v] & variety of her preeminence could only have been possible after long & intimate knowledge, to any one not on the same exalted level as herself. To me, so inferior in nature & so widely different in all previous discipline, a complete or adequate appreciation of her is impossible, & such approach to it

---

[44] whose friendship has been . . . be] *HM underlined "existence" and "many years of confidential intimacy", and wrote at left:* & who after twenty years of the most valuable friendship of my life became

[45] as early as 1830.] *HM deleted "as early as" and added at left:* when I was in my 25th she in her 23d year

[46] Its origin or rather occasion . . . for] *deleted by HM, who wrote at left three sentences that Mill copied into fol. 115r almost verbatim:* With her husband's family . . . lasting impression. (*see p. 151*)

[47] & must have made her approbation . . . greatness] *deleted by HM*

as I have made has only been the effect of the long course of education derived from the knowledge & contemplation of her.[48]

It is not to be supposed that she was, or that any one, at the age at which I first saw her, could be all [49] that she afterwards became. Least of all could this be true of her, with whom self-improvement, progress in the highest & in all senses, was a law of her nature; a necessity equally from the ardour with which she sought it, & from the spontaneous tendency of faculties which could not receive an impression or an experience without making it the source or the occasion of an accession of wisdom. Up to the time when I knew her, her rich & powerful nature had chiefly unfolded itself according to the received type of feminine genius. [RII.2r] To her outer circle she was a beauty, and a wit, with an air of natural distinction, felt by all who approached her: [50] to the inner, a woman of deep & strong feeling, of penetrating & intuitive intelligence, & of a most meditative & poetic nature. Morally she was already so perfect that even she could not add anything to her type of perfection in after life.[51] Every noble & beautiful quality seemed in its turn to be her leading characteristic so long as only that side of her character was looked at. The passion of justice might have been thought to be her strongest feeling, but for her boundless generosity & a lovingness ever ready to pour itself forth upon any or all human beings however unlike herself, if they did but shew a capacity of making the smallest return of feeling or even a wish to have feeling bestowed on them. Her unselfishness was not that of a taught system of duties, but of a heart which thoroughly identified itself with the feelings of others, & even, imaginatively investing others with an intensity of feeling equal to its own, [RII.2v] often [52] took great suffering upon itself to save others from pain which would have been comparatively small. She was by nature one of those who would have had most excuse for thinking first of themselves, for her impulses were tenfold stronger, her pleasures & pains tenfold more intense than those of common persons: yet to receive all pleasure & all good from the love of

---

[48] to any one not on the same exalted level . . . her.] *marked with a line in the margin by HM*

[49] all] *underlined by HM*

[50] with an air of natural . . . her:] *in one of several earlier attempts Mill wrote and HM deleted:* & a most distinguée woman

[51] Morally she was already . . . life.] *marked with a line in the margin by HM*

[52] often] continually

others would to her have been the only congenial state, & when
she took concern for herself or asserted any claims of her own,
every one [53] felt that the impersonal love of justice was speaking in her neither more nor less than it would have spoken in behalf of a stranger or an enemy. All the rest of her moral characteristics were those which naturally accompany these qualities
of mind & heart. The most genuine modesty combined with the
loftiest pride; a simplicity & sincerity which was absolute, towards
all who were fit to receive it; the utmost scorn of everything mean
or cowardly, & indignation at everything brutal or tyrannical, faithless or dishonourable in conduct or character; while making the
[RII.3r] broadest distinction between *mala in se* & mere *mala prohibita,* between acts giving evidence of intrinsic badness of feeling & character, & those which are mere violations of conventions
either good *or* bad, & which whether in themselves right or wrong,
may be done by persons otherwise loveable or admirable.

Such a woman could not, except by the rarest destiny, be otherwise than alone in the world, especially in a world like England.
Married at a very [54] early age, to a most upright, brave, & honorable
man, of liberal opinions and good education, but not of the intellectual or artistic tastes which would have made him [55] a companion for her, though a steady & affectionate friend, for whom
she had true esteem & the strongest [56] affection through life & whom
she most deeply lamented when dead; shut out by the social disabilities of women from any adequate exercise of her higher faculties in action on the world without, her life was one of inward
meditation varied by familiar intercourse with a small circle of
friends, of whom one only (a woman) [57] was a person of genius,
or of capacities [RII.3v] of feeling or intellect kindred with her
own, but all had more or less of alliance with her in sentiments
& opinions. Into this circle I had the good fortune to be admitted,
though it was many [58] years before I could be said to be at all intimate with her. But from the time when I could really call her
my friend I wished for no other.[59] All other persons whom I had

---

[53] every one] *altered by HM to read:* every good observer must have
[54] a very] an *altered to final form first by HM*
[55] and good education, but not . . . him] but of no intellectual or artistic
tastes, nowise *altered to final form first by HM*
[56] the strongest] *interlined by HM, then written over in ink by Mill*
[57] (a woman)] *deleted by HM*
[58] many] *interlined by HM, then written over in ink by Mill*
[59] But from the time when I . . . other.] *deleted by HM*

known either had not the opinions or had not the feelings which were necessary to make them permanently valuable [60] to me. In her [61] complete emancipation from every kind of superstition, & an earnest protest both against society as at present constituted, & against the pretended perfection of the order of nature & the universe, resulted not from the hard intellect but from strength of noble & elevated feeling, & coexisted with a [62] reverential nature. In general spiritual characteristics as well as in temperament & organization I have often compared her, as she was at this time, to Shelley: but in thought & intellect Shelley, so far as his powers were developed in his short life, was but a child to her. I have never known any [RII.4r] intellect in man or woman which, taken for all in all, could be compared to hers. All other intellects when looked at beside hers [63] seem to be but special talents,—a peculiar knack acquired by study & practice of dealing with some one particular thing. On all subjects on which she thinks, that is on all great subjects of speculation & on all near subjects of important practice, she goes quite down to the very heart & marrow of the matter, severing & putting aside all irrelevancies & nonessentials, cleaving through at one stroke all entanglements of verbal sophistry & haze of confused conceptions. Alike in the highest regions of philosophy & in the smallest practical concerns of daily life her mind is always the same perfect instrument; always seizing the essential idea or principle, the cause on which the effect depends, the precise end, & the precise obstacle to its attainment. The same exactness & rapidity of operation pervading all her senses as well as her mental faculties, would with her gifts of feeling & imagination have made her [64] a consummate artist in any department in which she had had the requisite mechanical instruction; [65] as her fiery & tender soul & her [RII.4v] vigorous eloquence would have made her a great orator, & her coup d'œil & power of practical combination might have made her a great general, if either carrière [66] had been accessible to women. But if I were to say in

---

[60] them permanently valuable] their friendship sufficient (*the last word altered to "valuable" first by HM*)

[61] alone *deleted first by HM*

[62] a] an originally *altered to final reading first by HM*

[63] All other intellects . . . hers] *altered by HM to read:* Most intellects

[64] made her] *altered by HM to read:* fitted her to be

[65] in any department in which . . . instruction;] *deleted by HM*

[66] would have made her a great orator . . . carrière] *altered by HM to read:* might have made an orator if any such carrières (*for "a great orator" Mill first wrote "one of the greatest of orators"*)

what above all she is preeminent, it is in her profound knowledge of human nature. To know all its depths & all its elevations she had only to study herself: her knowledge of its varieties she owes to an observation which overlooks nothing, & an activity of mind which converts everything into knowledge. Hence while she sees farther than, as it appears to me, any one else has done into the possibilities & capabilities of the future,[67] the thoroughness of her insight into & comprehension of human beings as they are preserves her from all miscalculations or illusions. Those who are dissatisfied with human life as it is & whose feelings are wholly identified with its radical amendment (as all the wisest & best of mankind are) have two main regions of thought in both of which her intellect is supreme & her judgment infallible: [68] One is the region of ultimate aims, the constituents of the [RII.5r] highest realizable ideal of human life; the other is that of the immediately useful & practically attainable. In both of these ever since I knew her well, I have been entirely & in the fullest sense her pupil.[69] And to say truth, it is in these two extremes that the only real certainty resides. My own strength, such as it was (apart from the capacity of appreciating & partly understanding things better & greater than myself, by which alone I was or am in any degree worthy of her) [70] lay wholly in the uncertain & slippery intermediate region, that of theory, or so-called [71] moral & political science: respecting the conclusions of which in any of the forms in which I have received or originated them, whether as political economy, analytic psychology, logic, philosophy of history, or anything else, it is not the least of my intellectual obligations to her that I have derived from her a wise scepticism; which while it has not prevented me from following out the honest exercise of my thinking faculties to whatever conclusions might result from it, has prevented me, I hope, from holding or announcing those conclusions with a con-

---

[67] than, as it appears to me . . . future,] into the possibilities & capabilities of the future than those who are reputed the most dreamy enthusiasts, *altered several times by both Mill and HM, the latter first writing the version that Mill accepted as final. She also marked the entire sentence with a line in the margin*

[68] in both of which her intellect . . . infallible:] *deleted by HM, who also underlined "infallible" and penciled "unerring?" at left*

[69] In both of these ever since . . . pupil.] *marked with a large X and a line in the margin by HM, who deleted the last eight words and interlined "derived &c" above "have been"*

[70] such as it was (apart from . . . her)] *deleted by HM*

[71] so-called] *deleted by HM*

fidence which the nature of such speculations does not warrant &
has kept my mind always open [RII.5v] to admit clearer perceptions & better evidence.[72] Everything in my later writings to which
any serious value can be attached, everything either far reaching
in speculation or genial in tone & feeling & sympathetic with humanity, everything to which the Political Economy in particular
owes its reputation & which is thought to distinguish it to its advantage [73] from other treatises under the same name, is in all essentials not my writing but hers: & still more will this be the case
with what remains to be written in order to bring our opinions
fully before the world.

It is [74] less obvious what even in the immaturity of her powers
& of her experience, could attract her to me, than me to her; or
what, peculiarly valuable to her, she could find in such a type
of character as mine: but a thorough agreement in opinion is to
any one, especially to a young person opposed to the reigning opinions,[75] always a support, especially when the concurring minds have
been very differently [RII.6r] formed & trained & have arrived at
their conclusions by very different paths. To her who had reached
her opinions by the moral intuition of a character of strong feeling,
there was doubtless help as well as encouragement to be derived
from one who had arrived at many of the same results by study &
reasoning. It was also a strong link between us that we felt alike
on that most vital question, the social position of women: whose
subordination, by law & custom, to men, we regarded as the last
remaining form of primeval tyranny & serfage, & whose equal ad-
missibility to all occupations & equal participation in all rights,
we deemed not only to be the clear dictate of justice, but to be an
essential condition of any great improvement in mankind either
individually or socially. It would give a totally false idea of her

---

[72] *The rest of the paragraph is marked with a line in the margin by HM, who
wrote some forty or fifty words at left, now erased and largely illegible, beginning:* "It is a subject on which we have often united as shewing [?]"

[73] to its advantage] *radically*

[74] much *deleted first by HM, who marked the entire sentence with a line in
the margin and wrote several words at left, now erased and (except for* "I
mention" *and* "attainments") *illegible*

[75] mine: but a thorough agreement in opinion . . . opinions,] mine. My
principal recommendation, besides that of strong admiration & desire for
sympathy with her, was our thorough agreement in opinion, which to any one,
especially . . . opinions, is *altered to final form first by HM*

character if I were not to say, that her strong feeling on this [76] point was the effect of principle, & not of any desire on her own part to mingle in the turmoil & strife of the occupations which the dominant sex has hitherto reserved to itself. Though her education had been masculine, her personal habits & tastes were all [77] peculiarly feminine; her feelings & inclinations all pointed to a life not of self-help or self-assertion but of loving reliance [RII.6v] on the love & care of others.[78] The importance she attached to the social independence & equal rights of women, arose from two of the principal features of her character, her love of justice & her sense of dignity. How indeed can either of these feelings, when a genuine outgrowth of the individual nature, & not a matter of arbitrary convention as much as any of the rules of deportment, tolerate that a human being should be marked out from birth to be the mere appendage of some other? Those most capable of the abnegation of any separate self, & merging of the entire being with that of another, which is the characteristic of strong passion or rather, which strong passion in its most passionate moments strives to realize,[79] are precisely those who would disdain to be the objects of this self-annihilating feeling unless the renunciation of any separate existence is equally complete on both sides [80] & unless it comes from the spontaneous impulse of individual feeling & not from social ordinances prescribing that one half of all human character shall develope itself in this way or have no developement at all. But men have first decreed that women shall have no passions except personal passions, & have then erected one of the natural promptings of strong personal passion into the ideal standard of womanly perfection, from which they endeavour to reap a double advantage: first, the pleasure, the convenience & the vanity of being all in all to [RII.7r] their nearest companion without her being all in all to them; & next that in the pursuit of their other objects they not only have not to contend with women as competitors but can *exploiter* their enthusiasm & their quick practical

---

[76] most essential

[77] Though her education had . . . all] Her education, her personal habits & tastes were all (*HM deleted "Her education" and "all", and wrote several words, now erased and illegible, at left*)

[78] *The next five sentences* ("*The importance . . . have been decided to be womanly.*") *are marked with a line in the margin by HM*

[79] or rather, which strong passion . . . realize,] *deleted by HM*

[80] the renunciation of any separate . . . sides] they give it in as full measure as they receive it

sagacity for the interests of their own success. And then because
the feelings of women being denied any other outlet, flow into the
channel dug for them with a force proportioned to the capacity of
strong feeling with which they are naturally endowed, the in-
ference is drawn that this is the channel demanded by their own
nature & that a woman who claims admission to any other, does so
because she has not the feelings which, by this kind of practical
petitio principii, have been decided to be womanly. If the commonest laws of human nature did not prove it, my wife is a sufficient proof by example that whoever has the greatest & fullest
measure of the feelings that produce self devotion to another or
others, is also the best qualified for any other field of action, great
or small, & must ever protest inwardly (unless her nature itself is
bowed to the yoke of her circumstances) against the stupid &
selfish social arrangements which compel her, if she acts at all,
[RII.7v] however the planning & originating mind & the com-
manding faculties may be on her side, to act solely through another.

The influence of this most precious friendship upon my own
mental developement was of a twofold nature. The first, & that
of which I earliest reaped the full benefit,[81] was her effect on my
ideal standard of character. My conception of the highest worth of
a human being, was immeasurably enlarged & exalted, while at
the same time this larger ideal was filled & satisfied by her [82] in a
manner in which no one had ever before satisfied even the far inferior ideal which I had conceived previously.[83] This first kind of
influence was not so properly her influence, as the [84] effect on my
own thoughts & feelings of new experience & new subjects of
contemplation.[85] The second was the direct operation of her intellect & character upon mine, & this [86] came to its full height only
gradually with the increasing maturity of her own thoughts &
powers.[87] But at a very early period of my knowledge of her she

---

[81] & that of which I . . . benefit,] *deleted by HM, who marked the rest of this
sentence and the next five sentences (to the bottom of RII.7v) with a line in
the margin*

[82] as a really existing character

[83] while at the same time this larger ideal . . . previously.] *deleted by HM*

[84] This first kind of influence . . . the] *altered by HM to read:* This was the

[85] subjects of contemplation.] objects of contemplation which she afforded to
me. (*HM underlined "objects" and wrote "Subjects" at left*)

[86] though considerable from the first *deleted first by HM, who wrote several
words, now erased and illegible, at left*

[87] *Originally continued after a colon:* as will be abundantly shewn in the
sequel.

became to me a living type of the most admirable kind of human being. I had always wished for a friend whom I could admire wholly, without reservation & restriction, & I had now found one. [RII.8r] To render this possible, it was necessary that the object of my admiration [88] should be of a type very different from my own; should be a character preeminently of feeling, combined however as I had not in any other instance known it to be, with a vigorous & bold speculative intellect. Hers was not only all this but the perfection of [89] a poetic & artistic nature.[90] With how eminent a practical capacity these endowments were combined, I only understood by degrees; but the rest was enough without this to make me feel that in any true classification of human beings such as I are only fit to be the subjects [91] & ministers [92] of such as her; & that the best thing I, in particular, could do for the world, would be to serve as a sort of prose interpreter of her poetry, giving a logical exposition to those who have more understanding than feeling, of the reasonableness of that which she either knew by the experience or divined by the intuition of one of the richest & strongest of natures guided by the most unselfish & highminded of characters.[93]

Accordingly the first years of my friendship with her [94] were, in respect of my own development, mainly years of poetic culture. It is hardly necessary to say that I am not now speaking of *written* poetry, either metrical or otherwise; though I did cultivate this taste as well as a taste for paintings & sculptures, & did read with enthusiasm her favorite poets, especially the one whom she placed far above [95] all others, [RII.8v] Shelley. But this was merely accessary. The real poetic culture was, that my faculties, such as they were,[96] became more & more attuned to the beautiful & elevated, in all kinds, & especially in human feeling & character & more capable of vibrating in unison with it.[97] In the same propor-

---

[88] object of my admiration] *underlined and marked with a question mark by HM*

[89] all this but the perfection of] *altered by HM to read:* this but in a high degree

[90] *The rest of the paragraph is marked with a line in the margin by HM*

[91] subjects] *altered by HM to read:* followers   [92] ministers] servants

[93] one of the richest & strongest . . . characters.] *altered by HM to read:* a rich & strong nature.

[94] my friendship with her] *altered by HM to read:* our acquaintance

[95] placed far above] *altered by HM to read:* preferred to

[96] such as they were,] *deleted by HM*

[97] & more capable of vibrating . . . it.] *deleted by HM*

tion, & by a natural consequence, I became less excitable by anything else. All [98] society & personal intercourse became burthensome to me except with those in whom I recognized, along with
more or less sympathy of opinion, at least a strong taste for elevated
& poetic feeling, if not the feeling itself. I gradually withdrew
myself from much of the society which I had frequented; [99] though
I still retained unabated [100] interest in radical politics & kept up
my connexion with such of the rising or promising politicians on
the radical side, as I had ever been intimate with. I even became
more involved in political & literary relations than I had ever been
before, through the foundation, as I have already mentioned, by
Sir William Molesworth of a new radical review, to be entirely
under my direction.

---

[98] In the same proportion . . . All] *deleted by HM, who wrote at left:*
"explain how what is called society always becomes burthensome to persons
of any capacity & therefore especially to those who require a real interchange
of ideas to make a change from solitude refreshing—not wearysome"
[99] I gradually withdrew . . . frequented;] *deleted by HM*
[100] still retained unabated] *altered by HM to read:* acquired increased

INDEX [1]

---

[1] In parenthetical documentation the abbreviations *WR* and *LWR* designate the *Westminster Review* and the *London and Westminster Review.*